Google™ Search & Re...
For Dummies®

D1441171

Standard Search Operators

+ (AND) Use before a keyword that must be included in search results. In the absence of any other operators, Google assumes that keywords are preceded by the *AND* operator. Example: *french +fries.*

- (NOT) Use before a keyword that must be excluded from the search results. Example: *soup stock -market.*

" " Use around keywords that must be matched as an exact phrase. Example: *american revolution "one if by land".*

OR Use to match either one keyword or another. When *OR* is placed between two keywords, Google is forced to include one of them. Example: *cheese cheddar OR swiss.*

Google URL Operators

link Finds incoming links to whatever URL you provide after the operator. The search displays sites that contain links to the specified URL. Example: *link:www.blogcritics.com.*

info When paired with a URL, this operator displays links to further information about the specified site. Example: *info:www.nytimes.com.*

cache Displays Google's cached (stored) snapshot of whatever URL follows the operator. Good for taking a short hop back in time. Example: *cache:www. usatoday.com.*

site One of the most important operators, this one restricts search results to a specified URL. Works with top-level domain extensions such as .edu and .gov by themselves in place of a specific site URL. Example: *yankees red sox site:www.nytimes.com.*

Google Keyword Operators

intitle Matches the following keyword against Web page titles in Google's index. Dramatically narrows results and makes them more relevant. For example, *intitle:dog training* displays Web pages with *dog* in the title and *training* in the title or page.

allintitle Forces all following keywords to match against Web page titles in Google's index. Narrows results even more than *intitle*. For example, *allintitle:dog training* displays Web pages with both *dog* and *training* in the title.

inurl Matches the following keyword against URLs (addresses) in Google's index. Severely narrows results and makes them highly relevant. For example, with *inurl:fleet online banking*, the results would have *fleet* in the URL and *online* and *banking* in the URL (not likely) or the page (likely).

allinurl Forces all the following keywords to match against URLs in Google's index. Ferociously restricts search results. For example, with *allinurl:yankees tickets*, the results would have both *yankees* and *tickets* in the page URL.

filetype Restricts the keyword search to results of a certain file type, such as Adobe Acrobat .pdf files or Microsoft Word .doc files. Excellent for conducting research. Example: *speed of light filetype:pdf.*

Getting Hidden Information

Google is not an encyclopedia, but it acts like one if you give it the right cues. Google Q&A answers nearly all questions framed as who, what, when, where, or why. Furthermore, Google can handle the following types of queries: UPS, FedEx, and U.S.P.O. tracking numbers; stock ticker symbols; and basic arithmetic calculations.

Google™ Search & Rescue For Dummies®

Cheat Sheet

Google Information Operators

define
When followed by a single word or single phrase, this operator brings up definitions culled from Web sites in Google's index. Example: *define:weblog*.

movie
Use this handy operator broadly, followed by any movie-related terms such as a film title or actor name, to bring up diverse information from a special Google database. Example: *movie:woody allen cannes*.

weather
Used with a cite or state combination or a zip code, this operator causes Google to deliver a brief four-day weather forecast. Example: *weather winter park fl*.

group
For use in Google Groups, this operator limits your search to a specific discussion group. Example: *john mcvey group:alt.binaries.music*.

author
Also for use in Google Groups, this operator should be paired with an e-mail address to find messages posted by an individual. Example: *author:jsmith@my-email.com*.

phonebook
When followed by a name (last name only) and either a state abbreviation or a zip code, Google displays the full address and phone number when available. Example: *phonebook:jones nj*.

rphonebook
Limits phone book results to residential listings. Example: *rphonebook:jones nj*.

bphonebook
Limits phone book results to business listings. Example: *bphonebook:starbucks 08542*.

Google Games

- Googlism
- Capture the Map
- Google Smackdown
- RandomWebSearch.com
- Google Art Creator
- Google time machine at Findforward.com

Copyright © 2005 Wiley Publishing, Inc. All rights reserved.
Item 9930-5.

For more information about Wiley Publishing,
call 1-800-762-2974.

Alternative Googles

Google these and try them out!

- GAPS, GARBO, and GAWSH
- Soople
- WebCollage
- Google Cartography
- Google Newsmap
- Babelplex
- TouchGraph Google Browser
- Google Ultimate Interface
- SketchWeb
- BananaSlug
- YahGoohoo!gle
- Elgoog

For Dummies: Bestselling Book Series for Beginners

Google™
Search & Rescue
FOR
DUMMIES®

Google™ Search & Rescue

FOR DUMMIES®

by Brad Hill

Wiley Publishing, Inc.

Goog Google search & rescue for dummies

Publi

Wiley Publishing, Inc.
111 River Street
Hoboken, NJ 07030-5774
www.wiley.com

WILEY

About the Author

Brad Hill has worked in the online field since 1992 and is regarded as a pre-eminent advocate of the online experience. As a best-selling author of books and in his columns, Hill reaches a global audience of consumers who rely on his writings to help determine their online service choices.

Brad's books include a *Publishers Weekly* bestseller and a Book-of-the-Month catalog selection. Brad's titles in the *For Dummies* series include *Internet Searching For Dummies, Building Your Business with Google For Dummies,* and *Yahoo! For Dummies*. He operates the Search Report Web site (www.TheSearchReport.com) and is a staff blogger at WeblogsInc (www.weblogsinc.com).

Brad is often consulted in the media's coverage of the Internet. He appears on television and radio Webcasts and is quoted in publications such as *Business Week,* the *New York Times,* and *PC World.*

Brad doesn't get outdoors much. Sunshine baffles him. As compensation, he is listed in *Who's Who* and is a member of The Author's Guild.

Author's Acknowledgments

Every book is a partnership of author and editor. Susan Pink is the editor of this book and a collaborator in other projects as well. Her keenness, careful reading, and incisive comments shine through every paragraph . . . except for the extra chapter I slipped in at the last second. You'll know it when you see it. Besides being an unusually fine editor who makes me look a lot better than I would without her, Susan has a gift for remaining calm during the most intense deadline crises. She also laughs at all the right times.

Colin Banfield had the challenging job of technical editor. His insights were invaluable.

Many thanks to Tom Stocky at Google for his unflinching willingness to answer my seemingly endless, detailed questions.

Melody Layne at Wiley Publishing nursed this project from the start, getting it off the ground quickly and helping shape its focus. I'm very thankful.

Mary Corder pulled me into the *For Dummies* family several years ago, and is, by now, sick of seeing her name pop up in my acknowledgments. But I am forever grateful, so she'll have to deal with it.

Many thanks to all the copy editors and production experts who pored over every page of the manuscript.

Finally, I'd like to thank the Pulitzer Committee for this fine honor. Oops . . . that speech is from an alternate reality.

Publisher's Acknowledgments

We're proud of this book; please send us your comments through our online registration form located at www.dummies.com/register/.

Some of the people who helped bring this book to market include the following:

Acquisitions, Editorial, and Media Development

Project Editor: Susan Pink

Acquisitions Editor: Melody Layne

Technical Editor: Colin Banfield

Editorial Manager: Carol Sheehan

Media Development Supervisor: Richard Graves

Editorial Assistant: Amanda Foxworth

Cartoons: Rich Tennant (www.the5thwave.com)

Composition Services

Project Coordinator: Adrienne Martinez

Layout and Graphics: Carl Byers, Barry Offringa, Julie Trippetti

Proofreaders: Leeann Harney, Jessica Kramer, Joe Niesen, TECHBOOKS Production Services

Indexer: TECHBOOKS Production Services

Special Help
Tom Stocky

Publishing and Editorial for Technology Dummies

    Richard Swadley, Vice President and Executive Group Publisher

    Andy Cummings, Vice President and Publisher

    Mary Bednarek, Executive Acquisitions Director

    Mary C. Corder, Editorial Director

Publishing for Consumer Dummies

    Diane Graves Steele, Vice President and Publisher

    Joyce Pepple, Acquisitions Director

Composition Services

    Gerry Fahey, Vice President of Production Services

    Debbie Stailey, Director of Composition Services

Contents at a Glance

Table of Contents

Introduction

*F*ew Internet phenomena have rivaled Google. Not even Yahoo! of 1994 and 1995 could claim the importance in so many lives that Google can claim. Amazon, eBay, Napster — all are milestones, but Google is a uniquely big wheel. It has been adopted quickly, its user base is of global scope, and it has influence on society at large. (A marketing survey reported that Google was a more recognized brand than Coca-Cola and Starbucks.) No online activity has become as deeply embedded in our culture and language as Googling.

The first wave of euphoria has ended. Google was launched, took over the world of Internet searching, became a public company, and settled down to life as an established Internet powerhouse. Google's millions of users were ecstatic over the uncannily useful search results and no-fluff interface, and *Googling* became part of the language and part of the Internet lifestyle. Google enlightened the online citizenry, and other Internet companies, by demonstrating that online searching could be profoundly rewarding and profitable. Google is now entering a second major phase of its existence.

Now a new stage begins. Users take for granted Googling and its great results. Competitors have wakened from their slumber and are battling Google fiercely for mindshare and search traffic. New search-related services are being introduced at a record pace. Innovation is in the air. Standards of search accuracy and relevance have been raised, and consumers know that the next great development might not come from Google.

The result of this increased competitiveness has been remarkable at Google. Always a brainy outfit that values invention for its own sake, regardless of what the marketplace seems to need, Google has expanded its Ph.D.-encrusted staff and dramatically increased the pace of its development of new products. Since the publication of *Google For Dummies,* Google has launched Google Local, Google Video, Google Suggest, Google Scholar, Gmail, Google Deskbar, and Google Desktop Search. The company has made extensive overhauls to Google Toolbar, Froogle, Google Groups, Blogger.com, and Google Free. Google has acquired photo-editing company Picasa and satellite-imaging company Keyhole. Google has been *busy.*

Google has matured and is driving forward quickly on all cylinders. Nearly from the start, more power has been under the hood than was generally recognized. Now, it is downright absurd to be using Google only as a simple Web search engine, hitting the home page with simple keyword strings, oblivious to the many features and services beneath the service and around its edges. It never fails: When somebody asks me how I can stretch Googling into an entire book, the conversation ends with them saying, "I didn't know that!" This book is that conversation.

About This Book

My intent in these pages is to reveal the inner depths and hidden features of the Googling lifestyle, and to rescue you from the overwhelmed feeling of information overload. Actually, this book's title has a double meaning: As Google rescues its users from a hopeless glut of online content, so does it save information from being lost in poor, wrongly worded searches. Google accomplishes that last part by providing many specialized features and tools, all of which are available to us, but many of which are not publicized much. Most people are unaware of Google's most powerful and precise tools. Even in the core service — the Web search engine — Google silently and without hype includes features that, when known, make daily Googling faster, more powerful, and more targeted.

Most people are astonished when they discover these brilliant Google features. Getting fast stock quotes or word definitions; finding shops in the local neighborhood; searching through pages in thousands of mail-order catalogues; finding files on government and military sites; locating certain file types; Googling over the phone; navigating search results without using the mouse; searching only the titles of Web pages; playing Google games at innumerable Google fan sites; plumbing the amazing Google Groups (one of the most remarkable reference resources in the world); using Google as a phone book; highlighting a word on any Web page and launching a Google search from that page; using the Google Toolbar to block pop-up ads . . . I could go on. And, in fact, I do for the next few hundred pages.

So, what is this book about? Without conceit, I can tell you that these pages are about your virtual life, your online intelligence, and your informed citizenship in the Internet nation. Whichever translation of this book you are reading, whatever country you live in, the beneficent informational power of Google belongs as much to you as to anyone.

Conventions Used in This Book

I despise conventions. All that walking; the bad food. Fortunately, that has nothing to do with the conventions used in this text, which are layout styles and typefaces designed to identify certain kinds of information. To make following along easier, this book is consistent in how it presents these items:

✔ Web addresses, also called URLs, look like this:

```
www.google.com
```

✔ When I use an unusual term for the first time, I *italicize* it.

✔ Google keywords appear *italicized* when embedded in text, and sometimes appear below a paragraph like this:

```
keywords google search
```

What You're Not to Read

This book is not technical, so I don't need to warn you away from difficult parts. But don't feel as if you must read straight through from start to finish. This isn't a novel. Google's many services fall naturally into distinct chapters, and it's natural to be interested in some things more than others.

For the Google beginner, Chapters 1 and 2 are probably the most important. But if you have lots of experience with basic Googling, those two chapters might be the least important. However, don't blow off Chapter 2 too quickly. It contains power-search information that can teach practically anyone something valuable about making Google's results more targeted and precise. That said, experienced users should pick and choose from the Table of Contents.

Many readers are probably interested in Google's new services, especially those introduced after the publication of *Google For Dummies*. They are Google Local, Google Maps, and Keyhole (all three bundled into Chapter 8, the local search chapter), Google Video, Google Suggest, and Google Scholar (packed into Chapter 11, the Google Labs chapter), the Google Deskbar (Chapter 12), and Gmail (Chapter 14).

Part V is mostly for Web site owners and bloggers, though it might be of interest if you aren't aware of Google's business services. The three chapters in this section contain a great deal of new information about AdWords, AdSense, and the general business of getting a site into Google, keeping it there, and pushing it up the results page. These topics are thoroughly summarized; for in-depth coverage of exhaustive (or is it exhausting?) detail, please look at *Building Your Business with Google For Dummies*.

If I were to point regular Google users to two chapters (and it looks as if I'm going to), I would say that Chapter 8, which covers local searching, and Chapter 12, which describes Google Toolbar, offer the most essential reading. But the back cover is also quite rewarding.

Foolish Assumptions

Google has so few requirements that, in writing about it, I don't need to make many assumptions. Which is a good thing, because I have a long track record of mistaken assumptions. For example, right now I'm assuming that you've taken this book to the bookstore coffee bar, and are dripping caramel macchiato all over the pages. That's what I'd be doing if I were you.

More realistically, I do assume that you can get on the Internet and operate a Web browser. Occasionally it's helpful to check which browser you're using, including the version number of that browser, and I blithely assume you can do that. Basic Internet navigation skills — such as visiting a Web site, filling in online forms, and following on-screen download instructions — are useful when exploring Google's many services. I'm quick to assume that you know all that stuff. You also need to know how to install programs if you are to use Google Toolbar, Google Deskbar, Keyhole, and a few others. Fortunately, most modern computers make installation quite easy, and Google provides instructions on its download pages.

So I guess I am assuming a fair amount about your ease of movement online, but honestly, nothing in this book is difficult. If Google were hard, it wouldn't be so popular.

How This Book Is Organized

This book employs a new and startling organizational system by which words are gathered into sentences, which in turn form paragraphs, and the whole shebang is printed on pages. Just turn the page, and . . . more words! I've collected thousands of the finest words in circulation, and strung them together in a manner that occasionally approaches coherence.

The book's chapters are organized into five parts, as follows.

Part I: Jumping Into Google

The two chapters in Part I present a detailed look at Google's most basic services — searching the Web from Google's home page. Here you get an overview of the entire Google landscape in Chapter 1, and then delve into basic and advanced searching in Chapter 2.

Throwing keywords hastily into Google is easy enough and delivers somewhat successful results. Studies have shown, however, that a surprising number of searchers are unsatisfied with the first page or two of results, and generally don't look deeper than that. Indeed, searching page after page of search results is often a waste of time; it's better in many cases to start a new search. That's where search operators and other tricks come in handy. These advanced (but easy) features give you better ways to narrow your search, often making that second attempt unnecessary.

This part is not merely a summary. To the contrary, I get very detailed about search operators (they can improve your life, trust me), finding certain types of documents, the Advanced Search page, and individualized preferences. Don't skim past these chapters if you know basic Googling! This part is stocked with tips and little-known facts about Google's underpublicized features.

Part II: Taming Google

In Part II you discover image search, Google Directory, Google News, Froogle, and Google Groups. In addition, Chapter 3 covers the many ways in which Google can be used as an answer engine. An answer engine differs from a Web search engine by directly delivering basic facts instead of links to Web pages that might, or might not, contain the basic facts you're looking for. Many people don't realize that Google can dish out answers and facts in ways that make your information-stoked life much easier.

Chapters 4 through 7 are focused on the main non-Web engines operated by Google — the ones linked from the home page. Those other engines are Google Images (photos galore), Google News (an interactive global newsstand), Google Groups (an archive of nearly twenty-five years of Internet discussion groups), Froogle (a shopping directory and search site), and Google Directory.

Part III: Specialty Searching

Part III goes somewhat farther afield to Google's outlying services. Chapter 8, which discusses local searching with three relatively new Google services, is particularly important and interesting. The other three chapters cover specialty categories of Internet searching such as universities and government sites, each of which has a dedicated Google engine; the Google Answers service, which delivers professional-level research for a small fee; and the sprawling cauldron of experimentation known as Google Labs. Google Labs contains the new services Google Video, Google Suggest, and Google Scholar, each of which is a distinct search engine.

Part IV: Putting Google to Work

Part IV starts by describing two ways in which Google can be put to work in uncommon fashion. First, and for many most importantly, Google can attach to Web browsers in various ways, offering one-click searching from anywhere on the Web. I venture to say that the Google Toolbar is the single most important Google service beyond the basic search engine, and I strongly recommend that you read Chapter 12. The second method of searching from afar is the Google Deskbar, which resides on your computer desktop, independent of the browser.

Speaking of the desktop, Chapter 13 explores Google Desktop, a major new service that allows users to search their own computers, Google style. Google Desktop requires an easy download and is free.

Gmail created more Google-related fuss than any other service to come out of Google in the last two years. There is good reason for all the commotion; Gmail provides a new way of tackling Web-based e-mail and offers a ton of storage. It works beautifully, and Chapter 14 explains all the ins and outs.

Finally, Chapter 15 illuminates the simple method by which site owners can put a Google search box on their pages and customize how search results appear.

Part V: The Business of Google

Part V is about Google's business services, so it is mostly about advertising. Chapter 17 covers AdWords (a way of advertising to searchers using keywords that relate to the advertiser's products), and Chapter 18 centers on AdSense, a way for professional Web sites of all types to run Google AdWords ads and make money doing it. Before those productive chapters, Chapter 16 explains how Google trolls the Web for sites to include in its massive index, and how your Web site can get favorable treatment.

Part VI: The Part of Tens

Part VI is almost all recreational. Chapters 19 through 22 take you all over the Web, trying Google-related sites developed by individuals who took advantage of Google's standing invitation to build alternate search interfaces. Google's index is available to any programmer, and some of the results are spectacularly successful — improvements, even, on Google's own pages. There are even Google-related games; if you've ever wondered what Googlewhacking is, head to Chapter 21. The book's final chapter (and I won't tolerate any high-fiving at the mention of the final chapter) points to sites and Weblogs *about* Google — even highly critical ones.

Icons Used in This Book

See how big these pages are? We have to put something in these wide margins, so we came up with icons. Figuring that they might as well be more than just decorative, we assigned meaning to the pictures you see marking some paragraphs.

This book is full of these things. They remind you to tip your waitress. Also, these icons indicate that the paragraph contains an especially usable nugget of information.

I throw in a lot of these, too, but I forget why. It'll come to me.

Rarely, I slip into the kind of technobabble that makes people avoid me at parties. Just slap me when I get like that. And feel free to ignore these paragraphs if you're not interested — they don't contain anything you need to know.

Using Google is considerably safer than leaping out of an airplane with a sack full of bowling balls, so I don't often have reason to issue warnings. But when I do, get the kids to a safe place and board up the windows.

Where to Go from Here

I don't know about you, but I'm going to lie down. It's 2 in the afternoon, for goodness sake, and time for a nap. If you're in the mood to keep reading, do it quietly.

Starting at the beginning never hurts, but if you're ready for the advanced stuff, I suggest leaping to the section on search operators in Chapter 2. In the mood for fun, straight off? Go to the chapters in Part VI. I know I've mentioned it before, but Chapter 8 is a great place to discover something new from Google — local searching.

Wake me for dinner, and happy Googling.

Part I
Jumping Into Google

The 5th Wave   By Rich Tennant

@RICHTENNANT

"I think you're just jealous that I found a community of people online that worship the yam as I do, and you haven't."

In this part . . .

*I*n the first part of *Google Search & Rescue For Dummies,* I introduce Google's basic search functions, which anybody can try by going to the Google home page. Ah, but by *introduce,* I mean that this part dives into keyword skills of which most people are unaware, to reveal dozens of ways to maximize your daily Google experience.

Google is good when you know just the bare minimum. Imagine how much better it can get for a laser-minded, Web-addicted power user who can blast apart a results page with a few simple search operators. Are you ready for this? Because that's what Part I is all about.

Chapter 1 sets you up with the overview; Chapter 2 goes way beyond basic keyword plodding by revealing search operators, the Advanced Search page, and Google Preferences. Get ready to hone your skills, sharpen your results, and project your mind over the vast global information matrix, diving down like a hawk to spear your personal bits of wisdom as they scurry through the tangled undergrowth of hidden knowledge. Oh, the power of simple tools . . . like the home cappuccino maker, for example, which I've been using rather too much lately. But forget that. The simple tools at hand are single-word commands that bend the mighty Google to your will and rescue once-lost information from the abyss of ignorance.

If you're a Google beginner — which is to say, either a newcomer or a long-time casual user — reading the two chapters in Part I will make you more knowledgeable about Google than anyone you know. More important, doing so will make you smarter, better informed, connected to sharper resources, and a more skilled online citizen. Brew your coffee and let's get going. [Editors' note: Brad Hill has promised to switch to decaf by the time you reach Part II.]

Chapter 1

Google Saves the Day, Every Day

. . . .

. . . .

*Y*ou're about to embark on an adventure that will stimulate your mind and gratify the most urgent desires of your soul. Then, when you've finished watching *American Idol,* you'll start discovering Google.

I know what you're saying: You've already discovered Google. Who hasn't? Not since the early Web days of 1994 and 1995, when everybody surfed through Yahoo!, have people flocked so overwhelmingly to a search engine as they do to Google. Google not only revitalized the search industry but also saved worthy information from obscurity and rescued countless users from the frustration of futile searching.

During the time since Yahoo! got the ball rolling, many keyword-oriented search engines have come. Many have gone. Some remain, offering specialty searches or emulating Google. (Imitation and flattery — you know the drill.)

Now, with *Googling* a common term in the mainstream vernacular, general searching of the Web has become standardized into a universal ritual. Anybody wanting to find an online destination follows this three-step process:

1. Go to Google.

2. Type a few words related to the search goal.

3. Click the search results to visit relevant Web sites.

All well and good. Google is lightning fast and devastatingly accurate. And the chapters in Part II dismantle general searching to help you maximize your basic Google experience. But as it turns out, general Web searching is just the tip of the Google iceberg.

Note: The Google home page is located, naturally, at this URL:

```
www.google.com
```

Any user, worldwide, can use that page to get the American version of Google. However, Google operates national versions of its service, using the domain suffix unique to those countries. Again, each of these national versions can be called up by anyone in any country. Here are a few examples:

```
www.google.ca (Canada)
www.google.fr (France)
www.google.co.uk (England)
```

Beyond Keywords

The term *search engine,* so apt for the lumbering, early-generation monsters that crunched through the Web looking for sites, seems only fractionally fitting for Google. Rather, Google should be called an information engine. Or a knowledge life-form. The stuff you get from Google might come from its vast and smart index of Web pages, or it might come from other indices seamlessly woven into the core data dump. Some of the usefulness that you can pry out of Google, such as Weblogging, comes from autonomous companies that Google has acquired and put under its service umbrella. However you use Google, greater awareness of what's under the hood is certain to make your online life easier, better informed, and more fluid.

The following sections furnish a quick survey of Google's information engine, including and beyond general keyword searching.

Finding all sorts of stuff

In Google, basic Web searching couldn't be simpler. The next chapter covers the basics, plus powerful ways of grabbing the information you want quickly. In addition to offering traditional Web searching, Google blends other types of searching into the basic keyword process:

✔ **Google Directory:** Yahoo! set the standard of integrated searching (through a keyword engine) and browsing (through a topical directory). In the beginning, Yahoo!'s search engine searched the directory, which was carefully hand-constructed by a staff of editors. Yahoo! still builds its directory manually. Google also presents a topical directory for browsing, and you can search it separately from the basic Web search. See Chapter 7.

Life without Google

In my life as an online citizen (no, I don't get out much), two destinations are indispensable. One is Yahoo!, a gargantuan domain that provides more free services than a sane person would try to count. The other is Google, which makes my virtual movements faster and more exact than ever. Online life without either is inconceivable. The amazing thing is that Google has been around only since the fall of 1999. Yahoo! has been building its reputation and service platform for more than ten years. (May 1, 2005, was Yahoo!'s tenth birthday.) And it can be argued that Google has embedded itself into the lifestyles of ordinary Internet citizens and the business practices of companies more profoundly and securely than Yahoo! has. Whereas Yahoo! spent millions on the "Do you Yahoo!?" ad campaign, everybody started saying "Google this" and "Google that" with little or no formal advertising from Google.

Yahoo! is certainly more diversified than Google, with a portion of its empire devoted to nearly every activity in which a person could engage online: playing games, booking travel, researching stocks, meeting a soul mate, chatting about nothing, watching music videos — on and on and on. Yahoo! operates the most popular G-rated, legal, free activity platform on the open Internet; in March 2005 Yahoo! had 165 million registered users and 345 million unique monthly visitors. With all this, Yahoo! has, until recently, forsaken its roots as a search engine and left the fertile field of keyword matching open to Google.

I wrote *Yahoo! For Dummies* and *Google For Dummies.* Each service is a cornerstone of the Internet. Prediction is a risky business, but when I'm in a divining mood, I can easily see Google becoming the most important online service in history, approaching the geek-idealist's dream of indexing every bit of human knowledge and virtual expression, with an awareness of the surrounding context and with each contribution ranked by its peers and instantly accessible. A foolish vision? The surprising part is how closely Google is chasing it already.

Life without Google? With each passing day, the thought becomes more inconceivable.

✔ **Newsgroup reader:** Newsgroups make up the portion of the Internet called Usenet, which is far older (and probably still bigger in some measure) than the Web. It has more than fifty thousand groups, organized by topic, covering everything from astrophysics to David Letterman. Usenet is a hangout for academicians, pornographers, armchair pundits, and nearly everyone else. It's a wild-and-wooly realm that's normally accessed through a dedicated computer program called a *newsgroup reader.* Outlook Express and other e-mail programs contain newsgroup-reading features. Google got into the act by purchasing the old Deja News, the groundbreaking company that first put Usenet on the Web. Google presents a deep archive of searchable newsgroup messages. Furthermore, it lets you establish an identity and post messages to groups, all through your Web browser. See Chapter 6.

✔ **Image finder:** The Web is a picturesque place. Every photograph and drawing that you see on a Web page is a distinct file residing at a specific Internet location, and Google knows how to search that tremendous store of images. See Chapter 2.

The mythical Internet library

The World Wide Web was developed to bring order to the chaotic Internet, which had been lurking in academia and the government since the 1960s. Because the Internet was regarded primarily as an information source — more than an entertainment medium or a community space — it was natural to imagine the quick construction of a universal, all-inclusive online library. Through the years, I've often heard people mistakenly speak of the Internet as an information realm in which one could find anything, read any book, and access all knowledge.

But the truth splintered away from that ideal. First, the Web became a distinct and autonomous entity with its own content, disregarding for the most part the academic material that was already online. Second, regular folks who stormed into the new virtual playground were interested in other, more recreational pursuits than learning. So the mecca of unlimited access to knowledge withered away from reality — and even from the imagination.

I am not going to imply that Google single-handedly manifests an Alexandrian library of human knowledge (yet). However, through the astounding accuracy of its search results, Google does ease access to an unprecedented breadth of knowledge. (And the nascent Google Print program, which seeks to digitize entire libraries of books for searching, certainly contributes to the "Internet library" ideal.) To whatever extent the Internet comprises the communal content of the human mind, Google illuminates the gray matter with clarity and usefulness. Want to know something? Google it. That's the modern recipe for learning in this information-saturated age.

✔ **Shopping assistant:** This is one of Google's huge, underappreciated strengths. For a long time, Froogle was unknown by just about everybody (who hadn't read *Google For Dummies,* that is). Then Google moved it from obscurity to the home page of the British and American sites, and everybody saw the light. Comparisons to Yahoo! Shopping are difficult to avoid. The two services differ crucially, in that you never actually buy things through a Google transaction system as you sometimes can in Yahoo!. (For example, Google has no Google Wallet for storing credit card information for one-click purchasing.) Google has two main shopping services, Froogle and Google Catalogs. You use Froogle to find shopping sites that sell things you want. Google Catalogs — arguably the more fun of Google's two shopping services — gives you a paper-free sense of accessing a mail-order universe. See Chapter 4.

✔ **Local search engine:** Most search pundits and consumer focus groups agree that local searching will eventually be just as important as global Web searching. By *local searching,* I mean a searching for stuff that exists in a physical neighborhood — on streets near your home. All the big search engines are getting into local action, and Google is flat-out winning the race as of this writing. I'm not saying so to sell this book; nobody else has put together a combination of local search, local mapping, and local photography as Google has — and this is just the beginning. See Chapter 8.

✔ **International newsstand:** In one of the most dramatic additions to the Google spectrum of features, Google News has replaced Yahoo! News as the default headline engine on countless screens. Almost unbelievable in its depth and range, Google News presents continually updated links to established news sources in dozens of countries, putting a global spin on every story of the day. See Chapter 5.

These features (except for Google Directory) hook into Google's home page, and it is easy to transfer a search from one of these engines to another. (Just click the links above the keyword box after entering a keyword.) At the same time, each of these engines stands on its own as an independent search tool. Other features, sketched next, exist more in the background but are no less important than the high-profile search realms.

Hidden strengths

You might be surprised to find what Google can tell you if prompted in certain ways. Active Googlers stumble across some of these features in the course of daily rummaging, because Google spits out information in unrequested configurations when it thinks you need it. (Yes, Google does seem like a thinking animal sometimes.) Other chapters describe exactly how to coax explicit types of search results from the site. Here, my aim is to briefly summarize power features you might not be aware of:

✔ **Document repository:** Most people, most of the time, search for Web pages. But many other types of viewable (or listenable) pieces of content are available on the Internet. For example, almost every modern computer comes with the capability to view PDF files, which are documents such as articles, white papers, research texts, and financial statements that retain their original formatting instead of being altered to fit a Web page. Google includes documents other than Web pages in its general search results and also lets you narrow any search to a specific file type. See Chapter 2.

✔ **Government and university tracker:** Not to get all paranoid on you, but if you're into watching your back, the first of these features could prove helpful. More benignly, Google reserves distinct portions of its search engine for government domains and another for university domains. This arrangement has uses explored in Chapter 9.

✔ **Scholarly resource:** If you ever imagined that Google was a sort of library card catalogue to the Web, Google Scholar brings that idea closer to home. This dedicated index digs up academic papers and scholarly books — though not to read, in all cases. The Google Scholar engine is great for finding both titles and citations to those titles in other papers and books.

✔ **Keyword suggestion tool:** One of the great (if unrecognized) difficulties of high-quality Internet searching is finding the useful keyword or keyphrase. Google Suggest offers productive keyphrase suggestions as you type in the keyword box.

These and other new aspects of the Google experience came from a dedicated technology incubation project called Google Labs. Remember when entire businesses were built solely on cultivating online ideas? Most of them crashed and burned, adding to the rubble of the exploded Internet bubble. Google is modestly, but importantly, continuing the incubating tradition by evolving ways of enhancing its information engine. See Chapter 11.

Answers of all sorts

One problem with the Web as an information source is the question of authenticity. Anybody can put up a Web site and publish information that might or might not be factual. True expertise is difficult to verify on the Web.

Two solutions exist to the verification problem: standard reference sources and on-demand professional research services. Neither is likely to be found on a typical Web site, professional and authoritative though that site might be. The desire for reference-style answers has given birth to dedicated *answer engines* such as Answers.com (formerly Gurunet).

Google, recognizing that its users sometimes need a quick answer rather than a list of Web sites that might (or might not) contain that answer, has built answer-engine capability into its Web engine. In some cases Google delivers the answer directly; in other cases it links you to an outside site that displays your answer. Some of the answers supplied by Google include eminently practical information such as stock quotes, the weather, movie show times, calculator functions, word definitions, phone book information, delivery service tracking, and airport status.

The second solution to the verification problem, on-demand professional research, is provided at Google Answers. Google Answers is . . . well, the answer. Staffed by a large crew of freelance researchers in many subjects, Google Answers lets you ask questions and receive customized answers — for a price. How much? That's up to you; an auction system is used whereby you request an answer for a specified price, and individual researchers either take on your question or not. See Chapter 10.

One nice touch: Google maintains a directory of previously asked and answered questions, sorted by topic. Browsing through the archives is a nice way to audition the quality of the service (it's good), and you might find that your query has already been solved.

Portable information butler

Google provides excellent results for the lazy, one-stop Internet searcher. And don't we all deserve a search engine that works hard on our behalf? Well, Google goes beyond the call of duty by following you around even after you've left the site. Only if you want it to, of course.

You can rip the Google engine right out of its site (so to speak) and take it with you while traipsing around the Web in three main ways:

- **Google Toolbar:** If you're aware of Google Toolbar, you're probably using it. You should be, anyway. If this is the first you've heard of it, today is the first day of the rest of your online citizenship. Internet life will never be the same. Google Toolbar bolts right into your browser, up near the top where your other toolbars reside. It enables you to launch a Google search without surfing to the Google site. I bet that in some dictionaries a picture of the Google Toolbar is next to the definition of *cool.* See Chapter 12.

- **Google Deskbar:** Deskbar takes independence even further by separating Google from the Web browser entirely. Google Deskbar sits right on your computer desktop, and displays search results in its own window. See Chapter 12.

Google searching is made easy and portable by Mozilla browsers — Firefox and Netscape, which incorporate search bars within the browser that are naturally configured (and can be customized) to take your search queries directly to Google.

Google's portable features insinuate the service into your online life more deeply than merely bookmarking the site. Google will take over your mind. But that's a good thing.

And now for something completely different

The Google empire is young and relatively small compared to the Yahoo! powerhouse. In building itself out, Google has made a few key acquisitions:

- **Blogger.com:** One of the most used platforms for Weblogging (easy online journaling), Blogger.com provides easy tools for creating online journals and amateur news sites.

- **Picasa:** Picasa is an image-sorting and image-editing program that was popular when Google got its hands on it, and then became much more popular when Google eliminated the price and gave the program away.

✔ **Keyhole:** A satellite-imaging company, Keyhole offers a subscription service through which users can view the earth and zoom down to see details with amazing precision.

All three of these companies operate somewhat independently of Google, while definitely being under Google's direction. For the Google user searching with Google, Blogger and Picasa don't play any part in the Google experience. Keyhole is somewhat integrated with Google Local (see Chapter 8).

Google the Business Partner

With the Google AdWords program, Internet advertising has been brought to the masses — and boy, people are eating it up.

AdWords (see Chapter 17) is a revolutionary system that lets anybody with a Web site advertise for a reasonable cost on the Google search results page. This exposure, on one of the Internet's most highly trafficked domains, was inaccessible and unthinkably expensive in the past.

AdWords is stunningly innovative but also complicated. Here's the gist: You hook a small ad to certain keywords and assign a price you're willing to pay. That price is based on *clickthroughs,* which occur when a Googler conducts a search with one of your keywords, sees your ad on the results page, and clicks the ad to visit your Web site. Other site owners might have hooked their ads to the same keyword(s); if they offered a higher price per clickthrough, their ads are listed above yours. No matter how much you pay, your final bill is determined by actual visits to your site, and you can set a limit to the total amount you pay.

All this is handled automatically, making AdWords a surprisingly sophisticated system. The complexities are explained in Chapter 17. AdWords isn't a search service, but the program is definitely part of the Google lifestyle for entrepreneurial types with Web sites ready for increased traffic.

Note: You might be wondering whether the AdWords system destroys the famous integrity of a Google search. Have hordes of Internet advertisers purchased placement in the search results pages, warping the accuracy of Google's engine? It's a good question because other search engines have been in public-relations trouble over this issue. The answer, emphatically, is no — Google AdWords don't pollute the purity of search results. The ads are placed over to the side, easily visible but not mingled with search results. And higher-priced sponsorships are placed above the search listing, in a manner that clearly differentiates them from the objective results.

Google for Programmers

All search engines operate by building an index of both Web pages and the content of those pages. This index is constructed with the help of *bots* (software robots), sometimes called spiders or crawlers. The index is a search engine's prime asset, the ever-shifting body of information that the engine matches against your keywords to deliver results. The formula that each search site uses to compile and search the index is a closely guarded secret.

Although Google doesn't breathe a word about its indexing formulas, it does do something else that's unprecedented and exciting. Google has released its application programming interface (API) to the public. An API enables software programmers to incorporate one program or body of data into another program. For example, Microsoft releases its Windows APIs to authorized developers who write stand-alone Windows software. Google's API lets software geniuses write programs that can access Google's index directly, bypassing the familiar interface at Google's site.

The public API is more important than it might seem at first. In the short time that the API has been available, many alternate Googles have sprung up, each a legitimate and authorized new method of Googling. A few people have created instant-message conduits to Google, so you can launch a search while chatting in certain IM programs. Some graphic presentations of Google search results that are being developed are, frankly, mind-blowing. These and many other Google stunts are explored in Chapters 19 and 20.

Google's expansion through third-party development lends variety to a search experience that is basically a rather drab chore — no matter how skillfully accomplished. And, like other Google innovations, the public API will probably serve to drive Google even deeper into the mass consciousness of the Internet community. Google will take over your soul. This, too, is a good thing.

If you're of a particularly geekish mindset or have some programming skills, you should know about Google Code, a clearinghouse for the publication of Google APIs. Check it here:

```
code.google.com
```

The Greatness of Google

In this chapter, I serve a sample platter of Google's buffet of services. But one central question remains: What makes Google so great in the first place? How did it become so rampantly popular that it started a new era of competition among search engines? Those, of course, are two questions, not one, and my inability to count is one reason Stephen Hawking doesn't return my phone calls. (In typing that little quip, I wasn't sure how to spell Hawking's first name. Naturally, I Googled it.)

Google's success depends to some extent on the size of its index, which has long passed the billion-page mark — Google claims to have the largest Web search index in the world.

But the big index is hardly the entire story. More important is a certain intelligence with which the index interprets keywords. Google's groundbreaking innovation in this department is its capability to not only find pages but also rank them based on their popularity. The legendary Google page rank is determined largely by measuring how many links to that page exist on other sites all over the Web. The logic here is simple and hard to refute: Page A links to page B for one reason only, and that is because page B contains something worthwhile. If pages C, D, E, F, and G also link to page B, odds increase that page B has something important going for it. If five-hundred thousand pages link to page B, it is without question truly important in some way.

This explanation is grossly simplified, and Google isn't divulging details. But the backlink feature is the advantage that makes Google search results so fantastic. Google can still dish up a clunker from time to time, frequently because of poor keywords entered by the user. And dead pages haven't been eliminated. But when it comes to finding basic information or Web destinations, Google delivers stunning results with incredible speed and accuracy.

Beyond Google's legendary indexing algorithm lies another aspect to its success. Users like Google not only for the quality of its results but also for the speed and reliability with which they are delivered. In Google's early days, as I was getting to know the service, my first and strongest impression was *speed!* Google receives hundreds of millions of daily search queries. It distributes the ponderous computing strain placed upon its system by using a gigantic global network of computers. How many? Google doesn't say, but the figure is certainly in the tens of thousands. Google values numbers more than pricey quality, and its computers are average machines. The software linking them keeps the system robust, and when a computer fails (which happens every day), others pick up the slack. So part of Google's winning formula lies in raw computing horsepower and resiliency to system failures.

Google calmly digests keywords in almost ninety languages. Googling is the one activity that unites the entire Internet citizenry, and Google has forever altered the Internet landscape and the ease with which we move through it.

Chapter 2

Reclaiming Your Time from Wasteful Searching

*T*his is where we get down to business. Searching for sites, finding files, wrangling with results, and generally raiding Google for all it's worth. You might be thinking, "I know how to search Google. You type a few words, press Enter, blink rapidly, and view the results." I won't comment on disturbing facial tics, but that process is essentially correct. And if you're impatient to explore more esoteric stuff, feel free to skip this chapter. I won't be hurt, bitter, or resentful. (And if I *am* hurt, bitter, or resentful, you'll never know it, so don't trouble yourself over my misery.)

Now, for those of you remaining, I'm going to send you each a million dollars. Which pales beside the wealth of useful information that follows in these pages. I get the basics out of the way quickly and lead you straight to the finer points of the search results page, advanced searching, narrowing your search results in various ways, and other life-altering techniques.

So read on. Your check is in the mail.

Setting Preferences

Many people breeze through Google umpteen times a day without bothering to set their preferences — or even being aware that there are preferences to set. A recent Internet study asked users whether they would rather set Google preferences or get bathed in chocolate syrup. Sentiment was overwhelmingly against setting Google preferences. But I'm here to tell you that the five settings on the Preferences page (see Figure 2-1) enhance the Google experience far more than the effort required to adjust them.

To adjust Google preferences, click the <u>Preferences</u> link on the Google home page or go here:

```
www.google.com/preferences
```

If you set your preferences and later return to the Preferences page by manually entering the preceding URL, your browser displays an unadjusted Preferences page (without your settings). That's because *your* Preferences page has a distinct URL with your preferences built in to it. For example, after selecting English as Google's default language for your visits, the URL appears like this:

```
www.google.com/preferences?hl=en
```

Figure 2-1:
Part of the
Google
Preferences
page. Its
settings
enhance the
Google
experience.

![Screenshot of Preferences - Mozilla Firefox]

File Edit View Go Bookmarks Tools Help

http://www.google.com/preferences?hl=en

Google Preferences   Preferences Help | About Google

Save your preferences when finished and **return to search**.   Save Preferences

Global Preferences (changes apply to all Google services)

Interface Language   Display Google tips and messages in: English
                          If you do not find your native language in the pulldown above, you can
                          help Google create it through our Google in Your Language program.

Search Language   ⦿ Search for pages written in any language (Recommended).

                       ○ Search only for pages written in these language(s):

☐ Arabic	☐ English	☐ Indonesian	☐ Romanian
☐ Bulgarian	☐ Estonian	☐ Italian	☐ Russian
☐ Catalan	☐ Finnish	☐ Japanese	☐ Serbian
☐ Chinese (Simplified)	☐ French	☐ Korean	☐ Slovak
☐ Chinese (Traditional)	☐ German	☐ Latvian	☐ Slovenian
☐ Croatian	☐ Greek	☐ Lithuanian	☐ Spanish
☐ Czech	☐ Hebrew	☐ Norwegian	☐ Swedish
☐ Danish	☐ Hungarian	☐ Polish	☐ Turkish
☐ Dutch	☐ Icelandic	☐ Portuguese	

SafeSearch Filtering   Google's SafeSearch blocks web pages containing explicit sexual content from appearing in search results.
                           ○ Use strict filtering (Filter both explicit text and explicit images)
                           ⦿ Use moderate filtering (Filter explicit images only - default behavior)
                           ○ Do not filter my search results.

Number of Results   Google's default (10 results) provides the fastest results.
                         Display 20 results per page.

Done

How Google remembers your preferences

When you set preferences in Google, the site is customized for you every time you visit it, as long as you're using the same computer through which you set the preferences. To provide this convenience, Google must place a *cookie* (a small information file) in your computer. The site and the cookie high-five each other whenever you visit Google, and then the site appears according to your settings. For this system to work, the reception of cookies must be turned on in your browser.

Some people are militantly anti-cookie, claiming that the data files represent an invasion of computer privacy. Indeed, some sites plant cookies that track your Internet movements and identify you to advertisers.

The truth is, Google's cookie is fairly aggressive. It gets planted when you first visit the site, whether or not you visit the Preferences page. Once planted, the Google cookie records your clicks in Google and builds a database of visitor behavior in its search results pages. For example, Google knows how often users click the first search result and to what extent they explore results lower on the page. Google uses this information to evaluate the effectiveness of its service and to improve it.

As to privacy, Google does indeed share aggregate information with advertisers and various third parties and even publicizes knowledge about how the service is used by its millions of visitors. The key word is *aggregate*. Google's privacy policy states that individual information is never divulged except by proper legal procedure, such as a warrant or a subpoena, or by individual consent. The privacy policy is published on this page:

    www.google.com/privacy.html

I have no problem with the Google cookie or with cookies in general. The convenience is helpful, and I don't mind adding to the aggregate information. It's rather comforting being a data droplet in Google's information tsunami.

Your best bet for reaching the Preferences page after first setting your preferences (when you want to readjust them, for example) is to use the <u>Preferences</u> link on the home page.

A single basic process changes one preference or several. Just follow these steps:

1. **Go to the Preferences page.**

   As mentioned, just click the <u>Preferences</u> link on the home page or go directly to www.google.com/preferences.

2. **Use the pull-down menus, check boxes, and radio buttons to make your adjustments.**

3. **Click the Save Preferences button.**

4. **In the confirmation window (which merely says "Your preferences have been saved" and is unnecessary), click the OK button.**

The next sections describe what you can accomplish on the Preferences page.

The international Google

If you're reading the English-language edition of this book, you probably enjoy Google in its default English interface. If you're reading the Icelandic edition of this book, please send me a copy — I want to see whether my jokes are funnier in a chilly language. Whatever your native language, you should know that you can get Google to appear in one of dozens of languages unpronounceable by George W. Bush (besides English, I mean).

Interface Language is the first Google preference, and it adjusts the appearance of certain pages — specifically, the home page, the Preferences page, the Advanced Search page, and many Help pages and intrasite directories.

Changing the interface language does not alter the language on the search results page or the search results themselves. (To change the language on those pages, you use the Search Language preference, up next.)

The Interface Language preference changes the Interface Language list in the pull-down menu! So if you choose an obscure language that uses an unfamiliar alphabet while playing around (it's irresistible), you might have trouble finding your way back to the mother tongue by means of the drop-down menu. But Google does provide a link to Google in English on the home page of most non-English language interfaces.

Google is nothing if not occasionally silly, and Interface Language offers a few must-try languages:

- **Elmer Fudd:** First on my favorites list, Elmer Fudd (or should I say Ewmew Fudd) capriciously changes all *R*s and *L*s to *W*s. On the home page, Groups is now Gwoups, and Directory has been cartoonized to Diwectowy. Most hilariously of all, the I'm Feeling Lucky button is denatured to I'm Feewing Wucky. Before changing the language menu back to its original state, be sure to ponder the difference between Twaditional and Simpwified Chinese.

- **Pig Latin:** Ouyay owknay owhay isthay orksway.

- **Hacker:** Changes alphabet letters to numerals and symbols wherever possible (pretty much everywhere), rendering a semicoherent page best comprehended after several bags of potato chips and a six-pack of soda. (See Figure 2-2.)

- **Interlingua:** A vaguely Euro blend of tourism-speak roughly understandable by nearly everyone.

- **Klingon:** If I have to explain it, you don't watch enough *Star Trek*. In fact, the folks at Google should bone up on their reruns, too, because the term is Klingonese, not Klingon. (Have they no honor?)

All right, stop playing around with the languages. Let's move on.

Figure 2-2:
Google in the mythical Hacker language.

Most non-English interface languages present a version of the Google home page tailored to that language. In some cases, the Froogle and Desktop links are missing, à la 2004 — or the Google News link might be missing. It's a shame, because I long to see "Fwoogle" in the Elmer Fudd language. If you usually navigate Google from the home page, have some familiarity with English, and are trying to decide between your native language and English, you might get more convenience from English.

Searching for non-English pages

After you have the Google interface speaking your language, you can turn your attention to searching for Web pages written in certain languages.

The language you search *for* doesn't need to match the language you search *in*. In other words, the first two preferences can be set to different languages. Furthermore, you can select more than one language in the Search Language setting, whereas the Interface Language preference, naturally, can be only one language at a time.

Use Search Language to narrow your search results by language. Choosing French, for example, returns Web pages written only in French. Use the check boxes to select as many languages as you want.

If you don't select any languages, leaving the Search Language preference in its default setting, your search results do not discriminate based on language. You're likely to see an international array of pages if you rummage through enough results.

G-rated searching

Google uses a filter called SafeSearch to screen out pornography from Web page and image searches. In its default setting (moderate), SafeSearch applies fairly strict filtering to image searches and leaves Web search results unedited. Change the setting to strict for harsher filtering of images and clean Web page searches. You can turn off the filter entirely for an unbiased search session. You select the filtering strength on the Preferences page, as shown in Figure 2-1.

SafeSearch operates automatically but can be modified manually by the Google staff. They accept suggestions of sites and images that should be subject to the adult-content filter. If you come across any objectionable material through a Google search (with SafeSearch set to moderate or strict), feel free to send a link to the offending page or image to the following e-mail address:

```
safesearch@google.com
```

Opening the floodgates

You can increase the number of search results that appear on the page, raising it from the default ten results. I think it's a good idea, so I keep my preference set at the maximum — one hundred results per page.

Google reminds you that shorter pages are displayed more quickly, which is a good point for people who hit the site for lightning-quick searches many times a day. Google's results are so uncannily accurate that you might usually need only ten results. Still, I like the higher number because the long page of search results arrives more rapidly than shorter pages at competing search engines. Furthermore, I have the impatient attitude of a demanding Web surfer, and I never like calling up a second page of search results. If the content I want isn't on the first page of results, I usually try new keywords, so stocking the results page with one hundred hits gives me a better chance of quick success.

You might not agree with my reasoning, in which case you should leave the number or results set to the default or choose a medium number of results from the drop-down menu.

Google is fast no matter how many results per page you request. The only thing that might hold you back is your modem speed. If you access the Internet using a high-speed connection (cable modem, DSL, corporate, or university connection), you might as well set the results number to 100 and be done with it.

New windows

The Results Window setting is an important preference setting in my life. It consists of a single check box which, when checked, opens a Web page in a new window when you click a search result. This is a useful way of staying anchored in the search results page, from which you might want to sample several Web pages that match your keywords. Without this preference, your browser opens the Web pages in the same window that Google is in, forcing you to Back-button your way back to Google if you want to see the search results again. And if you drill deeply into a site, it becomes even more difficult to get back to Google.

If you dislike multiple browser windows cluttering your desktop, leave the Results Window box unchecked. If you prefer a hybrid experience in which you sometimes want to anchor at Google while exploring several search hits, leave the box unchecked and get in the habit of right-clicking search result links when you want a new window. Choose Open in New Window from the right-click (shortcut) menu that your browser displays.

If you use a browser that displays Web pages in tabs within a master window, such as Firefox, Netscape, or Opera, Google can still open results in a new window for you. The Google search aids in Firefox (one of which is built in to the browser and the other of which is a version of the Google Toolbar called Googlebar) also can be set to open Google's search results in a new tab — my favored setting. But that setting works only when you enter keywords into the built-in Google keyword box or the Googlebar. See Chapter 12 for the whole deal about Google toolbars.

Basic Web Searches

Searching the Web is when you draw close to the life-form called Google. Entering a keyword is like venturing near the multilimbed Goddess of Knowledge and basking in the blazing glory of her wisdom. Or something. It's just a Web search, but with results so astute that you can't help wondering whether a person — a person who knows you very, very well — is lurking inside the machine.

The Google home page is a reactionary expression against the 1990s trend that turned search engines into busy, all-purpose information portals. (See Figures 2-3 and 2-4.) Yahoo!, Lycos, Excite, and others engaged in portal wars in which victory seemed to depend on which site could clutter the page with the most horoscopes, weather forecasts, news headlines, and stock market bulletins. This loud and lavish competition resulted from the failure of plain search engines to earn the traffic and money necessary to keep their businesses afloat. They piled more features onto their pages and, in some cases, ruined their integrity by selling preferred placement in search results. During this mad gold rush, some specialty engines retained their primary focus on Web searching.

These days, in the reborn era of pure search, Google is not the only engine with a streamlined, gunk-free home page. In fact, major competitors such as Yahoo! and MSN Search have followed Google's design lead on their search engine pages. In the former case, it's not too much to say that Yahoo! has explicitly copied Google, as you can see here:

```
search.yahoo.com
```

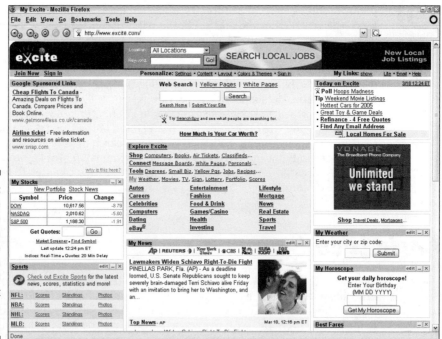

Figure 2-3: Yikes! The 1990s-style search portal is like an urban jungle. And you're not seeing the pop-up ads.

Figure 2-4:
By contrast, Google is a clean mountain stream with just one purpose: to quench your thirst for search results.

Google has embraced the purity of searching with an ad-free, horoscope-absent home page that leaves no doubt that searching is the task at hand. And its search results are so good that it has singly reshaped the search industry. Lycos, Excite, Netscape, and others barely register on anybody's radar as search engines, attractive though they may be as broad Internet portals. Some of them use the Google engine to deliver Web search results. In fact, until 2004, Yahoo! used Google search results in response to user queries. Since then, Yahoo! has developed its own search engine. Still, for millions of people who discovered or rediscovered the rewards of Internet searching through Google, to search something is to Google it.

How insensitive!

Rules dictating when to use uppercase or lowercase letters have taken a beating in the Internet's linguistic culture. The prevailing dialect of chat rooms, message boards, and e-mail discards the uppercase start to sentences as if it were an outgrown fad. Fortunately, nobody has to spruce up their typing habits for Google's sake because the search engine is oblivious to case issues — the technical term is case-insensitive.

Choosing the right keywords

Google is possibly the most forgiving search engine ever created. You can type just about any darn thing into it and get good results. Sometimes you can even get away with sloppy spelling — Google often catches it and suggests the correct spelling. Much of the crafty keywording I wrote about in *Internet Searching For Dummies* goes out the window in Google, which turns vague hints and plain-English queries into gold. Still, the first reason for disappointing search results is poor keyword choice, so some tips apply.

The golden rule in Internet searching is that more keywords deliver fewer results. So pile them on to narrow your search. With that technique, however, you run the risk of having conflicting or obfuscating keywords, creating a mixed bag of search results. Ideally, you want to concisely convey to Google what you need.

I've found that two or three is the golden number of keywords to use in Google searches. Tracking software on my Web sites tells me which search queries get to my pages, and usually the two-word strings reach my best stuff.

On the other end of the spectrum, many people get good results by typing entire sentences in the keyword box. Google eliminates certain little words such as *what* and *why,* which might seem to devalue questions but doesn't in practice.

Beware of words that have more than one meaning, especially if you search for one keyword at a time.

For power searching, in which the goal is not more results but fewer, better results, use the Advanced Search pages or the search operators, both described later in this chapter.

So let's get to it. A six-year-old would find the Google home page easy to use. When you log on to Google's home page, the mouse cursor is already waiting for you in the keyword search box. Type a word — any word. Or more than one. Or type a sentence in plain English. Press Enter or click the Google Search button. The results are on your screen within seconds.

Note the I'm Feeling Lucky button next to the Google Search button. Clicking it instead of the Google Search button takes you directly to the top search result's Web page instead of to the search results page. Only Google could dare to invite its users to skip the search results page and make it work out so well, so often. Try it. Remember: It's not a random-search button, and it works only when you've typed a keyword.

The links atop the keyword box — Web, Images, Groups, News, Froogle, Local — take you to the home pages of those sections when clicked. (A Desktop link also appears if you've installed Google Desktop, described in Chapter 13.) If you're on a search results page and click a tab, however, you get results from that link's engine instantly. So, the tabs shuttle between home pages when you don't have search results yet and shuttle between search results pages when you have one set of results in any area.

On to the search results page. That's where the action is.

Understanding the Google Results Page

Every Google search results page for a Web search includes at least three basic types of information:

- ✔ A summary of the search results
- ✔ The search results themselves
- ✔ A few things you can do with the results

Note: Many (but not all) search result pages contain additional types of information, such as sponsored links (text ads on the right side of the page and sometimes also above the search results), news links from Google News when your keywords are newsworthy, Froogle results when Google interprets your keywords to be oriented toward products, and results from your own hard drive if you are running Google Desktop (see Chapter 13).

As you can see in Figure 2-5, a Google results page can bristle with information when operating on all cylinders. The results summary is located in the shaded bar, above and to the right of the results list. The summary tells you how many total results for your keywords exist in the Google index and how long the search took. (Rarely does a Google search require more than two seconds.)

Next to the results summary, your keywords are displayed as links. When you click one of those links, you go to Answers.com for a definition of the word. This seems a bit gratuitous — if you didn't know what a word means, why would you use it as a keyword? But don't underestimate the variety of ways that people use Google, including as a dictionary. Answers.com also functions as a thesaurus, so if a certain keyword isn't delivering good results, perhaps a synonym (derived from Answers.com) would. Note that the links to Answers.com appear only when Google's language is set to English — naturally enough, because Answers.com is primarily an English dictionary.

The search results consist of the page name, which is hyperlinked to the page itself. Below that is a short bit of relevant text from the page. Below the text you can see the page's URL, which is there for information value and is not a link. Next to the URL is a number indicating the size of the page. Glancing at the page size helps you decide whether or not to visit it; pages more than 50K (that's 50 kilobytes) are too large for a quick visit if you don't have high-speed Internet access.

The Google staff doesn't compose the page title or the accompanying text, which explains why they're a little goofy sometimes and incoherent other times. The page title is created by the page developer. Some page designers forget how important the page title is, or they pack in lots of words to try and get the page higher on the search results pages of search engines such as Google. (The tactic generally doesn't work in Google, as I explain in Chapter 16.)

Name of the page   Results summary

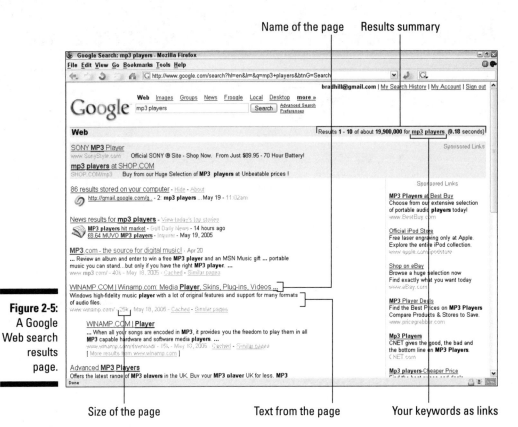

Size of the page   Text from the page   Your keywords as links

Figure 2-5:
A Google
Web search
results
page.

The text below the result link is not necessarily descriptive of the result page or even cogent. Google clips sentences and fragments that contain your key-words and presents them as evidence that you have a good hit. This is more useful than you might think. In fact, it's absolutely amazing how often a glance at the first few results and their accompanying text answers a search query without even visiting an outside page.

Note: The result link does not identify where on the result page your key-words are located. Not uncommonly, you link to a page and must then search in that page for relevant information — a headache when the page is long. You can always use your browser's Find feature to locate specific words on any Web page. However, the problem is solved more elegantly by the Google Toolbar, as described in Chapter 12.

Breaking Down Web Search Results

Three other elements are found on nearly every search results page. They are

- The Google cache
- Similar pages
- Indented results

These features enhance the value of the results page. The first two, in particular, represent hidden power that many people don't take advantage of.

The Google cache

A *cache* (pronounced "cash") is a storage area for computer files. Google maintains an enormous cache of Web pages. Don't confuse the cache with Google's Web index (which I describe more fully in Chapter 16). Actually, for practical purposes, it doesn't matter whether you confuse them or not, but they are different.

The index is a database of Web page content, stripped of its formatting. The cache contains the pages themselves. By and large, clicking the <u>Cached</u> link provides a quicker display of the target page because you're getting it from Google's computer instead of from the Internet at large.

So why would you ever *not* use the <u>Cached</u> link instead of the main page title link? Mainly because the cached page is not necessarily up-to-the-minute, especially with pages that change frequently (such as Weblogs and news sites). If you view the cached version of a page that you know changes frequently and is dated, such as the front page of a newspaper site, you can see that Google's cache is a day or more behind. For users without high-speed Internet access, it's more convenient to pull from the cache when looking for a big page (about 50K or so) that doesn't change much. You might also use the <u>Cached</u> link if the page title link refuses to display the page for some reason.

One disadvantage to pulling up a cached search result is the Google notice that appears atop all cached pages (see Figure 2-6). That is one bulky notice, taking up about two vertical inches of screen space on a screen resolution of 800 x 600. Besides being an eyesore, the notice sometimes makes additional scrolling necessary if you want to see the entire page. If you get tired of the notice, click its link to the uncached page.

Figure 2-6:
Viewing a
Google-
cached
page.
Notice that
the search
terms are
highlighted.

The cache link comes in handy when you want to take a brief trip back in time, to view a Web page that you know has changed or has been taken away. Once, David Letterman, on his late-night show, complained that the CBS site displayed a picture of Letterman's rival, Jay Leno. Letterman's show is taped in the afternoon, and by the time the show aired CBS had removed the offending image. Many people, including myself, wanted to preserve the amusing gaffe, and we did so by calling up the old page in Google's cache.

Similar pages

The Similar Pages link is interesting although not always tremendously useful. Clicking this link starts a new search for pages that somehow resemble the original search result. Sorry to be vague, but Google isn't very talkative about its Similar Pages formula.

The results are interesting and more diverse than you might expect. You'd think the search would yield a narrowed set of results, but my experience is to the contrary. Search for Britney Spears, for example, and you get a solid set of results including fan sites. Click the Similar Pages link under britney spears.com, and you get a far-ranging assortment of pages, including unofficial fan pages and sites dedicated to other singers and bands.

Searching with Similar Pages is a bit of a crapshoot — or perhaps I should say it's an adventure. Sometimes a pointless one. So when should you use Similar Pages? It's useful to get a sense of the network lurking around a Web page. Part of what the engine does with Similar Pages is explore outgoing links from the target page. On my site, for example, if I have a link to an article I wrote on another site, Similar Pages for bradhill.com will list that other site. Last time I checked, though, Similar Pages to my site also listed a Web page titled Amish Tech Support. There's no connection that I can see, though I respect the Amish and some day would like to try plowing a field. So, whenever you use Similar Pages, do so with an open mind.

Indented results

Some search results are offset from the main body of results with an indentation (look back to Figure 2-5). These indented sites are located in the same domain as the target page above them. (In Figure 2-5 the domain is www. domain.com.) They are indented to remind you that it might be redundant to click both the target page and an indented site.

Google refrains from listing all pages in a single domain that match your keywords. But you can see more results from that domain by clicking the More results from www.*domain*.com link in any indented search result. Doing so is a great way to perform a minisearch within any domain that has already proved useful to you.

Searching in a large Web site (also called a domain) can be accomplished another way: by using a special search operator called the *site* operator. This operator tells Google to apply your keywords to a specified domain. You type the *site* operator, the domain, and the keywords in a single glop of instructions. For example, if you want to search the *New York Times* for stories that mention Condoleeza Rice, you could do so with a single entry:

```
site:www.nytimes.com condoleeza rice
```

You can reverse the order of the syntax by placing the keyword(s) before the *site* operator and domain, without affecting the search results.

Using Advanced Search

Later in this chapter, I cover the use of special query terms (similar to the *site* operator just described), general search operators that can be used with keywords, and searching for specified types of documents. All these tricks and more are consolidated on the Advanced Search page, which is shown in Figure 2-7. To get to this page, click the Advanced Search link on the Google home page.

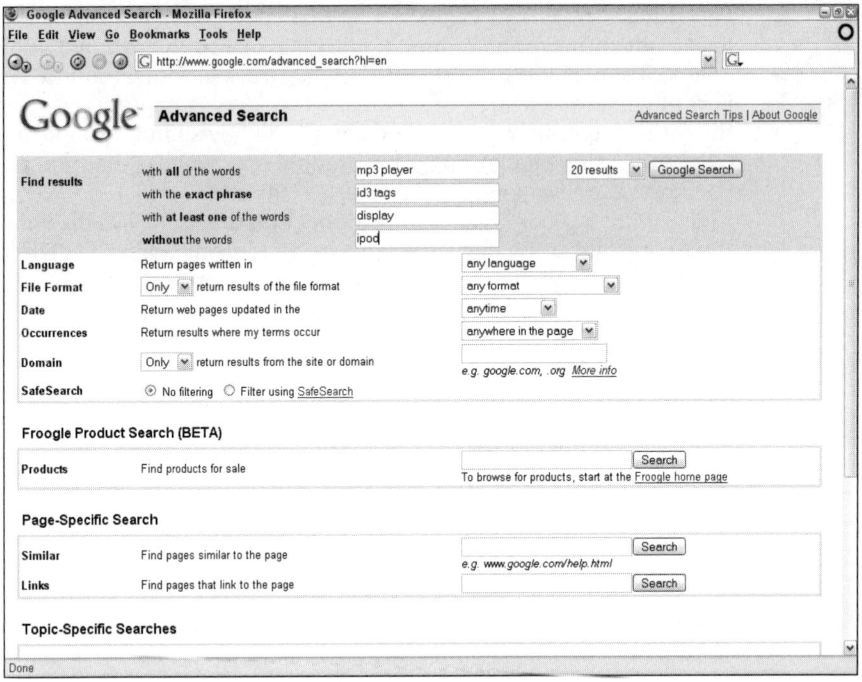

Figure 2-7:
Google's
Advanced
Search
page for
Web
searches.
Image
search has
its own
advanced
page.

Use Advanced Search for any one of three reasons:

✔ You want to focus a search more narrowly than a general keyword search.

✔ You don't want to bother with the complexity and thorny syntax of search operators.

✔ You want to combine more than one search operation.

As you see in Figure 2-7, the Advanced Search page bundles many keyword boxes and drop-down menus to launch a finely targeted search. You don't have to use everything this page has to offer. In fact, you may conduct a simple, one-keyword search from here, although that would be like using a race car to buy groceries.

Following is a review of the Advanced Search features. After setting any combination of these features, click the Google Search button to get your results.

Using multiple keywords

At the top of the Advanced Search page are a series of keyword boxes grouped in a shaded area called Find results. (See Figure 2-7.) You use the four keyword boxes in this area to tell Google how to manage multiple keywords. If you have just one keyword, type it in the top box. The instructions next to each keyword box correspond to *Boolean operators,* which are typed shorthand instructions covered later in this chapter. The Advanced Search page gives you the laser exactness of Boolean searching without all the typing.

Use these keyword boxes in the following ways:

- ✔ **With *all* of the words:** Putting keywords here forces Google to scour for pages that contain every word, with no exceptions. It has the effect of narrowing search results. For example, if you type *alan greenspan federal reserve,* you won't see irrelevant pages that contain only *alan* or only *federal.*

- ✔ **With the *exact phrase*:** This is like using quotation marks in most search engines and delivers pages that contain your keywords in the exact order and with the exact spelling that you used. You might use this option for people's names (*david hyde pierce*), sport teams with their cities (*los angeles dodgers*), and colloquial phrases (*jump the shark*).

- ✔ **With *at least one* of the words:** This option is useful when you're less picky about matching your words. It has the effect of widening search results. For example, if you're conducting broad research about building string instruments, you might type *violin cello viola* in this box, with *instrument building* in the top box.

- ✔ ***Without* the words:** Much confusion can be avoided with this keyword box, which instructs Google to eliminate matches that contain certain words. This command is useful when one of your keywords is often associated with other words. It has the effect of narrowing search results and making them more accurate. For example, if you're looking for pages about giants in fairy tales, you can stack words into this box that would match with pages about certain sports teams, such as *new york san francisco baseball football.* You'd also need to place the *giants* keyword in the top box and *fairy tale* in the exact phrase box.

Here's something to keep in mind: Google's general search results are so useful that Boolean commands are usually unnecessary. It all depends on your level of searching. If, during a general search, you find yourself looking beyond the first page of results (given thirty or fewer results per page), the Advanced Search keyword boxes might speed your searches along. Using the Advanced page is also simply fun and helps focus the search goal in your mind.

You can see how your Find results entries translate into Boolean operators by looking in the keyword box atop the search results page (and also in the blue summary bar). In the preceding example about instrument building, the Boolean search string comes out as

```
instrument building violin OR cello OR viola
```

Examining the search string on the results page is one way to get the hang of Boolean language on-the-fly. The appearance of the string also gives you a chance to adjust it for a new search without returning to the Advanced Search page.

Other Advanced Search features

The central portion of the Advanced Search page contains six settings designed to narrow your results. They are

- **Language:** Similar to the Search Language setting on the Preferences page (see the "Setting Preferences" section previously in this chapter), this pull-down menu instructs Google to return search results only in the specified language. The default setting is any language. Whereas the Preferences page has check boxes, allowing you to select multiple target languages, this menu limits your choice to a single language (or all languages). And whereas your settings on the Preferences page affect all your Googling until you change them, the Advanced Search setting affects just one search at a time.

- **File Format:** Google recognizes certain distinct file formats, such as Microsoft Word documents (which end in the .doc extension) and Adobe Acrobat (pdf) files. You can use the File Format setting to include or exclude selected file formats. Use the drop-down menu to select Only (to include your selected format) or Don't (to exclude your selected format). Then use the second pull-down menu to select the format. Feel free to ignore this setting if you're conducting a general Web search. When Any Format is selected in the second drop-down menu, your search results include all file types recognized by Google and will mostly consist of Web pages. When you get a search result in non-Web format, you can read it in its original form if you have the program associated with the file type. Or, conveniently, you can view Google's translation to Web-page format (HTML).

- **Date:** Google's index crawler can determine when a page was last changed. A page update might be as trivial as changing one word, or it might involve a massive content revision. The drop-down menu for this feature doesn't give you fine control over the update time — you may select pages updated in the past three months, past six months, and past year. That might seem useless, but one purpose of choosing three months over the default setting (anytime) is to reduce the occurrence of dead links (pages that no longer exist) in your search results.

- **Occurrences:** This powerful and useful setting whisks away questionable search results and gives you control of how important your keywords are to the matched page. The purpose is not to determine where your keywords exist in the page's text (that is, how near to the top of the page they occur), nor is it to help you avoid scrolling the page. This feature culls pages in which your keywords appear in the page title, in the page URL, or — amazingly — in the page's incoming links. (Again, Google's capability to sense the network surrounding each page is astounding and helpful.) Use the title or URL choice to powerfully narrow the search results, returning high-probability matches.

✓ **Domain:** Like the Occurrences setting, you can use this feature to include or exclude matches with certain properties. In this case, you're allowing or eliminating a certain domain, which is the portion of a site's URL after *www.* When typing the domain, you may type the *www* or leave it out. So, for the *New York Times* domain, you could type *www.nytimes.com* or *nytimes.com.* Use the first drop-down menu to choose Only (includes the selected domain and no others) or Don't (excludes the selected domain and admits all others).

✓ **SafeSearch:** The default position of this setting turns off SafeSearch if you have it turned on in your preferences. You can activate SafeSearch on a per-search basis by using this feature of the Advanced Search page. No matter what you do here, it doesn't affect your preference setting for Google searches launched from the home page.

Following are the two page-specific Advanced Search features:

✓ **Similar:** Identical to the Similar Pages link on the search results page, this feature finds pages related to the URL you type in the keyword box.

✓ **Links:** This one is addictive and shows off Google's extreme network awareness. Type a URL here, and Google finds Web pages that contain links to that page. The URL of your specified page is the keyword you type in the box. Because most large sites link to their own home pages from every other page, these searches yield a lot of tedious results from within the domain. However, it's fun to try with an inner page from a site.

Google provides the Advanced Image Search page for fancy picture searching. I describe it later in this chapter, in the "A Picture Is Worth a Thousand Keywords" section. The Advanced Search page just described relates to Web searches, not image searches.

Note: Google started including a Froogle keyword box on the Advanced Search page in 2004, after moving the Froogle link to the home page as one of Google's primary engines. Froogle is a product-based shopping engine. You may certainly start a Froogle search from here, but there is little reason to, save in those moments when you suddenly must find the cheapest Razor scooter in the midst of a search for articles about Condoleeza Rice in the *New York Times.* Chapter 4 is all about Froogle.

Searching Shorthand: Using Operators

There's no need to detour to the Advanced Search page if you know about keyword modifiers called *search operators.* Standard search operators are not unique to Google; most search engines understand them and require the same symbols and syntax when typing them. Search operators are typed with the keywords right in the keyword box. You do have to type neatly and make sure you don't add spaces in the wrong places or use the wrong case (small letters instead of capital letters).

Standard search operators fulfill the same functions as the Find results portion of the Advanced Search page. (These operators are known as Boolean operators, or Boolean commands. Dr. Mellifluous Boolean was a 17th-century explorer who discovered the island of Quiqui, brought lemons back to the Old World, and prophesied the Internet. None of which is true.) You don't need to learn search operators to get advanced results. But they're not hard to master, and doing so saves you the trip to Advanced Search and the bother of finagling with all those keyword boxes. Using operators, you can quickly type an advanced search query in the simple keyword box on Google's home page (or in the Google Toolbar or Google Deskbar, both described in Chapter 12).

Google understands standard search operators that have been in common use for years, but it also provides special commands for Google only. These unique keyword modifiers take advantage of Google's extraordinary index and bring to life Google's under-the-hood power. The next section covers standard Boolean commands. The section after that details the unique Google operators.

Typing standard search operators

If you're familiar with Boolean search operators and use them in Google or other search engines, feel free to skip this section. (Like you need my permission. By the way, be home by 11:30 tonight.) The four major Boolean operators work in Google's keyword boxes as follows:

✔ **AND:** The *AND* operator forces Google to match the search results against *all* your keywords. The operator is signified by a plus sign (+). The effect is to narrow search results, giving you fewer and more accurate hits. Place the plus sign immediately *before* any word(s) you want to force into the match, without a space between the symbol and the word, for example: *dog +chew +toy +slobber.* Keep in mind that Google naturally attempts to match all keywords without being commanded to. It always lists complete matches first, followed by Web pages that match fewer keywords. So the *AND* operator is well used with long keyword strings to force a single-word match even when other words in the string are not matched. An example of the latter is *recipe cookbook ingredients +vegetarian.* In this example, vegetarian is the main focus, and every matched page must contain that word. Whether it's a page about recipes or cookbooks or ingredients is less important.

✔ **NOT:** The *NOT* operator excludes words that might otherwise bring up many undesirable page matches. The effect is to narrow search results. The symbol is a minus sign (-). Like the *AND* operator, place the symbol immediately before a word. In using it, you should think of anti-keywords that would thwart the mission of your pro-keywords. For example, you might type *kayak lake -canoe -whitewater.* (Nothing against canoes, but if you haven't tried kayaking, what on earth are you waiting for?)

✔ **OR:** Not as wishy-washy as you might think, the *OR* operator is helpful when using obscure keywords that might not return much of value if used singly. It also neatly divides a search along two concurrent avenues of exploration. There is no symbol for this one; simply type *OR* (use capital letters) before a keyword and leave a space between the operator and the following keyword. Google then accepts matches to the keyword preceding the operator or following the operator, such as *wintry climate maine OR antarctica.*

✔ **Quotes:** Identical to the Exact phrase feature of the Advanced Search page, the quote operator tells Google which keyword sequence or keyword phrase to leave untouched. Google can't assume you have misspelled something, and it can't change the word order to create a match. Whatever you type within the quotes is interpreted and matched literally by Google. The quote operator is best used with keyword groups in which each word could return its own set of irrelevant results, for example: *"old town" canoes prices.*

If you forget to close the quotation at the end of the quotes-applied keywords, Google will extend the quote operator to the end of your keyword string, possibly reducing your matches to zero.

One operator that stands between basic and special functionality is the synonym operator, which is activated by typing a tilde (~). Placing a tilde immediately before a keyword (no space) commands Google to match not only the keyword, but its synonyms. So this keyword string:

```
~auto ~purchase
```

would match Web sites as if you had typed, for example, *auto buy* or *car purchase.*

Mix up search operators as much as you like. Here are a few examples:

```
television -cable -satellite "rural living"
"brad hill" +dummies -idiots
chocolate +dark OR bittersweet
stepdaughter +delinquent OR evil "why me"
```

Understanding special Google operators

Now this is fun. Google has invented its own search operators that work in the Google index. They enable fancy search tricks, some of which are also represented on the Advanced Search page. Knowing these operators takes a bit of memorization, and using them gives you power over the Google home page, circumventing Advanced Search.

Google-specific operators use a colon to separate the command from the keyword string. The format is like this:

```
operator:keyword string
```

Some Google operators require that you leave no space between the colon and the first keyword, as in the preceding. It doesn't matter with other operators. Because I don't want to remember which is which, I always crush the first keyword up against the operator's colon (this sounds like a medical condition).

You may use Boolean operators in the keyword string when the string is preceded by a Google operator, like this:

```
allintitle:new times -york
```

There are several Google-specific operators:

- ✔ **cache:** If you know the Web page address, use this operator to pull up Google's cache of that page. By itself, not too useful. But the *cache* operator has an intriguing hidden feature. If you type a keyword after the page URL, Google highlights that word throughout the cached document that it displays. For example, try *cache:www.lycos.com music.*

- ✔ **link:** This operator performs the same function as the Links feature on the Advanced Search page, finding pages that contain a link to whatever URL you specify. For example, *link:www.dummies.com* displays sites that contain a link to `www.dummies.com`. If you operate a site, running a search with this operator lets you check who is linking to your site — a great tool if you operate a Blogger site.

- ✔ **info:** An operator that consolidates informational links about a site, *info* is paired with a URL keyword. The result is the Google index entry for that page, plus links to view the cached page, similar sites, and pages that link to that URL. For information about the Google home page, for example, type *info:www.google.com.*

- ✔ **filetype:** Google can search for twelve types of document besides HTML documents that make up Web pages. One of the most common file types people want to find is PDF, a format that you can read with Adobe Acrobat Reader. Many official forms and academic papers are created in the PDF format. Finding tax forms using the *filetype pdf* operator command is a breeze when that command is part of a keyword string that also contains the form name or number. Other commonly searched file types are text (txt), Microsoft PowerPoint (ppt), Microsoft Excel (xls), and Microsoft Word (doc). Google can't find MP3 or video files with this operator.

✔ **related:** Use this operator in place of the Similar Pages link. The *related* operator is paired with a site URL. A keyword string including this operator might look like this: *related:www.cdbaby.com.*

✔ **site:** Use this operator in your keyword string to limit results to a specified domain. It's a good way to search online newspapers, such as *alan greenspan site:www.usatoday.com.* Combined with the quote operator, you can get pretty specific results in a newspaper site, for example, *"axis of evil" site:www.nytimes.com.* This operator even works with domain extensions, such as *.gov* and *.edu,* without using a domain. Knowing this, you can search for keywords matching university or government pages, such as *"code orange" site:gov.*

✔ **intitle** and **allintitle:** These operators restrict your results to pages in which one or more of your keywords appear in the page title. The *intitle* command affects the single keyword (or group of keywords in quotes) immediately following the operator. All other keywords following the first might be found anywhere on the page. For example, *intitle:tiger woods golf* assures that result pages are about Tiger Woods, not Bengal tigers. The *allintitle* command forces Google to match all your keywords with page titles. This operator can severely narrow a search. For example, the last time I checked, the *allintitle:carrot top nobel prize* search string returned no results. On the other hand, it's great for homing in on useful pages, as when searching for product reviews (see Figure 2-8).

✔ **intext** and **allintext:** Using these operators, Google restricts the search to the text of pages, excluding the URL, title, and links. Use the *intext* operator mainly for single keywords: *intext:labradors.* Use *allintext* for keyword strings: *allintext:labrador retrievers.* Had the *intext* operator been used in the second example, Google would have matched only the keyword *labrador* to the text of found pages.

✔ **inanchor** and **allinanchor:** Restricting a search to *link anchors* is a potent search technique. Link anchors are the visible portions of hyperlinks that you see on Web pages. If a link appears as Click this link, the phrase "Click this link" is the anchor. You can restrict your search to the link anchors of pages. Fascinatingly, this puts your results one step back from normal keyword matches. Instead of matching pages that are rich with your keywords, you are likely to match pages that explicitly *link* to keyword-rich pages. Use *inanchor* with single keywords and *allinanchor* with multiple keywords when you want each keyword in the string to match link anchors.

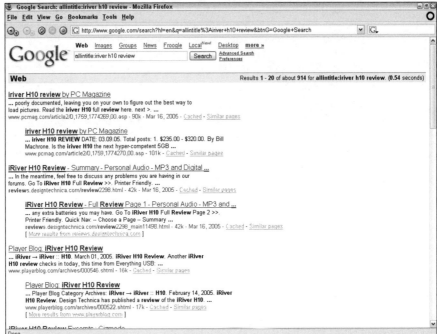

Figure 2-8:
Using the
allintitle
operator to
find product
reviews.
Every hit is a
good one.

> ✔ **inurl** and **allinurl:** These function similarly to *intitle* and *allintitle* but restrict search results to pages that contain one or more of your keywords in the page's URL. The result is a drastic narrowing of search results, but it's an interesting way to discover new sites with great domain names. For example, *inurl:diaper* returns *www.dog-diaper.com* as the first result. Another example is *allinurl:purple elephant,* which displays results, believe it or not. Note that using *allinurl* with two or more keywords is likely to match pages deep within Web sites with very long URLs.

Power Googling is all about knowing the operators and skipping the Advanced Search page. The more authority over the Google index you can wield on the home page, with its simple keyword box, the quicker you'll be on your way with great search results.

A Picture Is Worth a Thousand Keywords

Image searching in Google is less complex than Web searching and is fun in different ways. For example, you can search for pictures of people you haven't seen in years, for postcard-like images of travel destinations, or for pictures of yourself.

Google's task is a tricky one. It must match your keyword(s) with pictures — a far harder task than matching words with text. At best, Google can make educated guesses about the identity or subject matter of a picture based on the file name of the picture, the URL address of the image, the surrounding text, and any caption. So the results are bound to be erratic. Fortunately, Google errs on the side of abundance, delivering truckloads of possible photos and other images in response to your keywords.

Simple searches are identical to Web searches. From the Google home page, click the Images tab, enter a keyword or two, and press Enter. You can even use the *site, intitle, allintitle, inurl,* and *allinurl* operators described in the preceding section when searching for images.

It's in the search results that things differ from Web searches. Image results come in the form of *thumbnails* — small versions of images. Click any thumbnail to see a larger version of the image, along with the Web page on which it resides. Google reproduces the image above the Web page containing the image — arguably a big waste of space. (Click the Remove Frame link at the top right of the page to get rid of it.) This second reproduction of the image is usually a thumbnail, too, albeit a somewhat larger one. You may click this thumbnail to see a full-size version of the picture. Or you can scroll down the page to see the picture in context.

In November 2004, some enterprising Google users began making noise about not being able to find images of the Iraq war in Google Images. They made enough noise to prompt a confession from Sergey Brin, one of Google's founders. "We are embarrassed that our image index is not updated as frequently as it should be," Sergey stated. "Expect a refresh in the near future." Indeed, the update came along, but the currency of Google Images was damaged. On the day I wrote this paragraph, Google Images failed to display a picture of the iPod Shuffle, a wildly popular MP3 player introduced two months earlier. If you can't find a current events photo in Google Images, try performing a photo search in the Google Web index, which turns up photos when asked for them. Use the word *photos* in your keyword string. This trick sometimes works, but not always — indeed, it failed to show the Shuffle.

Advanced Image Searching

As with Web searches, Google provides a collection of enhanced search tools on the Advanced Image Search page (see Figure 2-9). Follow these steps to reach that page:

1. **Go to the Google home page.**
2. **Click the Images tab.**
3. **Click the Advanced Image Search link.**

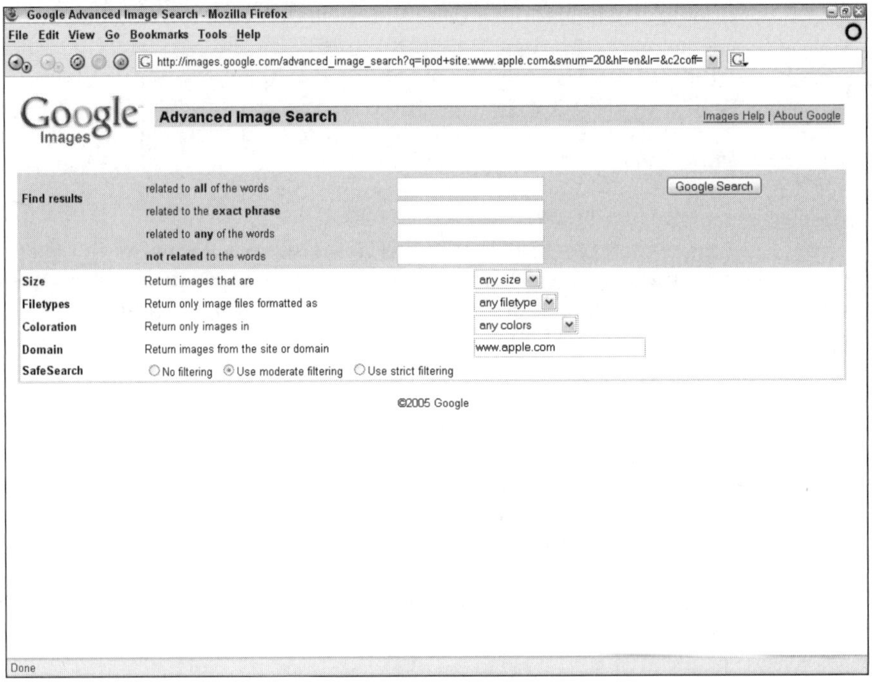

Figure 2-9:
The
Advanced
Image
Search
page.

The Find results portion of the Advanced Image Search page is nearly identical to the Advanced Search page for Web searches. (See the "Using Advanced Search" section earlier in this chapter.) The difference is that the keyword modifiers here relate to images by matching file names, captions, and text surrounding the images. Use the keyword boxes to add search modifiers to your keywords, but don't expect exact textual matches as with a Web search because images are not text.

Below the Find results portion of the Advanced Image Search page are five settings that determine the type and location of the images you are seeking:

- ✔ **Size:** Use the drop-down menu to restrict your search to images of certain sizes. Admittedly, the choices are vague: icon-sized, small, medium, large, very large, and wallpaper-sized. By themselves, these choices are nearly meaningless. They refer generally to image dimensions, not file size. A wallpaper-sized picture can be contained in a smaller file size than a medium picture.

- ✔ **Filetypes:** Use this drop-down menu to select JPG, GIF, or PNG files. As a practical matter, these file formats are nearly interchangeable. Whatever you plan to do with your found images, you can probably do equally well with any one of those three types. Accordingly, I always leave this feature set to its default, which is any filetype.

- ✔ **Coloration:** Here you can choose to locate black-and-white pictures, grayscale images, or full-color art. Full-color images are usually the largest file sizes.

- ✔ **Domain:** Use this keyword box to specify a Web domain that you want to search for images. This is a helpful way to search online newspaper graphics.

- ✔ **SafeSearch:** With the three SafeSearch options, you can determine the level of filtering Google will apply to your image search. The choices are identical to the SafeSearch preference settings (see the first section of this chapter), but apply to only one search at a time.

In nearly all cases, the images you find through Google are owned and implicitly copyrighted by other people. There is some buzz among copyright scholars about the capability of search engines to display other people's property on demand. Google itself puts a little copyright warning about using the images dished up in its search results. If you're wondering whether you can download and apply a photo as desktop wallpaper, for example, the quick legal answer is no in most cases. The search results are meant to be informational, and Google is not intended as a warehouse of downloadable images.

How you choose to approach online intellectual property is your business, but respect for the property of others strengthens the online community. Besides, in Google of all places, it's not too hard to find images whose owners invite downloads. Try using the keywords *public domain* or *free download* on the Advanced Image Search page to find images that you can legally reuse.

You may use search operators in Google Images, just as you do in Google Web searches. Some Web search operators, such as *intext* and *info,* don't apply to images. The best image operators to use are

- ✔ **intitle:** Find photos in Web pages that contain certain keywords in the page titles.

- ✔ **filetype:** Use this operator to find certain image file types, specifically JPG, GIF, and PNG. (Most people find no practical value in discriminating between these file types.)

- ✔ **inurl:** Find images in Web pages whose URLs contain your keywords.

- ✔ **site:** Restrict your image search to certain site domains or specific pages.

These operators help narrow a search but do not eliminate the fundamental problem, which is that most photos posted online are not named in a way that allows Google to easily identify them or match them with intelligent keywords. Constant experimentation and persistence are required.

Part II
Taming Google

The 5th Wave   By Rich Tennant

"No Stuart, I won't look up 'rampaging elephants' on the Internet. We're studying plant life and right now photosynthesis is a more pertinent topic."

In this part . . .

*P*art II explores the small collection of select Google services linked to the Google home page. Those links are important because they enable you to throw your search query into any of the engines described in this part with a single click — no need to retype keywords or surf to another site.

Chapter 3 is a revolution all by itself. (Not to mention a revelation.) You get acquainted with single-word commands that make Google divulge practical information such as word definitions, stock prices, weather forecasts, calculations, and phone numbers. No longer must you call up entire Web sites to get simple answers. Chapter 4 takes you into Froogle and Google Catalogs, where your consumer lusts will be inflamed and directed to the destinations where they may be sated. Chapter 5 rebuilds your life around Google News, an interactive, customizable global newsstand that has altered the virtual lives of sunshine-deprived souls everywhere. Chapter 6 navigates the rocky shoals of the incredible Google Groups and spits you out safely on the other side. Chapter 7 drills into the Google Directory.

This part isn't about sharing pictures of your kids on AOL. This is a life-enhancing skill set designed to rattle your matrix and supercharge your relationship to the living global network writhing on the other side of your computer screen. So shift your eyes to the right and start the first moment of a new virtual life. [Editors' note: Brad Hill claimed to be out of decaf, but we noticed a trail of unused coffee beans leading to his garbage can. We promise to get a handle on his caffeine dosing before Part III.]

Chapter 3

Recovering the Facts: Using Google as an Answer Engine

*U*nrecognized power. That's what this chapter is about, because most people I talk to have no idea that Google is so smart in so many ways. Some of the features highlighted in this chapter have been talked up since the publication of *Google For Dummies,* and you might be aware of them. But others, like instant stock quotes and the valuable Google Q&A, have been introduced recently. I think this chapter holds something new for every reader.

Most of the features in this chapter demonstrate Google's ability to deliver factual information directly to the results page, rather than forcing you to click through to another page. A few features still require clicking through to another site, but are useful nonetheless. Every feature represents Google's attempt, when faced with a factual question that would normally be answered by a reference source, to behave more like an answer engine than a Web search engine.

Search Engines and Answer Engines

Google is a search engine. You know that. But there exists another species of keyword searching called an *answer engine.* Answer engines differ from search engines by displaying direct answers to queries, as opposed to lists of Web sites. When using a search engine, your hope is that you'll find some useful pieces of Internet content. You might be seeking information or entertainment, knowledge or communication. Web sites offer many experiences, and search engines such as Google specialize in cataloguing Web sites.

Answer engines sometimes acknowledge the Web by presenting links to other sites in search results, but those links and other sites are not the main course. Answers are the main course, taken either from Web sites or from reference sources. Either way, the distinguishing characteristic of answer engines is that you don't click search results to get what you want; the information you're after is given to you directly.

One simple example of an answer engine's function is a word definition. If you look up a word in a dictionary, you don't want the book to direct you to another book — you just want the word's spelling and meaning. By the same token, you don't want a search engine pointing you to another site for a simple answer. Google used to link its users to another site for simple word definitions; now it defines the word directly. That's an example of Google taking on the characteristics of an answer engine.

It has become competitively important for search engines to provide quicker answers to reference queries of many sorts. The following sections describe several (sometimes surprising) ways that you can hit Google with a fast query and move on with the answer in hand, without unnecessary linkage.

What, Where, When, and How in Google

After introducing a variegated selection of fact-based services, Google launched a highly informed, nicely integrated answer service called Google Q&A in April 2005. Don't confuse Google Q&A with Google Answers, the paid answer service described in Chapter 10. Google Q&A is an automated service that you access directly from Google's home page (or from the Google Toolbar or Deskbar); Google Answers is staffed by human researchers and is located on its own pages. Google Q&A is not a well-defined service; it works to one degree or another depending on the wording of your query. Basically, if you ask a question in the right way, Google delivers an answer above the regular search results. Figure 3-1 shows Google Q&A in action.

Note that you do not need to put a question mark in your keyword string to denote a fact-based query. Pretend you're a zombie asking the question with no inflection whatsoever. A zombie with a thirst for knowledge.

If at first Google does not succeed, keep pestering it. In the example shown in Figure 3-1, the query is *who is van cliburn,* referring to the legendary American pianist who achieved stardom by winning the Tchaikovsky Competition in Moscow in 1958. Alternate queries, including *when did van cliburn get famous* and *when did van cliburn win the tchaikovsky competition,* got me nowhere. With a little bit of knowledge, you can get better instant information with a non-questioning keyword string. Figure 3-2 shows the Web results for *van cliburn moscow.* If you know that Van Cliburn did something important in Moscow, the first search result in Figure 3-2 gives you more information than the *who is van cliburn* query.

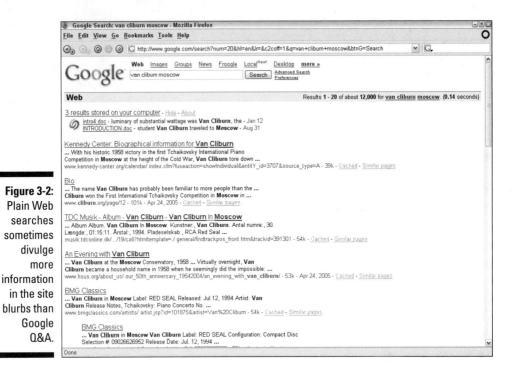

Figure 3-2:
Plain Web searches sometimes divulge more information in the site blurbs than Google Q&A.

Preceding all your Google Q&A questions with questioning words such as *what, where,* or *who* helps Google understand that you're asking a question. A question mark is not necessary. In some cases (try *population of japan*), questioning words are also not necessary. But they never hurt and often help.

Leaning on Wikipedia

Where do Google's answers come from? From a range of reference sources, not least of which is Wikipedia. In fact, if you use Google Q&A several times, it becomes apparent that Wikipedia enjoys prominence in the answers. (As Figure 3-1 illustrates, the answer source is cited immediately below the answer. Click that link to see a complete entry from which Google extracted the answer.) Wikipedia is a remarkable online encyclopedia written and edited by its readers. Anyone can post an entry, add to an entry, or edit an entry. With everybody chipping in and no formal editorial control, you might wonder how authoritative Wikipedia is as a reference source. The truth is that it's pretty good, thanks to dedicated work by some enthusiastic volunteers. Certainly good enough for basic Q&A.

Answers.com, a more traditional collection of reference sources, and a partner site to which Google turns for word definitions (described later in this chapter), is not used for Google Q&A answers as of this writing.

Knowing Your Words

The most elemental type of reference question involves word definitions. Google provides three methods of finding out what words mean:

- ✔ Using the *define* operator
- ✔ Using the *glossary* keyword in a keyword string
- ✔ Using the definition links that appear on nearly every search results page

The *define* operator is fast and useful. Its presence before a keyword forces Google to reach into its glossary (which is not really a built-in glossary, but don't worry about that) and pull out relevant definitions. Figure 3-3 shows Google responding to the keyword string *define:blade server,* a type of computer. Note that multiple definitions are presented when available. Often the competing definitions give a rounded understanding of the word without clicking through any of them. Note, also, the presence of Wikipedia as a source (see the "Leaning on Wikipedia" sidebar).

Figure 3-3:
Using the *define* operator brings up word and phrase definitions from multiple sources.

The *define* operator generally works best with words and phrases that have specific meanings, but you can get lucky using it with search phrases. For example, the keyword string *define:labrador dog* works well, as does *define: labrador retriever*. You can also use the operator to flesh out your knowledge of something — for example, if you're familiar with memory cards but don't know the names of available types, search this: *define:memory card*. More than a dozen definitions spill the beans on Compact Flash, SmartMedia, and other types.

Using *glossary* as a keyword brings up useful results, but of a different type. The word isn't a search operator, and you're not using it with operator syntax (the colon following the word and preceding other words). So, the results are links to Web pages that probably contain explanations of your words. Using the *memory card* example in the preceding paragraph, try this keyword string: *glossary memory card*. Figure 3-4 illustrates the results, which link to Web-based definitions. This method of discovering word meanings is not as concise as using the *define* operator and often requires clicking through to an outside page. The upside is that you might get a deeper discussion or examination of your words.

Figure 3-4:
Adding the word *glossary* to the keyword string displays definitions within result sites.

The final method of defining words is to rely on the definition links that appear in the summary bar of most search results pages. Look at Figure 3-4, in the shaded area just above the results, on the right. Each word — *glossary, memory,* and *card* — is linked. Those links take you to Answers.com, a great reference and word-definition site. The fact that each word is individually linked demonstrates the downfall of relying on this method. Google is providing the opportunity to define each of those words, including *glossary,* which, of course, was used merely to bring up Web sites with definitions. And *memory card* is treated not as a phrase but as two unrelated words. (Even if you had used the phrase operator, putting *memory card* in quotes, Google would have ripped the words away from each other and linked them individually.)

Because Google's link to Answers.com doesn't recognize the meaning of phrases, the Answers.com links are best used with individual keywords, after the act of searching when you want clarification of a keyword's meaning. Let's go back to the *blade server* keyphrase. Search on this string: *glossary blade server.* Figure 3-5 shows the results. At this point, perhaps you realize that you need to enhance your understanding of the term *server* to fully appreciate definitions of *blade server.* Click the linked word <u>server</u> in the summary bar. Figure 3-6 shows the Answers.com page that comes up — the fifth definition is the one you need.

Figure 3-5: Google links your keywords to Answers. com and separates two words of a phrase when doing so.

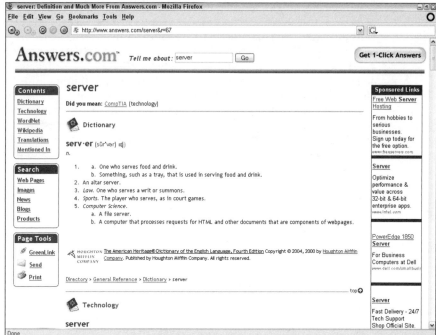

Figure 3-6:
Answers.
com is an
excellent
reference
site used by
Google to
define
keywords.

Invading People's Privacy

This should be fun. Two of Google's great and long-standing features are its phone book and reverse phone book. And they are drastically underused; even people who turn to Google ten times a day don't know they exist. (The features, not the people.)

If you type a person's name and address into the keyword box, Google will divulge the phone number — listed numbers only. You don't even need to know the entire address. Or the entire name. Last name and zip code do the trick. So do other combinations, including:

- ✔ First and last names, plus city or state or area code or zip code
- ✔ Last name, plus city and state or area code or zip code

Note that if you don't know the first name, you need the city *and* state, not either by itself. You should also know that Google understands names in order, but wimps out if you put the last name first.

Now for the good part. Google reverses the process, delivering a name and address if you can dredge up the phone number. The area code is required. Don't put any prefixes (such as 1) before it, and don't type parentheses around the area code, and don't worry about putting in spaces. Just type ten straight digits.

Google is at least one year behind in phone listings. There's no gentle way to say it. The feature is useless for new numbers.

Forget about names and phone numbers; try typing an address. Google recognizes addresses even when they're incomplete, and offers to link you to a map. (With egalitarian spirit, Google offers a choice of its own mapping service and two others.) Zip codes by themselves trip the map invitation, as do street names without numbers (followed by city and state or zip code). Even telephone area codes work by themselves. In some cases, an address brings up phone book results, especially of businesses whose names contain a street name, such as East Street Bistro. Figure 3-7 shows an example of this dual result: map and phone book results.

Figure 3-7:
Google sometimes delivers map and phone book results.

Tracking Packages

Many online retailers allow their customers to track the delivery of packages, either by providing a tracking service at the e-commerce site or by linking them to UPS, FedEx, or the U.S. Post Office site. Google simplifies these multiple destinations by providing a single location for putting in numbers related to all three delivery services. Google doesn't display the tracking information on its own pages; it merely provides a link to the appropriate service when you enter a tracking number.

Of course, you must have a tracking number for Google's feature to work. When supplied by an e-tailer, the number is usually on an order confirmation page or in an e-mail sent by the online store. You can also track outgoing packages that you've sent; the tracking number is found on the receipt you get after dropping off the package. Simply type the number into Google's keyword box.

Google at the Movies

Google's involvement with movie information started recently. You can get movie information in a standard Google search in three ways:

✔ Display movie times for theaters in your location

✔ Display information about a particular movie

✔ Use the *movie* operator to find movie-related information about your keywords

The simplest movie search you can perform is to type *movie* as a keyword. Google prompts you for a location by zip code. After you enter the zip, Google displays movie showtimes by film or theater — the latter usually being the more useful (see Figure 3-8).

Typing a movie title likewise cues Google to deliver movie-specific information, in the form of movie times for that title in the zip code you typed before. (If you didn't yet enter your zip, Google asks for it.)

The *movie* operator is the most productive path into the Google movie index. You can be fairly imprecise with your keywords and get good results. For example, at the time of this writing, Woody Allen's latest movie (*Melinda and Melinda*) was playing, and I wanted to read reviews but couldn't remember the title. Was it *Melissa and Melissa?* That didn't turn up anything useful. The keyword string *movie:woody allen's latest* delivered the page shown in Figure 3-9, which is representative of the type of result obtained with the *movie* operator.

Click the movie title and you get something like Figure 3-10, which is a handy resource. Google sorts reviews into positives, negatives, and neutrals, and links to actors associated with the movie.

Figure 3-8:
Google's
display
of movie
showtimes
by theater.

Figure 3-9:
Google
displays
results from
an extensive
database
of movie
information.

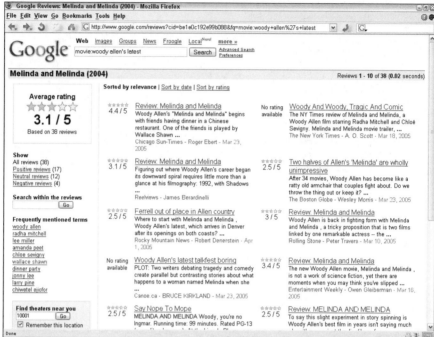

Figure 3-10:
Google sorts
a wide
range of
movie
reviews.

Stock Quotes, Math, and the Weather

Google has always dabbled in stock quotes, but until recently it merely linked
to finance sites when you entered a ticker symbol as a keyword. It's a bit of a
mystery why Google didn't deliver the information directly sooner, but no
matter — Google eventually came around. Now you can see stock quotes and
simple price charts atop the Google results page, as shown in Figure 3-11.

The Google calculator is another widely unrecognized feature. Using your
keyboard to type numbers and arithmetical operators, you can perform algebraic, trigonometric, and logarithmic equations. I can hardly believe I just
used the words *algebraic, trigonometric,* and *logarithmic* in a sentence. I must
lie down for a bit, but before I go, make note of this page:

```
www.google.com/help/calculator.html
```

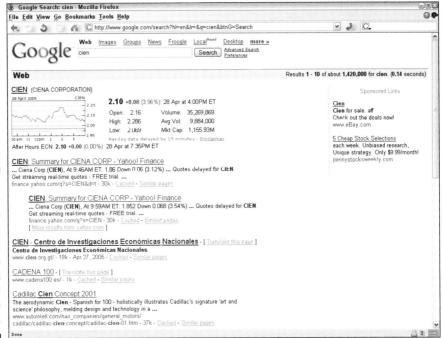

Figure 3-11:
Enter a ticker symbol and Google delivers stock quotes and simple price charts.

That page gives complete instructions in using the Google Calculator. Some operations are simple enough to be intuitive, such as *2+2,* typed directly into the keyword box. (You never need to type an equal sign; Google knows you want the answer.) Other operations are more complicated, and if I attempt an explanation I'll have to nap for the rest of the week.

Handily, Google Calculator performs conversions from one measurement system to another. For example, the keyword string *5 feet in centimeters* yields the result in centimeters. The word *in* informs Google that you're asking for a conversion.

One final Google informational perk: the weather. Use the *weather* operator paired with a zip code to get a four-day forecast, as shown in Figure 3-12.

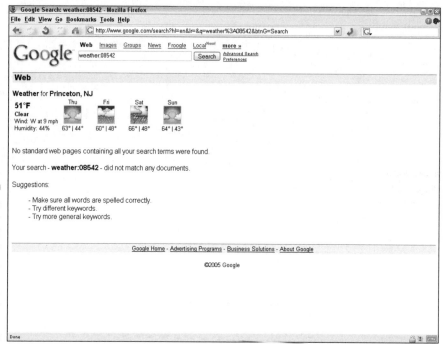

Figure 3-12:
No need for
a dedicated
weather
page;
Google
delivers
four-day
forecasts.

Chapter 4

Froogle and Google Catalogs Rescue Your Gift List

· ·

In This Chapter

▶ Introducing the Google shopping portal

▶ Searching and browsing in Froogle

▶ Special Froogle search operators

▶ Advanced searching in Froogle

▶ Introducing the dazzling Google Catalogs

▶ Browsing mail-order catalogs with the Google Catalogs control bar

· ·

*G*oogle, the world's most intelligent search engine, has an academic, ivory-tower sheen. The science behind its index and the insightfulness of its results lend Google an otherworldly feeling. Except . . . shopping! Shopping is a common denominator of the Web — everybody likes to buy stuff. Google turns its all-seeing eye to the swarming, steamy jungle of e-commerce.

Yes, Google is a shopping portal, but not of the sort you might be familiar with in AOL and Yahoo!. Google provides two shopping directories and applies its insightful, destination-ranking intelligence to them. The result is a sharp, objective, results-oriented, virtual window-shopping experience.

This chapter covers the details of Froogle, a keyword-empowered shopping directory, and Google Catalogs, an online mail-order browsing environment. Both are delightful — and more powerful than many people realize. The following sections cover basic keywords and clicks, and then introduce a few tricks I use in Froogle and Google Catalogs.

Neither Froogle nor Google Catalogs is a new service; earlier versions of both were covered in *Google For Dummies,* which was published when most people had not heard of either one. Froogle has become much more recognized and used since Google moved its link to the home page. Most people I speak to are still unaware of Google Catalogs.

Froogle and Google Catalogs are still in *beta,* meaning they are still being tested by Google and its users. There's no danger here, because nothing new gets installed in your computer. If you have specific suggestions, complaints, or words of adulation about Froogle or Google Catalogs, voice them by using these two e-mail addresses:

   ✔ For Froogle: `froogle-support@google.com`

   ✔ For Google Catalogs: `catalog-support@google.com`

Google's Approach to Online Shopping

The main difference between Google's shopping services and those in other major portals is that Google doesn't get its hands on the money. You don't buy anything through Google. Both Froogle and Google Catalogs function purely as directories to products, sending you elsewhere to buy the goods. Google has no revenue-sharing association with e-commerce retailers (in Froogle) or mail-order companies (in Google Catalogs). The search results you get in both services are pure; Google does not sell preferred placement in the search results lists.

The inevitable comparison is between Froogle and Yahoo! Shopping. (Google Catalogs is unique and can't be compared to anything else online.) Yahoo! Shopping is a virtual mall whose directory and search results list Yahoo!'s stores and non-Yahoo! stores. Banners for featured stores hog a portion of the front page. Yahoo! hosts many of the most important online retailers in the business. Yahoo!'s search engine shows off some smarts, breaking down many searches into brand listings. It also has a nice price-comparison engine.

Keeping a multitude of stores under one virtual roof has other advantages, first among them being a shared shopping cart and payment wallet. You can load up products from multiple stores, and then pay for them all at once. You provide your credit card and shipping information just once; the information is then stored on Yahoo!'s computer. AOL and MSN have similar programs. Systems like this are purchase oriented, whereas Google is search oriented. Google is not (currently) interested in handling purchase transactions, taking payment information, or hosting stores. There is no "Google Wallet."

When it comes to buying through Google, *through* is the right word (as opposed to *from*). Froogle search results are like Web search results, insofar as they link you to target sites, in this case e-commerce sites with their own shopping carts and payment systems. Google Catalogs provides mail-order phone numbers and — where possible — links to Web sites.

Searching and Browsing in Froogle

Your Froogle experience starts on the Froogle home page:

```
froogle.google.com
```

Before Google moved Froogle to the home page on Google's American site, Froogle displayed a directory-style browsing interface. Things have changed — I suppose because Google discovered that people were searching with keywords more than browsing directory categories. It's worth noting that Google has removed the Web directory link from its home page. Certainly, in Froogle, it is easier to cut to the chase, querying directly for the type of product you seek, than to drill slowly through directory levels.

As you can see in Figure 4-1, Froogle now presents a bare search engine, with a constantly changing array of recent Froogle searches, presumably for inspiration.

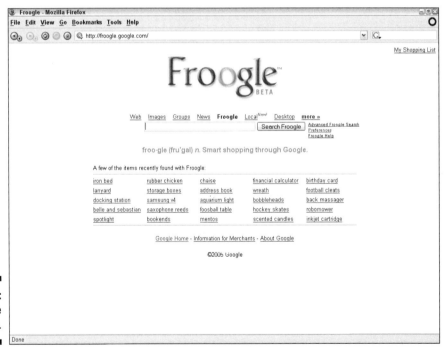

Figure 4-1:
The Froogle
home page.

Actually, a Froogle directory still exists, and you can dive into it from the Search within portion of the left navigation bar on search result pages. That explanation is a bit opaque, so let me step through finding the Froogle directory using a sample search for the keywords *tennis rackets:*

1. **Go to Froogle and search for *tennis rackets.***

2. **On the results page (see Figure 4-2), look for the Search within header in the left sidebar.**

    Three directory categories are listed: All Categories, which is the level of your current search (Froogle's entirety); Sports & Outdoors; and Tennis & Racquet Sports.

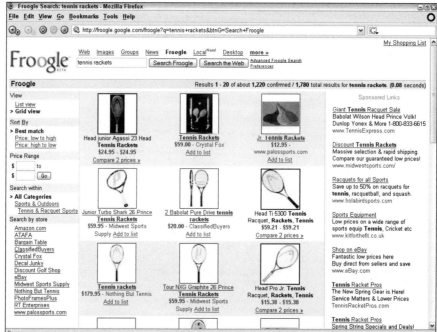

Figure 4-2:
A Froogle results page. Note the many sorting options in the left sidebar.

3. **Click the Sports & Outdoors category.**

    Clicking the category performs another search of Froogle, this time restricted to that category. The results might not change much, since Froogle is good at delivering properly categorized results from the home page. (You could also have clicked the Tennis & Racquet Sports category; either will get you to the next step.) Remember: If you conduct a new search with new keywords from this page, you remain in the

Sports & Outdoors category. Shifting gears with non-sports keywords on this page would lead to interesting and baffling results.

4. **On the Sports & Categories page, click the <u>Browse Sports & Outdoors</u> link.**

This click brings up a directory page, as shown in Figure 4-3.

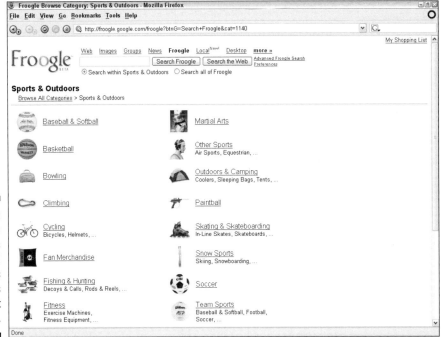

Figure 4-3: The Froogle directory is hard to find and not as useful as direct searching.

Once in the directory at any level, you can stay in the directory and surface to the top level by clicking the <u>Browse All Categories</u> link. There, you see an overview of the whole Froogle product universe.

After you get into the directory, your search options change. From the home page, your search encompasses all of Froogle. On any directory page, you may opt to limit your search to the subcategory at hand. The options below the keyword box (see Figure 4-3) default to limiting the search, but you can search all of Froogle by clicking the other radio button.

In Froogle, a keyword search is by and large more rewarding than directory browsing. Presumably, when shopping, you have an idea of what you're looking for, and using a keyword gets you to that product page faster than pushing down into the directory.

Search results in Froogle

Whether through browsing or keyword searching, you eventually reach a Froogle product page (refer to Figure 4-2). The product page is where you see individual items for sale. They are for sale only through their host sites — not through Google.

The product page contains several main features:

- **Keyword box:** You may launch a new search from any Froogle directory or product page.

- **Results summary:** This familiar feature tells you how long the search took and how items were found. Most searches reveal two result totals: confirmed results and total results. Confirmed results represent those products submitted by merchants, not found by Froogle during its Web crawl. Total results include everything — submitted and found results. Confirmed results are more valuable because of their near-guaranteed accuracy, so Froogle always presents them first.

- **View:** You may display the results in a list or a grid. Figure 4-2 shows the grid display, which I prefer because it shows more results on the screen. These controls are on the left side of the page.

- **Sort by:** The default setting here is Best match, which brings up results that most closely match your keywords, regardless of price. Use the other links to order the results by price: low to high or high to low.

- **Price range:** This is useful, especially when gift shopping with a budget in mind. Specify a price range and click the Go button.

- **Search within:** This feature invites you to enter new keywords that search within the current results.

- **Search by store:** Results pages list the top stores selling the products matching your keywords. Click a store to see all matching items sold by that store.

- **Product name and photo:** In the main portion of the page, the product name is the main link to its page in the host store. You may also get there by clicking the photo.

- **Product price and store name:** Here you find the basic stats: price, store name, and short product description.

- **Sponsored links:** In the right sidebar, text ads related to your keywords are displayed. These ads are of the same type as on the results pages of Web searches. In Froogle, the ads tend to be exceptionally relevant and useful; you can sometimes get better search results by clicking a Froogle ad than you can from nonsponsored Froogle results.

Price comparisons in Froogle

Froogle can become a handy price-comparison search engine if you know the brand and model number of the item you're shopping for. Even if you don't know that information going in, Froogle can help you compare prices of any product you find while searching. Here's how it works:

1. **On the Froogle home page, start a search for some type of product.**

   To follow along with the example, search for *digital camera.*

2. **On the search results page, identify a product you're interested in.**

   Suppose the product is the CANON Powershot A95. (This is not an endorsement of the CANON Powershot A95. That camera

showed up first on a recent results page. Of course, if CANON were to send me an A95 in consideration of this publicity, it would be rude of me decline it.)

3. **In the search box, type the product brand and model number.**

   To follow along with the example, type *canon powershot a95.*

4. **Press Enter or click the Search Froogle button to launch your search and view the results, as shown in the figure.**

The search results list contained 393 hits on that product name. Scanning down the list gives you a good idea of the range of retail prices. You can further hone the results by identifying a small price range in the Price Range fields.

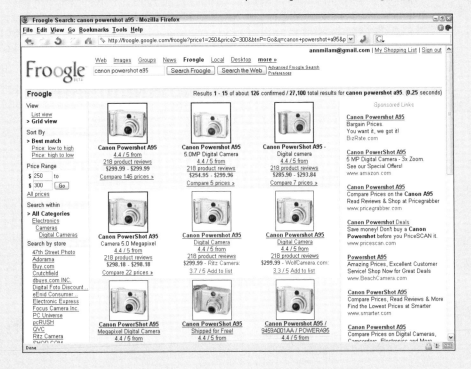

Froogle notices and obeys your general Google settings on the Preferences page (see Chapter 2). If you've set Google to display the maximum one hundred listings per results page, Froogle will do so too. Also, if you follow my recommendation and set Google to open a new browser window for the target page, Froogle will do so when displaying an online store that carries the product you clicked. This keeps you anchored at Froogle while you shop around in the target site.

This issue of loading one hundred listings per page could be a problem for telephone modem users because Froogle results pages display thumbnail pictures next to nearly every product. A one-hundred-item page is likely to contain ninety to one hundred pictures, slowing down the page load considerably. Adjusting your preferences just to use Froogle might not be worthwhile. My advice is to press the Esc key on your keyboard (which stops the page load in most browsers) when you get impatient with a page-loading delay. In most cases, you will have loaded all the listings but only some of the accompanying pictures. You can always click the Reload button (Ctrl+R in most browsers) if you decide you need the entire page with pictures.

The downfall of sorting results from low price to high price is that you're likely to get accessories to the product you want, not the product itself. This phenomenon occurs often when searching for moderately expensive stuff, such as iPods or digital cameras. Sort those search result pages by price, and the low end is likely to be glutted with earphones or camera cases. In this case, use the Price Range feature to determine a low price that is above the price of the accessories. (You don't need to fill in the upper portion of the price range.)

Any Sponsored Links that appear above or to the right of your search results are not part of Froogle's objective search. They are ads purchased by online retailers and information sites and keyed to appear on certain search results pages. However, that's not to say you should necessarily ignore them.

Froogle search operators

Froogle adds a new entry to Google's arsenal of search operators. Chapter 2 introduces Google-specific search operators: words in your keyword string that tell Google how to interpret your keywords. Standard operators that work in all search engines (*AND*, *OR*, *NOT*, and the quotes, or exact phrase, operator) mix with Google-specific operators listed in Chapter 2 to yield highly targeted search results.

In Froogle, three operators (one of them peculiar to Froogle) narrow your shopping search with great effectiveness:

✔ **store:** The *store* operator limits matches to particular stores. The *.com* part of a store's address is not required by this operator; for example, it understands *amazon* or *tigerdirect*. But Froogle does need correct spelling and spacing — for example, *tiger direct* (with a space between the two words) does not work. (This is not an endorsement of TigerDirect. But if that fine establishment were to send me all the items in its catalog in consideration of this publicity, it would be rude to decline them.)

✔ **allintext:** The *allintext* operator limits matches to product description text.

✔ **allintitle:** The *allintitle* operator limits matches to product names.

We'll consider the *store* operator first because it is special to Froogle and is one powerful little bugger. Using it, you can instantly browse one store's inventory in any product category. For example, type

```
"digital camera" store:bestbuy
```

That search returned 188 results, which can be narrowed by price or by model number. Figure 4-4 illustrates the results after narrowing the preceding search to a price range between $199 and $250. Searching this way saves you the effort of searching in many steps; you can leap from the Froogle home page directly to a list of items in you price range and sold in a specific store. (This is not an endorsement of Best Buy, but I'm never rude about receiving gifts.)

Figure 4-4: A tightly honed search in two steps: use the store operator and then narrow by price range.

The *store* operator is designed to work when the keyword following it is mashed up against it. In other words, don't put a space between the operator and the keyword.

To effectively use the *store* operator, you must know the Internet domain name of the store. Froogle doesn't understand store names per se if they differ from the domain names. For example, Home Shopping Network has an e-commerce Web site, and its URL is www.hsn.com. Froogle doesn't know anything about Home Shopping Network as a store name, but it does recognize *hsn* as a keyword related to the *store* operator.

You can use the *store* operator in a general way, without using keywords to define a product type, like this:

```
store:bestbuy
```

This search displays every Froogle listing for *bestbuy,* which isn't practical. If you want to search the entire store, it makes more sense to visit the BestBuy site.

The *allintitle* operator forces Froogle to match your keywords to product names. I find this more useful when using descriptive keywords than when using identifying keywords. For example, the identifying keywords *digital camera* are likely to be in relevant results titles anyway. But if I'm searching for a certain type of digital camera, using the following search string narrows the results beautifully:

```
allintitle:4 megapixel
```

In fact, the preceding search string is all you need to get a nicely target list of digital cameras because *megapixel* is a term closely related to digital cameras. You can further narrow the search to a single store like this:

```
allintitle:4 megapixel store:opticsplanet
```

This string yields two 4-megapixel digicams currently on sale at OpticsPlanet.com. (Not an endorsement, but if gifts arrive, you know what I'm going to do.)

The *allintext* operator works similarly to *allintitle* but forces Google to look in the product description when matching your keywords. Going for the text instead of the title widens the search and lengthens your results. Use it when you're using keywords that describe product features and those features aren't likely to be part of the product name.

Note that many retailers squeeze lots of information into their product headers in an attempt to get the product positioned higher on search results lists, because Google and other engines are swayed to some extent by whether keywords appear in titles. So when using *allintext,* your keywords might appear both in the text and in the title. Don't be frustrated — this reality merely encourages you to associate more esoteric keywords with the *allintext* operator.

Think in plain English when you're considering *allintext* keywords. Imagine you're talking to a salesperson in the store, describing features you want to see in a product. Here's an example that continues the digital camera expedition:

```
allintext:preprogrammed exposure mode
```

That search recently delivered 122 confirmed results, ready to be narrowed by price or store.

You may combine the store operator with *allintitle* and *allintext.* Doing so hones your results effectively. Try this:

```
allintext:preprogrammed exposure mode store:megacameras
```

At the time of this writing, that search string delivered a streamlined page with ten confirmed results (see Figure 4-5). Remember, though, that your search results with *allintext* are not conclusive of what's available. A lot depends on how stores describe their products and, therefore, how their listings appear in Froogle.

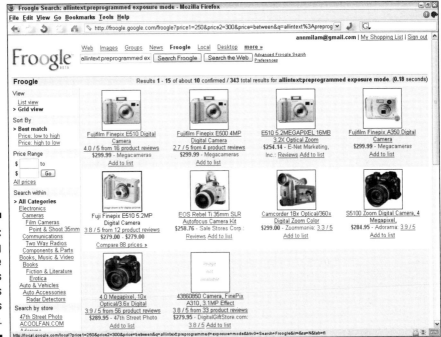

Figure 4-5: Combining Froogle operators narrows searches radically.

Froogle Advanced Search

If you prefer avoiding the use of search operators typed by hand but want to make your searches more powerful, go to the Froogle Advanced Search page. (See Figure 4-6.)

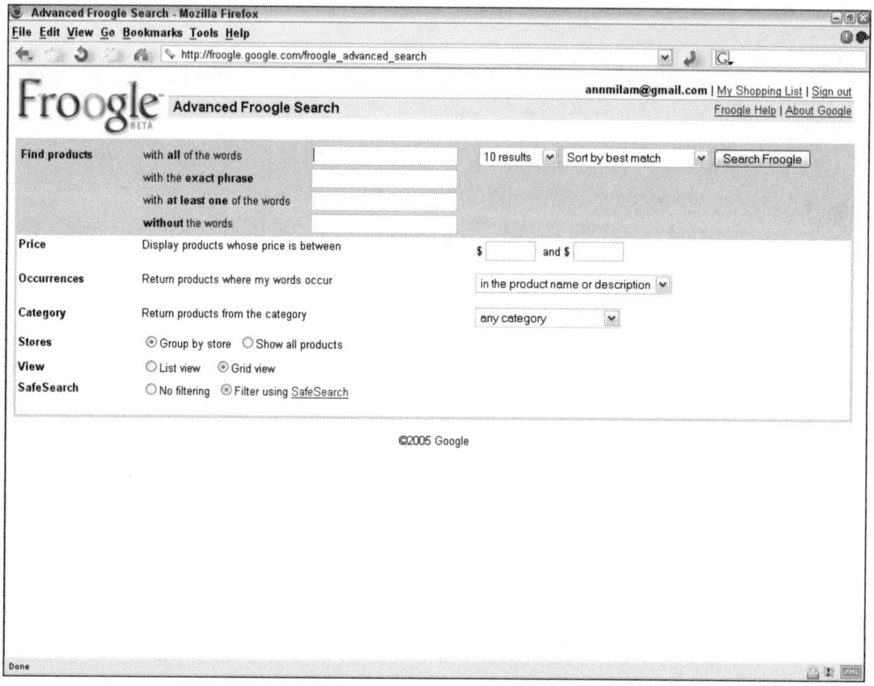

Figure 4-6:
Froogle
Advanced
Search
provides the
power of
search
operators in
keyword
and drop-
down
options.

The first section of the page, shaded in green and labeled Find products, operates identically to the Advanced Web Search page described in Chapter 2. This section employs standard search operators to include, exclude, and group keywords in certain ways.

The next five Advanced Search features jockey your keywords in ways described earlier in this chapter:

✔ Use the Price fields to define a price range within which products must fall to enter your search results.

✔ Use the Occurrences drop-down menu to specify whether your keywords should appear in the product name *and* description (the default selection), or just one or the other (the *allintitle* or *allintext* operator, respectively).

✔ Use the Category menu to limit searches to a single Froogle directory category.

✔ Choose List view or Grid view.

✔ Choose SafeSearch filtering to exclude results that might violate G-rated sensibilities.

About Google Catalogs

Most of Google's great ideas depend on behind-the-scenes technology. But one Google service relies more on hard work and continual maintenance than great programming: Google Catalogs, a searchable directory of mail-order catalogs, is brilliant in conception and execution. And keeping it going requires a monumental scanning effort.

Unlike Google's Web index, which crawls through Web sites and reduces their content to a tagged database controlled by retrieval algorithms, the Google Catalogs index leaves the content in its original format. What you see in this directory are scanned catalog pages, laid out exactly as they would appear at home. Well, you probably are at home. But you know what I mean — you're reading the catalog magazine on the screen.

But there's more. Merely presenting scanned catalog pages would be interesting but ultimately frustrating and unproductive. Google can search every word of the scanned catalog pages, deliver targeted results, and even contrive to highlight your keywords when they appear on the pages. Google has also designed a control bar for thumbing through the catalogs, turning your browser into a specialized e-zine reader.

All in all, Google Catalogs is one of the most underrated features Google offers. You almost never hear people talking about it. Part of the reason is that Internet shopping is sexier than old-fashioned mail-order. But mail-order is thriving, partly in reaction to the impersonality of e-commerce.

And here's the beauty of it: Google Catalogs is most useful to people who already get a lot of catalogs and enjoy shopping that way. Why? Because nobody gets the range of catalogs Google makes available. (If you do receive all the catalogs Google does, you need to reconsider your life. Seriously.) And Google Catalogs solves the one problem of catalog shopping — namely, the passiveness of an experience that depends on *waiting* for a catalog to arrive, and then reading it through to find what you want. Google brings searching to a realm that has always been limited to browsing. So whether you're using the Google Catalog viewer to examine a catalog that you receive regularly or one you've never heard of, you get more out of that catalog.

I can't hide the fact that, at the time of this writing, Google Catalogs was slipping into a state of neglect. In the spring of 2005, I could not find a single catalog with a 2005 cover date. Google was behind in its scanning. The service is still useful enough and cool enough (in my view) to warrant coverage here.

The tremendous scope of mail-order firms represented in the Catalogs database is valuable, and it's easy enough to link from an outdated catalog to the company's Web site. Perhaps it's no surprise that Google is sloughing off in the Catalogs service; it was always a quirky blend of old media and new media.

Searching Google Catalogs

As in Froogle, Google Catalogs presents a topical directory and keyword searching. After you get into the directory, you can limit further searching to that directory category or launch a global Catalogs search. Start at the Google Catalogs home page (see Figure 4-7):

```
catalogs.google.com
```

The directory tempts by listing a few mail-order companies in each main category. Feel free to leap into the directory by clicking either a catalog or a topic on the home page. (Clicking a store name on the home page brings up a one catalog for that store, not a list of catalogs; in most cases, that one catalog is not the most recent. I don't recommend clicking store names on the home page.) Drill down to subcategories.

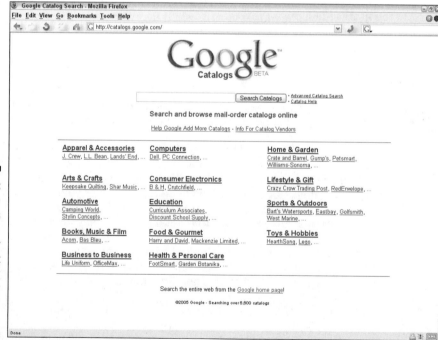

Figure 4-7:
The Google Catalogs home page. Search by product keyword or browse by mail-order house.

Figure 4-8 shows the directory page for Photography in the Consumer Electronics category. Note that each catalog is represented by its cover, title, short description, date, and Web link. Google maintains an archive of past catalogs, which can gum up the works when browsing the directory. The Advanced Search page (described shortly) lets you specify current catalogs, but some of them are a bit dusty, too.

Click any catalog cover to see the catalog in the Google Catalogs viewer (see Figure 4-9). You get miniature presentations of each two-page spread. Notice, also, the viewer control bar atop the page. Some control bar features appear dimmed in Figure 4-9, but they spring into action when you click one of the pages to see a full-screen representation. I get to that in a minute.

Searching by keyword provides a somewhat different experience. Starting at the Catalogs home page, I entered the keyword string *digital camera,* which displayed the page shown in Figure 4-10. Here, for each result, you get the catalog cover, a thumbnail of the page matching your keywords, and a zoomed-in shot of the portion of that page containing your keyword. Keywords are highlighted in the Catalogs viewer.

Figure 4-8:
A Catalogs directory page, showing covers, dates, and Web links.

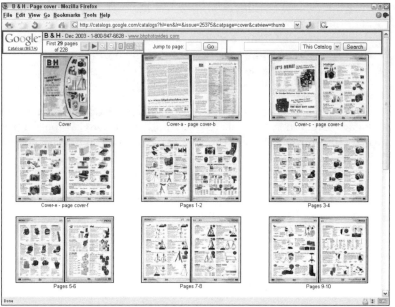

Figure 4-9:
Each catalog directory page contains thumbnails of that catalog's two-page spreads. Click a thumbnail to zoom in.

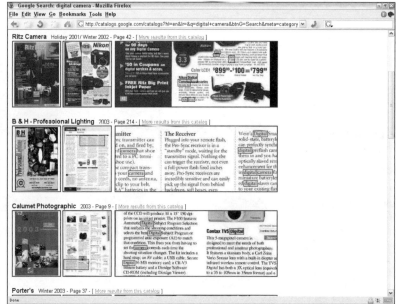

Figure 4-10:
A Google Catalogs search results page, showing catalog pages containing keyword matches with keywords highlighted.

Google Catalogs normally displays just one search result from each catalog. Click the <u>More results from this catalog</u> link above the items that *do* offer more hits to see a complete list.

Let's look at the larger view. Click the second or third thumbnail to get the entire page, as in Figure 4-11. Things get really interesting on this page because the Google Catalogs *control bar* kicks into action. This viewing assistant appears at the top of each page as you browse the catalog, allowing you to turn pages, jump to a page, zoom, choose one-page, two-page, or four-page view, jump to a particular page, and conduct new searches.

Title bar   Search menu

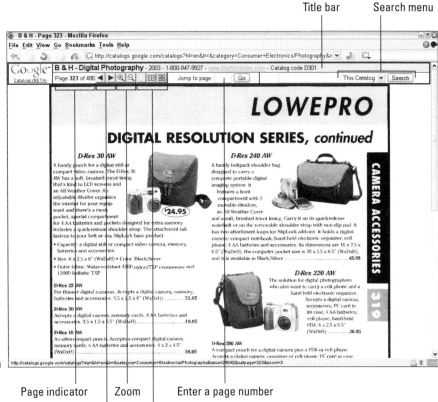

Figure 4-11: An expanded catalog page with the Google Catalogs control bar ready for browsing.

Page indicator   Zoom   Enter a page number

Move backward or forward   Page view

Here's a rundown of the control bar's features:

✔ **Title bar:** Atop the control bar is a summary of where you are and how to purchase things. It includes the catalog title, its publication date, the company's mail-order phone number, and the company's Web address. Remember that the Web sites for mail-order companies are not necessarily e-commerce sites. Even when they are, the Web site sometimes carry different inventory and prices than the catalog.

✔ **Page indicator:** To the left of the control buttons, this indicator tells you what catalog page you're currently viewing.

✔ **Page buttons:** Click the arrow buttons to move forward and backward by one page. (Or move by two pages, if the two-page view is selected, or by four pages if the four-page view is selected.)

✔ **Zoom buttons:** Use these buttons to zoom in to, and out of, the page. Zooming in (the plus sign) magnifies a portion of the page. Click any portion of the page to zoom in this fashion. You can zoom in twice.

✔ **Page view buttons:** You can view one page at a time, two-page spreads, or thumbnails of four pages at once. I prefer the two-page spread, zooming in as necessary. Large monitors running at high resolutions (at least 1024 x 800) are particularly suited to the two-page view (see Figure 4-12).

Figure 4-12:
The two-page view makes catalog browsing easier. Click a page or use a zoom button to magnify a page.

> ✔ **Jump to page:** Enter a page number and click the Go button. Using this feature is akin to flipping through a published catalog. If you're viewing in two-page or four-page thumbnail view, Google keeps that view, with your selected page as the first page of the spread.

> ✔ **Search:** Using the drop-down menu, you can launch a search of the catalog at hand or all catalogs — or you can leap over to a general Web search.

Google Catalogs recognizes your general preferences settings, which govern the behavior of Google Web search. If you set the number of results per page at one hundred (the maximum), you'll get one hundred search results in Google Catalogs, which is probably the most graphics-intense portion of Google. Even with a high-speed connection, loading a results page with three images per result can cause delays. The solution, as I suggested previously when describing Froogle, is to stop the page load before it's finished (press the Esc key in Internet Explorer), and reload the page if you end up needing the entire page of results.

You can request the addition of any catalog you don't find in Google Catalogs. Use the online request form located here:

```
catalogs.google.com/googlecatalogs/add_catalog.html
```

Or you can mail a request, using an archaic institution called the post office, to this address:

Google Catalogs

171 Main St. #280A

Los Altos, CA 94022

Before requesting additions to the Google Catalogs index, be sure your request doesn't already exist in the index. Don't count on browsing or haphazard search results — search directly for the catalog by name. In fact, searching for catalogs, not products, is a good way to review all recent issues of that catalog.

Advanced Searching in Google Catalogs

The truth is, advanced searching in Google Catalogs isn't as powerful as other Advanced Search pages. The reason for the simplicity of advanced searching is that the Google Catalogs search engine doesn't offer any special search operators. So the Advanced Catalogs Search page, shown in Figure 4-13, is useful mostly for invoking standard search operators without having to know them. Chapter 2 describes these operators (*AND, OR, NOT,* and the quotes operator) in detail.

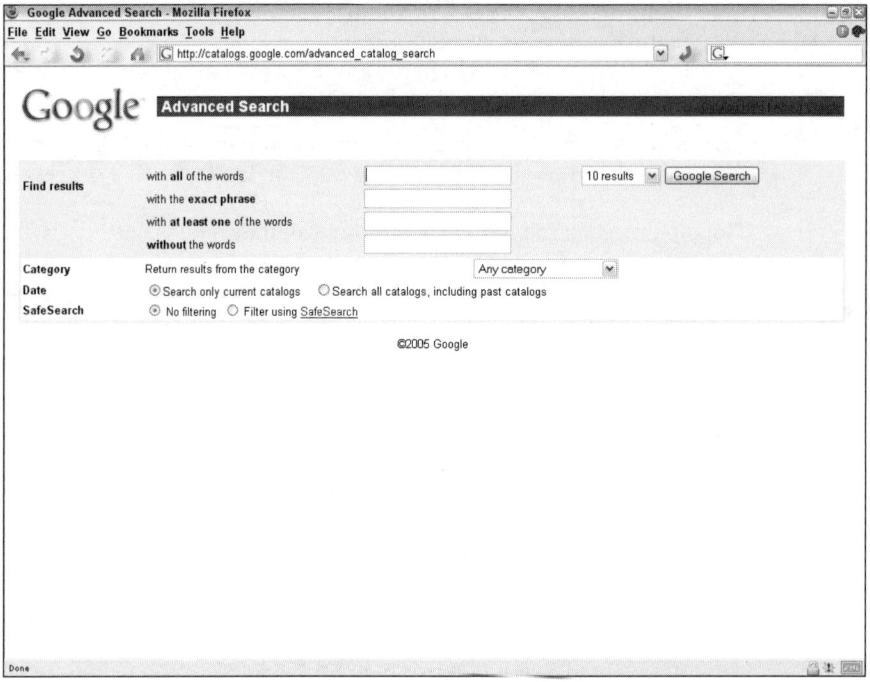

Figure 4-13:
The
Advanced
Search
page for
Google
Catalogs.

The instructions in the Find results portion of the Advanced Search page might be self-explanatory. If they aren't, please refer to the detailed description in Chapter 2.

Chapter 5

Saving Yourself from TV News with Google News

*W*e have more ways of receiving news than ever before, online and offline. Nearly every print publication runs an online edition, and a new breed of amateur journalists publishing Weblogs adds a powerful new voice to professional news reporting and commentary. In addition, the mechanics of news distribution have evolved rapidly over the last ten years. New, free tools such as RSS feed aggregation and podcast downloading have made it ever easier to receive a highly customized selection of news sources onto your screen (and into your ears). Don't worry if you aren't aware of RSS or podcasts; you don't need to know them.

Google News is a virtual newsstand of astounding scope. It was revolutionary when first introduced, and now, if not as novel, it continues to be as important in the areas in which it specializes. Google News is a completely automated search engine for daily news. That automation sets it apart from a major competitor for your eyeballs: Yahoo! News, which uses a combination of news crawlers and human editors. (Google News is not 100 percent automated, because humans can add sources to the engine. But the selection of stories and the arrangement of those stories on the Google News site are accomplished entirely by software.)

Google News sticks to its strong points and does not attempt to keep up with new trends. This means if you're deeply into reading Weblogs and assembling RSS feeds in a newsreader (again, don't panic if you've never heard of RSS), Google News might not be a big part of your day. But as a news portal and keyword news searcher, Google News remains unparalleled. Its index holds new and dated news stories from more than forty-five hundred publications around the world. It's all free, and it's all available with a few clicks.

Remarkably for such a mature and stable service, Google News remains in beta (official test mode) as of this writing. Other Google services, such as Google Desktop, flew through beta quickly, but Google has earned a reputation for withholding official releases seemingly forever. Google News sits at the forefront of that reputation, but don't be fooled by its beta status. Google News has been ready for primetime for years, and there's no risk in using it.

Googling the Day's News

Google News is amazing — in certain ways. At the time of this writing, Google News had not become involved with RSS news feeds, which represent a distinctively useful method of gathering news from many sources into one window on your screen. But Google News is, itself, an extraordinary portal that pulls news from many publishers, without any effort on your part. Furthermore, Google News furnishes keyword search of articles from an astounding number and range of publications.

There's a good reason why the Google Toolbar (see Chapter 12) contains a dedicated button linking to the News section. After you get a taste for Google's news delivery style, you'll go back for more throughout the day. The front page (see Figure 5-1) is a good place to turn for headlines or in-depth current events. And I don't mean just among Web sites. I prefer Google News to TV, radio, newspapers, and magazines. No other news portal approaches its global scope, intelligent organization, and searchability.

Figure 5-1:
The Google News home page is updated every few minutes.

Start at the beginning — the front page. It contains five main features:

- ✔ **Searching:** As in each of Google's main information areas, Google News presents a keyword box for searching. (More on this in the next section.) Use the Search News button to confine the search to Google News. Use the Search the Web button to toss your keywords over to the Web index.

- ✔ **News categories:** The left sidebar contains seven main news categories: World, U.S., Business, Sci/Tech, Sports, Entertainment, and Health. Each of these subject divisions has its own portion of the front page — scroll down to see them. Clicking a sidebar link takes you to a dedicated news page for that news topic.

- ✔ **Headlines and leads:** When you click a headline, the source page opens. This method differs from Yahoo! News, Google's main competitor, which reformats its sources in the Yahoo! style. Google does not pursue the same type of licensing arrangement as Yahoo! does, preferring to simply link to a large pool of online newspapers and magazines. Accordingly, your browser's performance when displaying Google News stories varies depending on the source's capability to serve the page when you click it. Slowdowns can also be the result of attempting to display a publication from halfway across the world (the Web is not instantaneous when thousands of physical miles must be traversed.). The brief description following a main headline is taken from the story's first paragraph. In a later section of this chapter I describe how to eliminate those leads if you prefer seeing only headlines.

- ✔ **Alternate sources:** Google selects a few different, and usually divergent, news sources below each headline. Click a source to see a story from that source's perspective.

- ✔ **Related stories:** This is where the scope and thoroughness of Google News shines. Click any related link to see an amazing range of publications covering that story. The related articles are listed on as many pages as it takes to fit them all (often there are hundreds), and each listing includes the first line or two of the published story. Figure 5-2 shows a portion of one of these pages. Observe the timing notes; Google News indicates how fresh the story is by calculating how long ago it was posted. Links in the upper-right corner invite you to sort the list by relevance or date. My experience is that the most recent hits are usually the most relevant.

Tracking a story over time

Using the related stories feature, you can track the evolution of a current event. Here's how:

1. **On the Google News front page, click the related link associated with any headline.**

2. **On the next page, click the Sort by date link.**

3. **After the page reloads, scroll to the bottom and click the last results page listed.**

4. **On the last page, view the oldest headlines related to the story.**

Move forward in time by clicking the Previous link at the bottom of each page.

Unlike Google Directory, your Google preferences do apply to Google News. This means that if you have Google Web search set to open a new window when you click a search result (recommended in Chapter 2), Google News likewise opens articles in new windows.

If you prefer a less graphic presentation of news, find the Text Version link in the upper-right corner. The text format has the same features as the graphical version, but without any photographs or columns, as shown in Figure 5-3.

Figure 5-2: Browsing related stories reveals divergent coverage of a story from all over the world.

Figure 5-3:
The text
version of
Google
News.

Searching for News

Searching for news really brings Google News to life. It's amazing, when you think about it; with a few keystrokes, you have keyword access to every article published by forty-five hundred news sources around the world.

You search Google News with the same set of tools described in Chapter 2 for searching the Web. Keywords go in the keyword box. (Click the Search News button or press Enter to begin the search.) Google attempts to streamline your results by filtering similar articles and presenting the top-ranked hits for your keywords. Figure 5-4 illustrates a News search results page.

When searching Google News, you may use the standard search operators (*AND*, *NOT*, *OR*, and the quotes operator) which are described in Chapter 2, as well as these Google operators, also described in Chapter 2:

  ✔ **intext** and **allintext:** Use the *intext* operator to restrict a keyword match to the text of a news article. Use the *allintext* operator to force a match of all your keywords.

✔ **inurl** and **allinurl:** Use the *inurl* operator to find a keyword in a story's Web address. This tactic narrows results and usually makes them extremely relevant. Use *allinurl* to further tighten results by forcing a match of all your keywords. The ultimate honing of results would be putting keywords in specific-phrase quotes, and limiting matches to the URL, like this:

```
allinurl:"social security reform critics"
```

However, this drastic measure usually eliminates all results. The problem with using *inurl* and *allinurl* is that story titles and keywords do not usually appear in the URLs of publication Web sites. For better results, use the *intitle* and *allintitle* operators, described next.

✔ **intitle, allintitle,** and **quotes:** The *intitle* operator works well because keywords representing news topics tend to appear in story titles — more so than in story URLs (see the preceding). Use *allintitle* to force a match of all your keywords, and use the quotes operator to ruthlessly narrow your results, like this:

```
allintitle:"podcasting popularity"
```

✔ **source:** This operator is specific to Google News and is useful for finding articles in certain publications. Not every publication in the world (or on the Web) is represented in Google News, so using this operator to find a specific source might be an exercise in guesswork. But many of the majors are in there, and of course you can narrow a search to any source you've spotted in Google News using this operator. Use the full title of the publication, and place underscores between words. Do not abbreviate, even if the source's Web URL is abbreviated, such as *www.nytimes.com.* The correct key string for finding stories in the *New York Times* is

```
keyword string source:new_york_times
```

✔ **location:** You may also narrow a Google News Search by region. Remember, you are determining the location of the source publication, not the location of the story. Google does not recognize municipalities more local than U.S. states. Use the Post Office's state abbreviations, like this:

```
princeton township budget location:nj
```

As you can see in Figure 5-5, that search string brings up plenty of stories in local Princeton newspapers, a nice solution to Google's inability to search a town's location as a region.

Figure 5-4:
Search
results in
Google
News.

Figure 5-5:
Use the
location
operator to
zoom in
to local
publications.

Submitting a news source

If forty-five hundred news sources just aren't enough, or if your favorite offbeat publication never seems to be represented, you can suggest a news source to Google. The submission method is informal. Just send your suggestion by e-mail to this address:

news-feedback@google.com

You may submit any site you like, but blog fiends (and bloggers) should know in advance that Google News scours few Weblogs, at least that I know of. Google concentrates on traditional news sources that publish on the Web. That includes online editions of newspapers and magazines and online news organizations such as CNET.

If the default U.S. version of Google News doesn't pertain to your geography or nationality, try one of the approximately two dozen other national editions linked at the bottom of the front page. (More country-specific versions are in development.) Alternatively, if you haven't done so already, change your Google preferences to your native language (see Chapter 2 to discover how to make the change). If that language is one that Google News uses, the news will automatically appear in that language. Changing the language from English might reduce the number of sources harvested for news, because Google is restricted to outlets publishing in that language. Figure 5-6 shows Google News in Spanish.

Figure 5-6: Google News in Spanish, one of about two dozen available languages.

Customizing Google News

Recently, Google added customization features to Google News. Customization allows you to personalize the look of the Google News home page by rearranging the display order of main news sections, eliminating sections altogether and inventing new sections based on search terms. It's a whoppingly (if I may use a technical term) useful improvement to the Google News experience.

If you refer to Figure 5-1, you can see a big Customize this page link on the right side of the Google News home page. Figure 5-7 illustrates what happens if you click that link: Your computer explodes! Kidding, kidding. You get upset too easily. The Customize this page panel opens, embedded in the Google News page.

Figure 5-7: The customization panel invites users to create personalized Google News pages.

Six customization options are available:

  ✔ **Drag news sections:** You can rearrange the order in which standard news sections are arranged in the window by simply clicking one and dragging it to a new position. (Drag by left-clicking a section and moving the mouse while holding down the mouse button.) Figure 5-8 shows a customized layout, but it is badly done. All the sections (except for the Top Stories section, which remains on the left side of the page) have been pulled to the right side, and Google translates this customization literally, placing all the headlines in a long column stretching down the

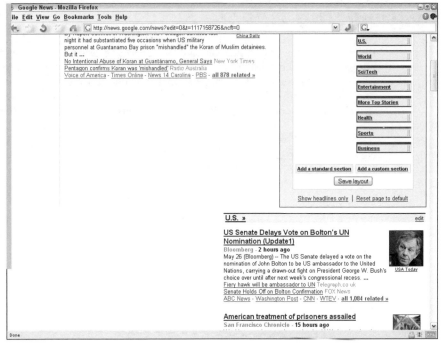

Figure 5-8:
Dragging
the news
sections to
one side
wastes
space on
the page.

right side of the page, wasting the left side. Better to rearrange the order of news sections in two columns, in the same general design as the default page display.

✔ **Delete a standard section:** This option is not immediately apparent on the customization panel, but you can do it easily. Click any standard section, and a new panel opens. Click the Delete section box, and then click the Save changes button.

✔ **Add a standard section:** Use this option when you've previously removed a standard section. Eight standard news sections are available.

✔ **Add a custom section:** This is the best part. Create an original news section to save any keyword search, and have that section appear on your Google News home page automatically. Click the Add a custom section link, and a custom section panel opens (see Figure 5-9). Enter your keyword(s), and then click the Save changes button. Remember, you may use any of the search operators described earlier in this chapter, or any standard operators discussed in Chapter 2. Figure 5-9 shows a key phrase with the quotes (specific phrase) operator.

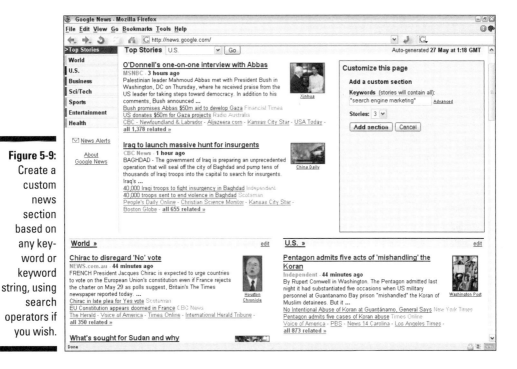

Figure 5-9:
Create a
custom
news
section
based on
any key-
word or
keyword
string, using
search
operators if
you wish.

✔ **Show headlines only:** This option clears out the leads below headlines. It streamlines the page, at the expense of not seeing snippets of the articles.

✔ **Reset page to default:** If you've created many topical news sections, and they're getting out of date, the quickest way to start over is to click the <u>Reset page to default</u> link. It's also the quickest way to erase a lot of hard work if you're not careful. So be careful.

When adding a custom section, use the <u>Advanced</u> link in the customization panel to see a few additional options, one of which is particularly useful: the label option. If your keyword string is on the long and complex side, assigning a label to the customized section keeps your display neat and coherent. See Figure 5-10 for an example.

When you've finished customizing your page, click the Save layout button. Doing so ensures that you will see the layout every time you return to Google News on the computer on which you created the customization. Click the <u>close</u> link to collapse the customization panel.

Figure 5-10:
You can assign a label for a customized section.

Figure 5-11 shows a fully customized page. Most of the standard news sections have been replaced by custom sections. The top stories on the right side of the page reflect the topics of the custom sections.

Figure 5-11:
A customized Google News page, with most standard news sections replaced by custom sections.

Chapter 6

Preserving Online Conversations with Google Groups

*W*hen I wrote *Internet Searching For Dummies,* I devoted quite a bit of space to a unique search engine called Deja News. Deja, as it was affectionately called by its devoted users, maintained a growing catalog of messages posted to Usenet newsgroups, which make up the native bulletin board system of the Internet. You could look up messages posted years ago, relive old flame wars, track down participants in e-mail, review somebody's entire Usenet output across all newsgroups, and perform a slew of other newsgroup tricks. You could even use the site to post messages to groups — an innovative, if clunky, departure from the traditional use of a stand-alone newsgroup program.

Then, disaster. Deja News crumbled, a victim of the Internet boom-and-bust period. Much grief was felt across the online nation. But redemption was at hand in February 2001, when Google purchased Deja News and its catalog. The renamed Google Groups performed essentially the same functions as Deja News did, but with Google's advanced searching sensibility and lightning-quick page delivery. Then, in December 2004, Google launched a second version of Google Groups (still in public beta testing when this book went to press), incorporating a massive overhaul of features and appearance.

Because of the word *beta* in the URL in this chapter's figures, you might think that you have a choice of using the new (beta) or old (not beta) version of Google Groups:

```
groups-beta.google.com
```

You don't. The official Google Groups URL takes you to the groups-beta thing:

```
groups.google.com
```

Don't ask me why. I don't know why. Stop asking. Some things in life must simply be accepted. This is one of them. Be at peace with it.

This is a large chapter that takes you through basic Usenet information before describing how to navigate Google Groups. If you're a newsgroup veteran, feel free to skip the first three sections without worrying about my crumbling feelings. If you're familiar with the previous version of Google Groups, you might want to take a hard look at this chapter because the new version is very different.

In Praise of Usenet

If you're unfamiliar with Usenet, this chapter might seem like a big nuisance. I implore you to mellow such a harsh attitude and ease into these pages with an open mind. Usenet is incredible. Google Groups is magnificent. The encompassing newsgroup culture is, to my mind, an indispensable part of online citizenship. Let me tell you a little story.

Some time ago, one of my Internet service providers, a local cable-TV company that provided high-speed Internet access through a cable modem, sold my town's franchise to another cable company. There was no problem with my TV service after the transition, but I suddenly couldn't log on to the old company's Usenet service, naturally enough. I called the new company and asked for the new server address that would enable me to get my newsgroups. To my astonishment, the representative told me that they would not be offering Usenet service to their inherited customers. This was like hearing they wouldn't be providing e-mail service. I immediately cancelled my account and got another ISP. Internet life without Usenet is inconceivable.

I won't do business with an ISP that refuses basic services such as Usenet, but the truth is I could have continued my newsgroup habit through Google Groups. So if this scenario happens to you, don't feel like you have to leave in a huff as I did. If you learn one thing from my tragic (well, annoying) experience, let it be to floss daily. Oh, and that Usenet newsgroups should be an important part of everyone's online lifestyle.

So, what the heck *is* Usenet and its newsgroups, anyway? Read on. This chapter gives you a bit of history, and then moves to the practical stuff of using Google Groups to begin — or, for the more experienced, to enhance — your Usenet participation.

Welcome to the Pre-Web

Usenet is older than the World Wide Web and quite possibly bigger. It's hard to measure their relative sizes because the Web consists of pages with text and pictures and Usenet consists of posted messages. Usenet is more closely related to e-mail, which is why many e-mail programs (such as Outlook Express) read public Usenet messages as well as private e-mail messages.

Usenet is the original bulletin board system of the Internet. You're probably familiar with some type of online message board. If you use AOL, you've most likely seen or used AOL's private message board system. If a favorite Web site includes a discussion forum, you've probably read or posted messages in that format. Both examples are bulletin boards, but neither is Usenet. The crucial difference lies in back-end technicalities that are unimportant here. However, it *is* important to understand the three major differences between Usenet and specially built systems such as AOL or a Web site forum:

- ✔ **Usenet is public:** Anybody with Internet access, on any computer, can view and participate in Usenet. Google makes it easy to stay connected with Usenet even if your ISP puts up a barrier, you don't have Usenet software, or you're traveling and are away from your home computer.

- ✔ **Usenet is threaded:** Threading is a layout style that clarifies conversational flow. On a threaded message board, you can see at a glance who is responding to whom. AOL's message boards are famously primitive in the threading department, discouraging depth of conversation. Many Web-based forums are likewise flat and unthreaded.

- ✔ **Usenet is unregulated:** This is a whopper. Nobody owns Usenet and nobody even tries to regulate it. Message board behavior is uncontrolled. Usenet is not a place for children. I am not being critical; the simple fact is that Usenet reflects the scope of human nature, in conversational format, much as society does in offline formats. People are mean, kind, ill-tempered, good-humored, stupid, smart, inarticulate, eloquent — and you see it all on Usenet. Language is spicy. Hundreds of groups are dedicated to pornography. Fortunately, the Usenet realm is organized and avoiding undesirable newsgroups is easy.

Usenet glossary

Know what you're talking about when the conversation turns to newsgroups. More importantly, know what I'm talking about in this chapter. Following are some essential terms regarding Usenet and newsgroups:

✔ **Alias:** see *Screen name.*

✔ **Article:** Traditionally, a newsgroup message is called an article. This terminology is a holdover from the days when newsgroups were about news and academic discourse. Now, messages are usually called *messages* or *posts.* This book doesn't refer to newsgroup articles, but the Help pages at Google Groups do.

✔ **Binaries:** Media files posted to Usenet. Discussion newsgroups usually discourage posting binaries such as pictures, music files, and video files. Even HTML posting is frowned on — plain text is the preferred format. But thousands of newsgroups are devoted to binary postings, from music to movies to software to pornography. These groups are usually identified by the word *binaries* somewhere in their Usenet address.

✔ **Cross-post:** A message sent to more than one newsgroup simultaneously. Although typically a low-level type of spam, cross-posting is sometimes used legitimately to ask a question or make a comment across related groups. Capricious or spammy cross-posts are loathed, partly because many people, when responding to a cross-posted message, inadvertently post the response to several newsgroups, compounding the disruption. Generally, cross-posting is bad form. If you do it, acknowledge the cross-post in the message.

✔ **Expired messages:** Usenet messages stay on their servers, available for viewing, for a certain time. Then they expire, which is sometimes called *scrolling off* or just *scrolling.* The amount of time varies from server to server and even from group to group on one server depending on the group's traffic. When messages expire, Google Groups swings into action by archiving the content that would otherwise be lost.

✔ **FAQ:** Frequently Asked Questions. Many newsgroups maintain a *FAQ file,* which is a long message spelling out the customs and basic facts of the group. It's acceptable to post a message asking where the FAQ file is located. Google Groups can also locate FAQs for individual groups — just search for *FAQ* within a group. Ignore the FAQ at your peril.

✔ **Flame:** A message posted with the intent to hurt. Flames are personal attacks, launched in response to spam or other behavior contrary to community interests or just because somebody is in a bad mood. Flaming is an art form and can be funny or frightening depending on the practitioner.

✔ **Lurking:** Reading without posting. In any message board community, lurkers greatly outnumber active participants. There's nothing illicit about lurking; newsgroups are for recreational reading as well as conversation. Anyone can delurk at any time to post a message and then slip back into lurker mode or stay out to talk.

✔ **Message:** Similar to an e-mail message and often composed in an e-mail program, a Usenet message is posted to a newsgroup, where it can be read by anyone in the group.

✔ **Newsgroup server:** Usenet newsgroups are distributed through a network of autonomous, networked computers called *servers.* That's how the entire Internet works, in fact, and newsgroup servers are a specialized type of Internet computer.

Each newsgroup server administrator decides which newsgroups to carry as well as the duration of messages in the groups.

✔ **Newsgroups:** Topical online communities operating in message board format. Newsgroups don't necessarily have anything to do with news; many groups are purely social. Technology companies such as Microsoft often use newsgroups to provide customer service.

✔ **Newsreader:** A stand-alone program interface to Usenet, often paired with e-mail functions. Outlook Express, primarily an e-mail program, is the best-known newsreader. Some specialized programs deliver only newsgroups, not e-mail messages. Google Groups provides a Web interface to Usenet and needs no program besides your browser.

✔ **Post and posting:** Posting a message (often called a post) places it on the public message board. Usenet software, operating behind the scenes, positions the post in correct thread order as long as you don't change the thread title.

✔ **Quote-back:** Portions of a previous message repeated in a new message, to sustain continuity in a conversation. Google Groups provides quote-backs automatically, indicated by the > symbol before each line of the quote.

✔ **Screen name:** The online identity of a Usenet participant, the screen name is also called an *alias*. You find a great deal of anonymity in newsgroups — and also lots of real names out in the open. In Google Groups, you set your screen name when establishing a Groups account.

✔ **Spam:** One message, usually promotional in nature, posted (or e-mailed) to many destinations simultaneously. Less formally, any repetitive and self-serving behavior is regarded as spam. Spamming is considered a diabolical sin in Usenet and is met with flames.

✔ **Subscribe:** Bookmarking a newsgroup in a newsreader is called subscribing. Unlike a newspaper subscription, there is no charge and nothing is delivered to your screen. Subscribing is an easy way to keep the newsgroups you follow handy. Google Groups doesn't have a subscription feature, but you can use your browser's bookmark function to tag your favorite groups.

✔ **Thread:** A series of messages strung together into a single newsgroup conversation. Sometimes called a *string*. A thread might consist of two messages or hundreds. Initiating a new conversation on a newsgroup message board is called *starting a thread*. Google calls threads *conversations*.

✔ **Threaded:** Online conversations whose message headers are graphically displayed to clarify the evolution of the discussion. Threaded message boards make it easy to see who is responding to whom.

✔ **Troll:** Newsgroup disrupters, trolls post deliberately offensive or off-topic messages in an apparent desire to get noticed at any cost. Some practitioners have taken the art of trolling to a high level of imagination and are regarded with some admiration and even occasional affection. By and large, though, trolls are reviled by Usenet inhabitants.

✔ **Usenet:** A network of Internet-based bulletin boards called newsgroups, used primarily as discussion forums and secondarily as repositories of media files.

The Usenet system contains more than fifty thousand newsgroups. The Google Groups archive holds about one billion messages and is expanding daily, even hourly. Size isn't everything, though, and the issue is really what value Usenet has, or could have, in your life. I find newsgroups irresistible in four major ways:

- **Community:** The online realm has long been prized for its capability to connect like-minded people without regard to geography, time zone, or any other factor that keeps people from meeting face-to-face. A newsgroup is created for practically every area of human discourse, from philosophy to specific television shows. Finding a home in one of these groups, and getting to know people from the inside out — without the distracting clues upon which we usually base our likes, dislikes, and judgments — is a unique experience. It is this quality of interaction that first drew me to online services many years ago, and it is still, despite the advances of the Web, the best thing about the Internet. Every morning I check my e-mail and my newsgroups, before setting foot on the Web.

- **Expertise:** When I have a technical question, especially about computers, Usenet is the first place I turn. Thousands of people hang out in the *.comp* groups (and others) for no purpose other than to help answer questions and share knowledge about computers. Some of those helpful souls are amateurs; others are professionals. A recent persistent glitch in my home network was solved by an expert at Microsoft, who posts dozens of newsgroup messages every day, outside his job, assisting people like me.

- **Recreation:** Newsgroups are just plain fun — the rants, the humor, the childishness, the astuteness, the complex threads. I browse through Google Groups sometimes, searching on various keywords that come to mind, just to get out of my well-worn newsgroup ruts and see what people are saying in other parts of the vast Usenet landscape.

- **Learning:** Besides getting technical questions answered, I regularly read certain newsgroups (especially in the *.sci* cluster) to eavesdrop on professional chatter. I have an amateur's interest in physics and cosmology — quarks and black holes and other unseemly phenomena — and it's fascinating to listen in on conversations among people who really know what they're talking about. Being a Usenet lurker in any knowledge field adds a dimension to learning that you can't find in books and magazines.

Google provides an excellent introduction to Usenet, and its searchable archive throws open the doors to Usenet history. You might not choose Google as your primary interface when posting, subscribing, and reading every day. Stand-alone programs are quicker and sleeker, and they have better tracking features than any Web interface can. But every longtime Usenet pilot I know occasionally uses Google Groups for searching or when traveling.

Accessing newsgroups on and off the Web

Some people use Google Groups as their only interface to Usenet for reading and posting messages. They have no choice in some situations, such as when a user doesn't own a computer and accesses the Internet on a public computer. When there is a choice, though, my recommendation is to perform most of your active Usenet participation using a stand-alone newsgroup reader. This program might not be the same as your e-mail program. (They're not the same for AOL users.) Outlook Express, probably the most popular e-mail program, offers full newsgroup functionality. In addition, many dedicated newsreaders are available as freeware and shareware downloads. The Netscape browser/e-mail/newsgroup program is free and quite advanced. X-News is another good (and free) one.

It might seem strange to advise against using Google Groups for your daily Usenet lifestyle. Let's be clear about its strengths and weaknesses. Google Groups is best at archiving and presenting a searchable database of Usenet history. It functions also as an interface for posting and daily reading, but its interactive features fall way behind those of a stand-alone program. Also, importantly, your ISP's newsgroup server is likely to be more up-to-the-minute than Google's server, and that factor definitely affects the Usenet experience.

So, my advice is to use Google Groups for searching and when traveling or forced away from your own computer. Otherwise, use a desktop program for subscribing to, reading, and posting to the current day's Usenet.

Usenet Newsgroups versus Google Groups

The new version of Google Groups incorporates several changes, the biggest being this: You can now create your own group. The first version of Google Groups served exclusively as a Usenet archive. The second version continues that tradition, but deemphasizes historical searching. The focus is now on current-day communicating, and group creation is designed to gather clusters of people who already know each other or who share an interest. Of course, that's what Usenet is for, and with more than fifty thousand existing newsgroups, you wouldn't think any more were needed. But creating a group gives you control, which is fun and useful. You determine who is in and who is out; you control the mailings that can go to the group's members.

The coexistence of Usenet groups and homemade Google groups adds a layer of complexity. One way to clarify this complexity would be to define it clearly by separating Usenet groups from Google Groups. The risk, though, lies in forcing users to approach Google Groups as if it housed two distinct domains.

Google prefers to offer an integrated experience, so it mixes the homemade groups right in with the Usenet groups. In fact, the word *Usenet* is not found much at the site — all groups are simply *Groups.* They are all bundled into the same interface, so when you build up a volume of favorite reading material, it is likely to come from a mixed bag of sources, some in Usenet and some in Google. You are not supposed to notice this, and indeed, there is no point dwelling on the difference.

However, there is one important distinction between Usenet newsgroups and Google groups: Homemade Google groups can't be seen outside Google Groups. Usenet newsgroups can be accessed in a stand-alone newsgroup reader and in many e-mail programs. Homemade Google groups can be accessed only through the Web-based interface of Google Groups (or through an Atom feed, which I get into later).

Signing In and Joining Up

Google Groups is all about membership. You have to start a Google account to post a message in any group. Furthermore, Google's homemade groups require individual memberships to post messages. In fact, when you subscribe to a Usenet newsgroup (see the "Usenet glossary" sidebar), Google says you have "joined" the group, even though no such thing as joining really exists in Usenet. Subscribing to a newsgroup is more like bookmarking than joining; it just keeps the newsgroup on your page so you don't have to search for it every day.

These are the two levels of joining in Google Groups:

✔ Using a Google account enables you to post in a Usenet newsgroup. Once signed in, you may post to any Usenet newsgroup without joining it (subscribing to it). Besides allowing you to subscribe to newsgroups, the account enables you to mark conversations (threads — see the "Usenet glossary" sidebar). You also must have a Google account to join homemade groups.

✔ Joining a homemade Google group allows posting to that group. (Some groups act only as announcement boards, and you can never post to those groups.) You must be signed in to your Google account before you join the individual group.

If you have a Gmail account (see Chapter 14), it serves as your Google Groups account. Gmail and Google Groups are closely allied and have similar interfaces. Google Groups prompts you to sign in, or create an account, if you try to post a message when signed out. Or cut to the chase by going to this account page:

```
www.google.com/accounts/newaccount
```

Browsing and Searching Google Groups

Just as with the Web, Directory, and News portions of the site, Google Groups allows you to both browse its content in directory style or search it with keywords.

Browsing the Groups directory

Because Google Groups has shifted its focus from the historical Usenet to a mix of Usenet and homemade groups, it has altered its Groups directory. This alteration is a major change since *Google For Dummies* was published. Now is a good time to look at Figure 6-1, which shows the Google Groups home page when a user is not signed in. (When you *are* signed in, the directory doesn't appear on the home page.) Note that the directory is organized by topics. In the previous incarnation of Google Groups, the directory was organized by Usenet address divisions, such as *alt.*, *sci.*, and *comp.* Those Usenet categories still exist, and it's possible to search Google Groups along those divisional lines, but doing so is not easy.

Figure 6-1: Google Groups as it appears when you're not signed in.

Topical browsing through the Groups directory turns up a mix of Usenet and homemade groups. Drilling into the directory, you begin finding homemade groups by the third level. At that level and lower (where the topics are fine-tuned), it's not unusual to find directory categories entirely populated by homemade groups. Creating a group in Google is much easier than creating a group in Usenet; as a result, homemade groups are nimbler in responding to current events that people want to talk about. Homemade groups about specific movies, music groups, and new TV shows are common. In Usenet, movie-specific newsgroups are rare, and a band or TV show must be long-running to get Usenet coverage.

Figure 6-2 shows a third-level directory page containing links to four groups — two Usenet groups and two homemade groups. Several aspects of the Groups directory page are evident here:

✔ Google tracks where you are in the directory in the common "Top Level > Second Level > Third Level" format. This linked display makes it easy to hop back to the top level or any higher level. In Figure 6-2, I selected high-traffic groups (the ones with most messages posted) in the Arts and Entertainment category. You can also select lists of groups from the Topic or Region category.

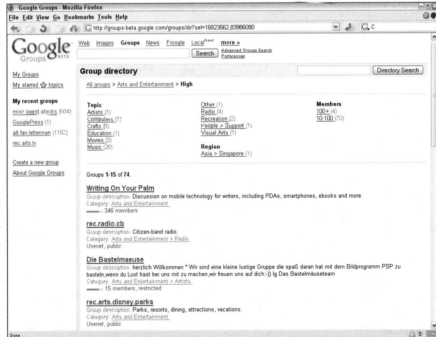

Figure 6-2:
A third-level
directory
page
showing
a mix of
Usenet
news-
groups and
homemade
Google
groups.

✔ Usenet groups are identified by the "Usenet, public" tag below the group listing. Usenet newsgroups are, by loose definition, public groups. (It's possible to set up a private group using Usenet technology, but those groups are mostly invisible.) Homemade groups are identified by their member counts; Usenet newsgroups do not have membership rosters. And homemade groups generally have longer descriptions than Usenet groups.

✔ Note that one of the groups is written in German, emphasizing the international reach of homemade groups (in this case) and all groups.

✔ Several groups are listed below My recent groups (in the left sidebar). The header is a misnomer, and Google should change it. Those are actually subscribed groups. Google does present a single recently visited group in the left sidebar, but only while you're visiting that group! Oh well, as of this writing, Google Groups is still in beta (the testing phase), so room for improvement can be expected.

Browsing Usenet exclusively

Although Google Groups goes to some length to hide the traditional Usenet structure of newsgroups, it's possible to browse Usenet exclusively, leaving out homemade groups. The link you need is <u>Browse all of Usenet</u>, which is located on the Google Groups home page. If you're signed in to Groups, that link (with the topical directory of mixed groups) is at the bottom of the home page. If you're not signed in, the directory and that particular link are in the middle of the page (refer to Figure 6-1).

Searching Google Groups with keywords

Using keywords in Google Groups is no different than in other Google indexes, but, of course, the results pages contain entirely different content. Keyword boxes are located at the top and bottom of pages. When conducting a simple search, it's important to remember that Google returns results that match all parts of a message. In a simple search, you're searching for messages, not for groups — though, of course, every message resides in a group. You'll likely find interesting groups through interesting messages. Google matches your keyword(s) against group names, message titles, message texts, and the screen names of people who posted messages.

Figure 6-3 shows a Groups results page. What you see is a list of messages. Each header links to an individual message. Below the header is an excerpt of the message that contains your keywords, and below that is a link to the front page of the message's group. You can also see a time stamp, the author's name, and the number of messages in that post's thread. Google helpfully lists related groups (usually homemade groups) atop the results.

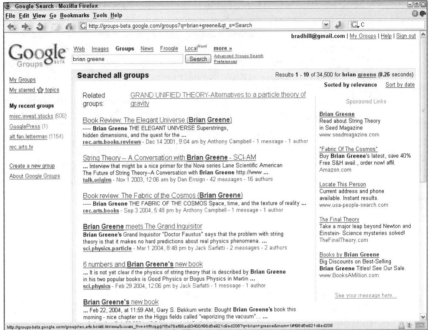

Figure 6-3:
Search
results link
to the
message or
to the front
page of that
message's
group.

A quick glance at Figure 6-3 shows outdated search results. Google sorts results by relevance first, and gives you the option to sort by date, with newer messages listed first. (Use the Sort by date link.)

When you sort by date, the quality of your results frequently goes all to hell: Google is no longer ensuring relevance as the first priority. Figure 6-4 illustrates this phenomenon; I was searching for references to the physicist Brian Greene, and the date-sorted results deliver many other Brians and Greenes. At this point either more specific keywords (such as *brian greene physicist*) or an advanced search is needed. The problem with changing the keyword string and searching again is that Google sorts, again by relevance first. Damn Google and its insistence on relevant results! Oh, wait, that's what makes it so great. But I wish Google Groups would stick to date sorting after that option is selected.

Using Advanced Groups Search

Google provides an Advanced Search page for Groups as it does for its other indexes. And, as with the others, it offers a user-friendly way to employ search operator functions without knowing the operators. As you can see in Figure 6-5, the Advanced Search for Groups page looks very much like the other advanced pages. The Find messages section works just as it does with a Web search (see Chapter 2). Use the four keyword boxes in this section in combination, forcing Google to treat your keywords in certain ways.

Figure 6-4:
Sorting by
date
sometimes
makes the
results less
relevant.
Either use
more
specific
keywords or
resort to
Advanced
Search.

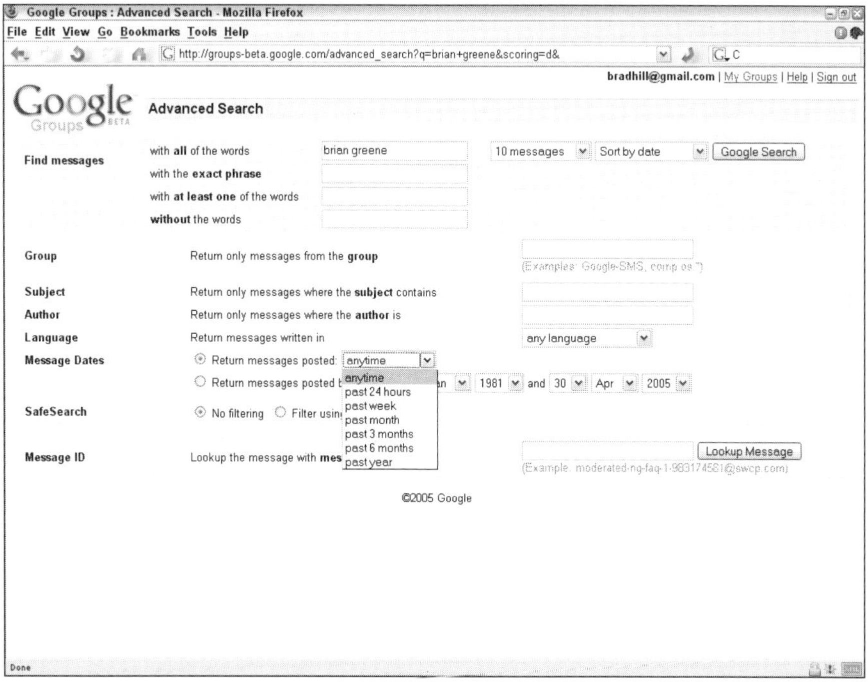

Figure 6-5:
The
Advanced
Search
page for
Groups
resembles
Google's
other
advanced
Search
pages,
but with
features
unique to
Groups.

The Advanced Search page also includes the following search parameters exclusive to Google Groups:

- ✔ **Group:** Use this box to specify a particular newsgroup for searching, or even part of a newsgroup name. Feel free to include the asterisk if you don't know the entire name. This feature replaces using the *group* operator.

- ✔ **Subject:** Use this box for keywords that you want to appear in the thread title. This feature replaces using the *intitle* and *allintitle* operators.

- ✔ **Author:** Use this box to specify an author's screen name or e-mail address. In the latter case, this feature replaces using the *author* operator. Using the *author* operator with a screen name yields uneven results, which this Advanced Search page works out through fancy operator syntax.

- ✔ **Language:** Usenet is international, just like the Web. Use the drop-down menu to specify a language.

- ✔ **Message Dates:** This is da bomb. Here's where the advanced action is in Google Groups. The Groups archive is precisely historical in a way that the Web index can't be because each one of the eight hundred million catalogued Usenet posts is stamped with a date and time. Use these drop-down menus to specify a date range for your search. Google Groups stretches back to 1981, though not all newsgroups are that old. This feature does not replace a search operator that can be typed into a keyword box. However, very handily, Google places the drop-down menus below the keyword box on the search results page (see Figure 6-6), so you can adjust the date range without returning to the Advanced Search page.

Figure 6-6: The specified date range appears atop the search results page, allowing adjustments on-the-fly.

✔ **SafeSearch:** This feature applies the same content filter as in Web searches. (See Chapter 2.)

✔ **Message ID:** This rarely used feature searches for a Usenet message ID, which you can glean from a message header.

Using operators in Google Groups

Chapter 2 covers search operators that sculpt Web search results in various ways. A search operator specific to Google Groups is the *group* operator. Using it forces Google to match your keyword(s) against newsgroups in a single group. Normally, the *group* operator is used to find content in Usenet newsgroups because remembering the name of a homemade group is difficult and unlikely. Usenet newsgroups have more generic names, and those names reflect how Usenet is divided into categories of groups — groups of groups, you might say. The most well-known example is the *alt* category, which contains thousands of recreational, community-oriented newsgroups. Some large technology companies operate customer-support newsgroups; Microsoft, for example, operates hundreds of them.

You can use the *group* operator to ferret out newsgroups in these divisions. For example, when searching for a Windows XP support group in the Microsoft newsgroups, this keyword string is effective:

```
windows XP group:microsoft.*
```

The result of this search is illustrated in Figure 6-7. The asterisk in the keyword string opens the door to results from all newsgroups in the *microsoft* division.

Up to the minute, more or less

Google puts a time stamp on every message it displays and every message it archives. The time stamp indicates the date and time (in Pacific U.S. time, regardless of where you're located) when the message traveled through Usenet and hit Google's newsgroup server.

Keep in mind that time stamps for the same message differ from server to server. Also, Google has a reputation for being slower than ISP (Internet service provider) servers. Since the great overhaul of Google Groups, I have monitored *latency* (which means the time delay between posting a message and seeing it appear in Google Groups) with uneven but improving results. When this beta test was first launched, the latency was a disastrous nineteen hours according to my testing, which compared selected newsgroups both in Google Groups and in a dedicated newsgroup reader. (That reader accessed the newsgroup server of a large national Internet service provider.) Since then, Google has really snapped to it, dramatically improving server performance. Delays are measured in minutes now, not hours.

Figure 6-7:
Searching
with the
group
operator
yields
targeted
and
intelligent
results.

When using the *group* operator, always place a period and asterisk after the division name you're searching for, if you know (or are guessing) an exact division. Neglecting the period-wildcard combination leads to quirky and less specific results.

Operators usually work in reverse as well (see Chapter 2). Such is the case with the *group* operator and the *-group* operator. The *group* operator, immediately preceded by a minus sign (no space), tells Google to exclude groups in the newsgroup division that follows. Suppose you want to find discussions about Windows XP and want to avoid Microsoft-sponsored newsgroups. The following string is productive:

```
windows xp -group:microsoft.*
```

I can't stop talking about the *group* operator. I want to make sure every reader understands that it's not just for defining top-level newsgroup divisions such as *alt., soc.,* and *microsoft.* You can use the operator to define a single newsgroup, if you know its name. Let's go back to the *windows xp* example. Perhaps you want to avoid Microsoft newsgroups, but you also don't want to trudge through a hundred miscellaneous groups in which your keywords might be mentioned. If you've received good results in the past from the newsgroup *comp.windows.misc,* your keyword string should look like this:

```
windows xp group:comp.windows.misc
```

Note that there's no need for the wildcard asterisk because you're defining the entire newsgroup name. Now if the reverse is true, and you want to eliminate results from that particular newsgroup, here's your search string:

```
windows xp -group:comp.windows.misc
```

TIP

Yet another special Google search operator lets you troll the Groups index for messages written by a single person. The operator in question is the *author* operator. This one is useful when searching within a single newsgroup or across Usenet globally. The operator needs to be paired with an e-mail address, *not* with a screen name. (You can, however, search for a screen name without an operator.) As usual with Google operators, don't put a space between the operator and the address. Here's the correct syntax:

```
author:name@email.com
```

Basic search operators in Google Groups

Google Groups understands most of the search operators you use when searching the Web (see Chapter 2). The standard operators — *AND* (+), *NOT* (-), *OR*, and " " (exact phrase) — work fine in modifying your keywords in Google Groups. The exact phrase operator (quotation marks around the phrase) is especially useful when searching Usenet, which is full of colloquial speech. Suppose you want to look back at Usenet posts about the famous *Seinfeld* episode that introduced "master of your domain" into the vernacular. This search string is productive:

```
"master of your domain"
    group:*seinfeld*
```

In addition to specifying the exact phrase, you are defining a *Seinfeld*-related newsgroup, even if you don't know any exact names of such newsgroups. The two wildcards (asterisks) allow Google to search for newsgroup names containing *seinfeld*. My results were 259 highly targeted messages, mostly from the *alt.tv.seinfeld* newsgroup and posted between 1993 and 1998.

One of the Google search operators discussed in Chapter 2 also works well in Google Groups. It is the *intitle* operator, which forces Google to find only search results whose titles contain your keywords. The *intitle* operator includes only the first keyword after the operator. Use *allintitle* to include all your keywords in the title. The simpler *intitle* operator also allows you to include entire exact phrases with quotes surrounding them.

Working with the *Seinfeld* example again, you can narrow the first search with the *intitle* operator, like this:

```
intitle:"master of your domain"
    group:*seinfeld*
```

That search string narrowed the original 112 results to a trim, extremely relevant 11 results, each of which contained the specified phrase in the thread title. I should mention that Google always attempts to find keywords in the thread title, assuming that they are the most relevant hits, and groups those results toward the top of the search results list. Using the *intitle* operator gets rid of extraneous results.

Reading Messages and Threads

When you click a message title, Google throws you into a different sort of page that shows an entire newsgroup message (finally!) and various options that affect how you perceive and interact with the entire thread. It's from this page that you can post a message (see the following section for posting).

Figure 6-8 shows a full Usenet post from the previous search on *brian greene "string theory"*. Note that the keywords are highlighted in the message. Note, also, that this particular message occurs in the middle of a long discussion thread, and the thread itself appears as a list of links in the left frame. You can click <u>No frame</u> to obliterate that list of links, but do so cautiously. The thread (which Google calls a tree) is a valuable aid to navigating the conversation. A few more things to note: The target message appears at the top of the page; the next message in the thread appears below the target message; and, if the target message is short, a few other messages might appear below it.

If the left frame showing the thread tree doesn't appear, click the <u>view as tree</u> link to conjure it up.

Figure 6-8:
A Google Groups message showing highlighted keywords and, to the left, the entire thread.

Keeping your own stuff out of the archive

You can restrict Google from including your Usenet posts in the Groups archive in two ways: by preventing Google from archiving a post to begin with or by removing an archived post.

You can use the Usenet software to prevent archiving by typing a single line of code either in the message header or in the first line of the message body:

```
X-No-archive: yes
```

The line must be typed exactly as it appears here, with a single space between the colon and yes. Placing the line in a message header is less conspicuous than positioning it in the message body but much harder for most folks to accomplish. So, when posting a message that you want to keep out of the archive, just place that line in the message itself. Make sure it is the *first* line, above the quote-back that Google places in all response messages.

Removing an already archived post is more complicated. Follow these steps:

1. **On the Google Groups home page, click the Help link in the upper-right corner.**

   The Google Groups Help page appears.

2. **Click the question, How do I remove my own posts?**

3. **Click the removal tool link.**

4. **Enter the e-mail address used to post the message you want removed, and then click the Continue button.**

5. **Enter the message ID(s) or Google Groups page address(es) of the message(s) you want removed, and then click the Continue button.**

   The easier of these two options is to find the offending message in Google Groups, click the show options link, and then click the Individual Message link. When the message appears alone on the page, copy the page address (URL) and paste or type it into the form here.

6. **On the verification page, click the Continue button.**

7. **On the validation page, fill in all forms and then click the Finish button.**

The size of a thread frame is adjustable. Position your mouse cursor over the border between the two frames until the double arrow appears, and then click and drag to the left or right. When dealing with long and complex threads that are sharply indented (as in Figure 6-8), the left frame needs to be widened to view the entire thread. Figure 6-9 shows the same page as Figure 6-8, but with the thread frame widened to clarify navigation.

In certain circumstances, Google displays messages without their corresponding threads in a left frame. When that is the case, a view as tree link snaps the left frame back into place.

Complicated? It sure is. Fortunately, most people never have cause to remove a message from Google Groups. And remember — doing so does erase your message not from the Usenet universe but only from Google Groups.

Figure 6-9:
Widen the
thread
frame to
make
navigation
within the
thread
easier.

Posting Messages through Google Groups

Google allows posting to newsgroups, but you must register as a Google Groups user to do so. This necessary step is not the typical Web site registration forced upon you to get an e-mail address, which is then sold to Internet marketing companies. The main reason you must register is to establish a screen name that is then used to identify your posts. I explain signing up for a Google Groups account earlier in this chapter.

This issue of posting messages in Google Groups, and reading them in Google Groups, can stir up confusion. Here are the essential points:

✔ You may post a message to a Usenet newsgroup from any Usenet access point — your ISP, for example, probably runs a newsgroup server and allows you to read messages on and post messages to that server using Outlook Express or a newsgroup program. (AOL has discontinued its newsgroup service. But I'm talking about *real* Internet service providers.) Messages posted in this manner are visible in Google Groups, as well as in your newsgroup program.

✔ Likewise, you may post a message to a Usenet newsgroup from Google Groups. This message is visible in Google Groups and in any other newsgroup program.

✔ You may post a message to a homemade Google group (after joining that group) only from Google Groups. That message would be visible in Google Groups but not in another newsgroup reader.

Registration is not required to browse, search, or read newsgroups through Google Groups. In fact, Google doesn't encourage or even display a path toward registration until you first attempt to reply to a newsgroup message or start a new thread.

You can post a message in two basic ways:

✔ Reply to a post

✔ Start a new topic

Replying to a message

When replying to a post, two methods present themselves, and, unfortunately, the more obscure of the two is the better option. Figure 6-10 shows a thread with two messages displayed. Each has a <u>Reply</u> link below it. Clicking that link opens a box in which to compose your response, along with Preview and Post buttons. This would be fine if only Google provided quote-backs of the original message — it's standard in groups to respond to a message phrase by phrase or at least by quoting the entire original message above or below your response. This technique allows readers to follow the discussion better.

In the preceding paragraph, it might seem as if I'm making too much of a small point. But let me tell you something. When AOL discontinued its newsgroup service in early 2005, many thousands of users decided not to dump AOL entirely, for some reason, and swarmed into Google Groups to satisfy their newsgroup cravings. Naturally enough, they started using the <u>Reply</u> link below messages, and the resulting epidemic of unquoted messages disrupted newsgroup communities right and left. I'm telling you honestly, you risk getting flamed to a cinder if you jump into conversations without quotes — people won't know what you're responding to and will thrash you for wasting their time.

So, now that I've frightened your socks off, here's the solution. Instead of clicking the <u>Reply</u> link below the message, click the <u>show options</u> link above the message (refer to Figure 6-10). Figure 6-11 shows the options displayed above both messages.

Figure 6-10:
The Reply
link offers
an easy way
to respond
to
messages
but not the
best way.

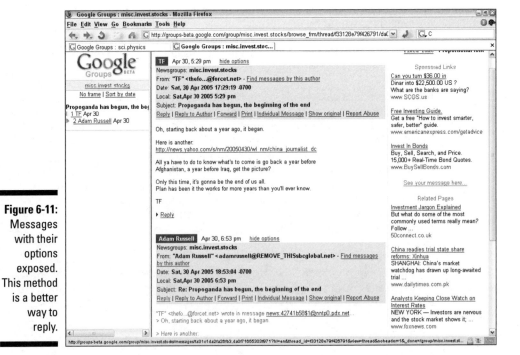

Figure 6-11:
Messages
with their
options
exposed.
This method
is a better
way to
reply.

Now look at Figure 6-12, which shows what happens when you click the <u>Reply</u> link in the exposed options panel. Note that the original message is quoted back, allowing you to compose a response above it, below it, or interpolating responses within it.

The other options revealed by the <u>show options</u> link are these:

- <u>Find messages by this author</u>: This link reveals other public messages by the person who wrote your target message.

- <u>Reply to Author</u>: This link provides a direct communication between you and the message author; your response is sent to that person's e-mail address.

- <u>Forward</u>: Click this link to send the message to anybody's e-mail address.

- <u>Print</u>: This, of course, prints the message.

- <u>Individual Message</u>: An option I rarely (okay, never) use, this link displays the message on an empty page, all by itself.

- <u>Show original</u>: This option strips the message of all formatting and reveals the entire routing header. Figure 6-13 shows the result. Most people find little reason to use this option.

Figure 6-12: Composing a response above the quote-back of the original message.

Figure 6-13:
An original message with all formatting removed. Ugly and, in most situations, useless.

✔ <u>Report Abuse</u>: This link displays a complaint form that, when filled out, goes to Google. It's important to remember that Google does not own or regulate Usenet newsgroups. The company can disable a user's Google Groups account, and it can remove messages from the Google Groups archive of Usenet. But those messages would still be visible through other interfaces and that excluded person would still be able to post by other means.

Starting a new topic

Anyone may start a conversation by initiating a thread in a Usenet newsgroup (or in a homemade group in which the person is a member). You must be on that group's page to start a topic — you can't do it from a search results page. Simply click the <u>Start a new topic</u> link on any group page. Doing so brings up a message composition page similar to the reply page shown in Figure 6-12. Simply fill it in and post it.

Fun and flames: newsgroup etiquette

To a greater extent than other portions of the Internet (except perhaps chat rooms), Usenet embodies a distinct, autonomous culture. Embarking on a Usenet journey is not unlike visiting another country. You might know the language, but that doesn't mean you know the customs. It's easy to make gaffes. And unlike polite society in many countries, Usenet citizens don't hesitate to pound your virtual self to the ground when you make a mistake. Rudeness? Yes, but it's more than that; Usenet is ancient, by Internet standards, and proud of its traditions. An unspoken requirement is that a newcomer must learn the local ways before opening his or her mouth.

Perhaps the most important rule is this: Lurk before you leap. Even if you've been around online communities before, get to know any individual group before jumping in with your own posts. Read the board for a few weeks to get the flow of inside jokes, to understand its topical reach, and to learn the personalities and social power structures of the group. Google Groups can compress this process by allowing you to read back in time, covering a lot of ground quickly.

Always put the community first. Newsgroup stars develop through eloquence and intelligence, not by pushiness. Don't ever use newsgroups to promote products — even free products such as Web pages. (Placing a link to a personal Web page below your signature is perfectly acceptable.) Don't spam, cross-post, or generally attempt to mine Usenet's traffic for personal gain. Go there to contribute to the common good. If your contributions are worthy, attention will accrue to your entire online package.

Flame with discretion. I am not a Usenet peacenik who believes that all flaming represents an abuse of online anonymity. But nothing is more foolish (or worthy of reciprocal torching) than a misinformed flame attack. Make sure you have some standing in the newsgroup, and get your facts right. The most cogent and entertaining flames go after another poster's content, not the other poster's personality.

Overall, keep a giving attitude. No matter how you manufacture your Usenet personality — caustic, loving, intellectual, argumentative, whatever — make contributions that somehow enhance the group. It's all about community.

Keeping Track of Your Groups Activity

Some people use Groups occasionally for research or to answer the occasional question; others use it daily (hourly, even) to engage with vibrant online communities. In all cases, and especially in highly participatory cases, Google makes it simple to track your groups, threads, and messages. The new system, in fact, is the single greatest improvement in the new Google Groups over the old version.

Google provides two convenient links for managing your Groups activity:

- My Groups
- My starred topics

These two bookmark lists are located in the left sidebar until you click a message header — then they disappear. To get them back at any time, click the Google Groups logo in the upper-left corner. Figure 6-14 shows the Google Groups home page as it appears to an active user immediately after signing in (or clicking the Google Groups logo).

The My Groups folder (it doesn't look like a folder, but that's a good way to think of it) displays message topics to which you have posted replies, if those threads have received more messages since you last signed in. The My starred topics folder displays threads that you've bookmarked by clicking star icons on group pages. Figure 6-15 shows a Groups page with two topics selected.

By using My Groups (for following discussions in which you take part) and My starred topics (for following discussion you're reading, without necessarily posting), Google provides a quick way to keep track of your Groups life without navigating to each group in which you're active.

Do not confuse My Groups with My recent groups; the latter is a list of groups to which you have subscribed. *My Groups* should be changed to something like *My Conversations,* and *My recent groups* should be changed to *My Subscribed Groups.* But has Google asked for my opinion? Nooo.

Figure 6-14:
The My Groups selection displays topics you've contributed to.

Figure 6-15:
A Groups
page; any
topic can be
selected
and
bookmarked
by clicking
its star.

Creating a Group

Creating a homemade group in Google is a three-step process, assuming you have a Groups account (see my explanation near the start of this rather long chapter). This is how you do it:

1. **On the Google Groups home page (be signed in), click the <u>Create a new group</u> link.**

2. **On the Create a group page, fill in the name, group description, and access level (see Figure 6-16).**

   Most groups are public, but some are used for mailing lists only; in fact Google itself uses that mechanism to send press releases. The Restricted option is good for a friends-and-family group that you wish to keep private and invisible to strangers. When you're finished, click the Create my group button.

3. On the next page, add members, select an e-mail distribution method, and write a welcome message, and then click the Done button.

You needn't add members right now; you can do that anytime. Everything you do on this page can be changed later by clicking the Manage group link within your group. It's probably a good idea to select No Email, at least to start; many group members do not like receiving e-mails of posted messages, and prefer to keep their Groups activity within the group.

A newly created group looks just like any other group in Google Groups — Usenet or homemade — except it contains no messages. Go ahead and post one. You don't want your members to be staring at a blank page, do you?

Chapter 7

Mapping the Web's Terrain

● ●

In This Chapter

▶ Understanding Google Directory

▶ Browsing and searching the directory

▶ Visiting Open Directory Project

▶ Submitting a site to the directory

● ●

*G*oogle is primarily known as a search engine, but it offers good browsing, too. You search Google with keywords, and you browse topical categories in the Google Directory. (You may also use keywords in the directory, in which case all results come from directory listings.) Searching is for when you know what you're after; browsing is for when you're in a less demanding mood. Searching is like going to the store for a gallon of milk; browsing is like strolling through town looking in all the windows.

Google Directory represents a landmark achievement in human cooperation and virtual cataloguing. Google takes its basic listings from the Open Directory Project database, a large volunteer organization determined to assemble the largest and most useful classified index of Web sites. More than twenty thousand real-life editors evaluate and select Web sites for this project, which was started in 1998. Listings created by Open Directory Project are used by certain other Web directory sites, including Google Directory (as well as Lycos, AOL Search, Netscape Search, and HotBot). Google takes Open Directory as a kind of raw ingredient, and cooks it by adding PageRank formulas. The result is an enhanced directory experience.

Relaxing into Browsing Mode

After a hard day of Googling, there's something comforting about putting on the slippers, lighting up the pipe, and cruising around Google Directory. And if that scenario isn't weirdly retro-tech enough for you, throw in a dog bringing you the newspaper. Browsing can be more relaxing than searching. Trolling the directory leads to unexpected discoveries as opposed to the routine precision of Google's Web search. Google's search index is so precise and uncannily helpful that it's easy to lose track of the directory entirely — especially since Google removed the directory link from the home page. Clearly, Google has been deemphasizing the directory since 2004.

Nevertheless, Google Directory and directories in general are fun. If you've been around the Web from the beginning, you probably remember the thrill of Yahoo! when it was a new directory mapping out the infant World Wide Web. The Web is hardly an infant now, and most of us — no matter how long we've been online — are somewhat jaded about our virtual activities. By encouraging newness and discovery, directory trolling enlivens an online life that has become just another rut in our lives.

If you liken Google searching to finding a needle in a haystack (and a whopping big haystack, at that), browsing the directory is like shining a giant spotlight on broad topic areas of Web content. Search the index to be productive; browse the directory for fun.

Google versus Yahoo!

The comparison is inevitable. The two best-known Web directories pitted against each other in a titanic struggle to the death . . . in my imagination, anyway. A competitive atmosphere *does* surround these two Internet giants generally and Web directories in particular. Yahoo! essentially invented the directory format that became standard, and Google is now the foremost search-and-browse site. Hence the battle imagery. And in this case, I give the edge to Google's Web directory.

Don't get me wrong. I wrote *Yahoo! For Dummies* and am the world's biggest fan of the Yahoo! experience. If Yahoo! disappeared, I'd turn off my computer and step outside for the first time in years. I pray it won't come to that. But when it comes to trolling Web directories, Google's ranking and general presentation put Yahoo! in second place.

Google prevails for two reasons. First, Google's directory listings come from Open Directory Project, a large Web directory maintained and updated by thousands of volunteer editors. Yahoo!'s in-house staff, diligent though it be, cannot crank the numbers competitively. Bigger isn't always better, but with Google's page ranking — which sorts the gigantic directory intelligently — I'll take the bigger directory in this case. Google Directory also displays more neatly and coherently than Yahoo!'s.

The other reason for Google's dominance is its PageRank system, which prioritizes and enhances the already stellar listings compiled by Open Directory Project.

So, Yahoo! Directory, I visit you only occasionally. You gave me my first tours of the Web in 1994, during a thrilling time that is no more. Now, when the urge to troll comes over me, I head for Google Directory.

The directory has its productive uses, too. In particular, Google Directory serves as an alternate search engine for those who don't like using search operators (see Chapter 2) to narrow the search field. The directory is all about narrowing, from broad category to thin subcategory. Drilling into the directory, and then using the within-the-category search function, is a fantastic way to bring up high-quality sites with a minimum of hassle and technical search knowledge.

Here's an example of directory productivity. If you're searching for an online edition of your hometown newspaper, you could drill into the directory's News category, select Newspapers, select Regional, and search for your town's name in the Regional directory. This method avoids search operators in the Web index.

Understanding Google Directory

First things first. Google Directory, like most other directories, is self-explanatory on the face of it. You just need to visit the Google Directory home page to get started. Google used to link the directory to the Google home page but removed the link in 2004. There is no question that Google has deemphasized the directory: no link on the home page and no directory links in search results, as once occurred. Now, you get to the directory by visiting the URL directly. Here it is:

```
directory.google.com
```

Note: You can also get to the Google Directory by clicking the <u>More</u> link on the Google home page, and then finding the directory on the following page, which lists all of Google's services. That <u>More</u> link is handy; I use it all the time so I don't have to remember specific Web addresses for Google pages.

Open Directory Project

Open Directory is open to the extreme. Modeled on the open source software movement, in which resulting software programs are not owned and anybody can contribute to their development, Open Directory is distributed free of charge to many of the most important Web destinations, including Netscape (which acquired the Open Directory organization in 1998 and oversaw development of this free directory), Lycos, and of course Google. Accordingly, you can view the nearly identical directory (allowing for minor differences due to distribution time lag) at several online destinations, including the Open Directory home page:

```
www.dmoz.org
```

Google adds unique value to Open Directory and makes it its own (as Randy Jackson would say on *American Idol*) by imposing its PageRank structure on the Open Directory template. That means the site selections in each category and subcategory are ordered by Google's popularity and importance formulas. In other locations, including its home site, Open Directory is organized alphabetically.

Directory preferences (not)

On the subject of preference settings for Google Directory . . . there aren't any. Lack of global settings isn't a problem because directory browsing is a simpler matter than Web searching, which *is* subject to preference settings (see Chapter 2). On one point, though, you might expect the Web-search preferences to cross over to the Directory experience: namely, the ability to open a new window when you click an outside Web link. This preference is extremely useful in the search engine because it keeps one browser window anchored on the search results while you're off in another window exploring a result site.

Don't expect Google to open a new window when you click a directory link, even if your search preference is set that way. Instead, right-click any directory link and choose the option to open a new window (or a new tab in the Netscape, Firefox, or Opera browsers).

Figure 7-1 shows the home page of Google Directory.

Click a main category link or a subcategory link to get started. Many more subcategories exist in directory strata beneath the Google Directory home page. However, you needn't dig deep before encountering results: Most main category pages list primary Web sites for that category in addition to the first level of subcategories for that topic. Figure 7-2 illustrates how this structure works.

Figure 7-1: Start exploring by clicking a category or subcategory.

Figure 7-2:
The main
News page,
showing
categories
of News
and, below
the cate-
gories,
primary
site links.

The directory runs deep — it's not hard to drill down six levels in many subjects. Don't give up early. Searching in a lower-level category can yield interesting results.

You might think that searching in a narrow subcategory is pointless because a
quick scroll down the page shows you what sites are listed. But when Google
searches a category, it doesn't match your keywords against only the words
on the category page; it searches the *content* of the listed pages. This throws
the door wide open, but in a small topic area. Searching in a narrow directory
category results in extremely rewarding hits.

Figure 7-3 shows a subcategory page, in this case a third-level page in the
Society category. Two items on subcategory pages are worth noting:

- ✔ The directory path is displayed above the Categories banner. Figure 7-3
  is a third-level page with a short path. Lower-level pages have longer
  paths, and each step you climb down is linked, so you can leap back
  upward along the path.

- ✔ The Related Categories section, under the Categories banner, links to
  directory categories that share some degree of topicality with your current category.

Figure 7-3:
A sub-
category
page with
related
categories
listed.

Submitting a Web Page to the Directory

Anyone may submit a site for inclusion to Google Directory or offer corrections of currently listed sites and their descriptions. When doing so, you deal not directly with Google but with Open Directory Project, from which Google obtains its listings. Google provides links for interacting with the Open Directory Project submission forms, but I think it's easier to operate from the Open Directory site.

Most people do not sit in front of their computers trying to find interesting sites that aren't represented in Google Directory. If you do find yourself burning hours that way, you might consider becoming an Open Directory Project editor. (Click the Become an Editor link at the bottom of any Google Directory page.) Site submissions are usually made by site owners hoping to get more exposure for their pages. Nothing wrong with that, but be aware that Open Directory Project is a hand-picked, edited directory, and it is not obligated to list a submitted site. Nor are the ODP editors known for their speed in accepting new listings. Some categories are quicker than others; it depends on the editor.

You submit a site by filling in an on-screen Open Directory Project application that asks for the site address, a description, the proposed directory category for inclusion, and your contact information. Google provides links to this application at the bottom of some category pages. Look for the <u>Submit a Site</u> link at the bottom of any directory page.

The <u>Submit a Site</u> link is convenient, but there's a problem. Open Directory Project is in charge of deciding which categories and subcategories are open to new submissions. Not all of them are — especially upper-level directory pages. Google doesn't distinguish between open categories and closed categories, so it places the <u>Submit a Site</u> link at the bottom of *all* pages. When you click that link on a category page open to new submissions, you get the application form with any special instructions that apply to that category. When the category is closed, clicking the <u>Submit a Site</u> link displays the general information page about submitting to Open Directory Project.

Because of this confusion, I recommend starting your submission from Open Directory's home base. Go to this URL for the Open Directory's home page:

```
www.dmoz.org
```

Figure 7-4 shows the Open Directory main page with its top-level categories. They're the same categories as in Google Directory, but the layout is different.

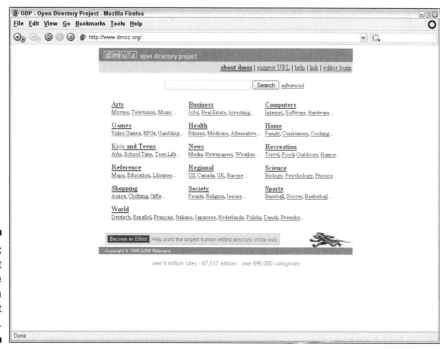

Figure 7-4:
Start your site submission project here.

As you drill into the directory, keep an eye on the upper-right corner of the page. Notice that some pages carry no reference to adding or correcting a URL, while others offer the <u>suggest URL</u> link, or both. Figure 7-5 shows a third-level directory page with both links. Click the <u>add URL</u> link to see the application for that subcategory.

Generally, the broad categories closer to the top of the directory are unavailable for new submissions. Open Directory is particular about where new listings are placed, and your submission is better received if you take the time to research appropriate categories.

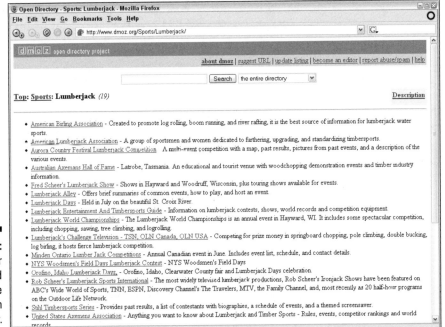

Figure 7-5:
Check for
links to add
or update
in Open
Directory.

Part III
Specialty Searching

The 5th Wave   By Rich Tennant

"This is amazing. You can stop looking for Derek. According to a Google search I did, he's hiding behind the dryer in the basement."

In this part . . .

This part deals with specialty searching, some of which is a bit quirky. Search through a university's Web pages when you're feeling studious. Limit your queries to government sites when you're feeling paranoid. Hey, indulge the mood.

Chapter 8 is anything but quirky; it introduces the hottest field in the Internet search industry: local search. This is where you grab the blazing spotlight that is Google, refine its wattage to laser-thin accuracy, and point it at your own little residential domain. Or somebody else's little residential domain. The point is to link online searching with offline results, and then get in your car and go buy something. Local searching in Google is an incredible experience. If you think I'm overstating the case, you *really* need to read Chapter 8.

Chapter 9 covers Google's preset specialty categories, which make your whole paranoia trip as easy as looking over your shoulder. Chapter 10 gets all professional on you by describing one of Google's most unusual and little-known services: Google Answers. This little corner of the Google realm features a staff of professional researchers standing (sitting, actually, and wearing tweed) ready to answer your research queries. Keywords are not necessary — you actually talk to these people on your screen — but money is required. You bid fairly small amounts for their attention and expertise. There's more to it than that, so don't skip Chapter 10. Chapter 11 delves fearlessly into Google Labs, where all sorts of weird experiments are curdling. Some are of dubious day-to-day value, but others, such as Google Suggest and Google Scholar, are delightful and promising.

You've come this far; in your soul's core you know you must not turn back. The transformation of online life is in process, and its momentum grips us all with the gleaming vision of new possibilities, new realities, new virtual selves. [Editors' note: Brad Hill has become clinically caffeinated. An intervention has been scheduled. We hope for a return to normalcy by Part IV.]

Chapter 8

Searching the Neighborhood

*T*he Internet has a disembodied quality to it. Useful as it is, and woven as it has become into our everyday lives, the Internet exists in a realm parallel to the physical world, representing it in ways but always floating above it autonomously. Sometimes I conceive of the Internet Nation as a real (if intangible) land with borders made of electrons and a citizenry that interacts without regard to real time or geography. In there, we even have a distinct written dialect (if u no wh4t I mean), specialized customs, different standards of acceptable behavior, and a particular sense of place defined by e-mail addresses and Web site URLs. The notion of locality has a bizarre Einsteinian relativity online, where everything is the same distance from everything else — one click away.

When we Google something, we usually are searching for information, for Web-stored content (such as a video clip), or for a service (such as an online travel agency). What we seek, and what we find, has little or no bearing on the location of our home, neighborhood, or town; the time of day, or other real-world factors that define life away from the computer. For a long time, Internet search engines were content to scour the virtual landscape. Recently, the idea of linking Internet search with physical locales has taken hold with a competitive frenzy. Local search is a new frontier of online search engines, and they are stumbling over each other to be the most accurate and easiest to use. If the idea is to make up for lost time, the engines have accomplished that; seemingly overnight, local search has matured as a power tool.

And going local is fun! This is one of the most entertaining chapters in the book, partly because local searching is so useful and partly because Google's tools are exquisite. Google approaches local searching with three discrete services that can be used individually and that link together in certain ways. These three services are

- ✔ **Google Local:** The flagship service for local searching, Google Local was launched in 2004 and is linked on Google's home page. Google Local is designed to find offline businesses and services that lack a Web presence — dry cleaners, restaurants, toy stores, dentists, and so on.

- ✔ **Google Maps:** Launched in 2005, Google Maps is a joy to use and is great for mapping a region of any size, from the entire United States to the intersection closest to your home. Google Maps is meant to compete with Mapquest and Yahoo! Maps, and like those two venerable services, it provides routes between two points and driving directions. Google Maps also duplicates Google Local in certain ways, though the graphics are different (and impressive). One can productively launch a search for a local business from Google Maps.

- ✔ **Google Earth:** Google Earth is a satellite-imaging and flyover service — and don't worry, this chapter totally explains what that cryptic description means. Briefly, Google Earth is a control panel that you download and install, and it lets you zoom into satellite pictures of any place on earth. You can see cities, streets, houses, and cars. Through this dynamic interface you can conduct Google Local searches, the results of which are overlaid on the terrain.

This chapter covers each of these three elements, in the order listed.

The promise and reality of local search

To be sure, finding brick-and-mortar stuff using the Internet is not new. Online yellow-page services have existed for years. Retail outlets have linked their in-store shopping with their e-commerce shopping (some better than others) for a few years. Local movie listings are a snap. But an idealized version of local search would enable the user to find anything related to the physical world, not just business listings or retail products. How about locating a state park in North Carolina, or all the elementary schools around Austin, Texas? Or perhaps you need a graphic layout of the local airstrips in central New Jersey. On a one-night layover in a strange town, it might be useful to see a map of all the convenience stores, gas stations, movie rental shops, coffee houses, and ATMs in the area.

This is the sort of local searching long promised (and unevenly delivered) by PDAs (personal digital assistants such as Palm Pilots and Windows CE devices) and GPS (global positioning system) receivers. The delivery isn't altogether consistent in Google or other search engines, either, but the exciting part is that local search is trickling down to ubiquity. You no longer need specialized equipment (a PDA or a GPS receiver) to launch effective local searches. And in the case of Google, the pieces are in place to weave the online and offline worlds to an amazing extent.

Finding the What and Where in Google Local

Google Local is basically a fancy online yellow pages. As with a normal Google search, you enter keyword(s) and browse results. In Google Local, the results are close to a location that you enter as keywords. Google claims to match your keyword against its gigantic Web index, and then filter the matches with business directory information (which means yellow pages databases from various sources) to display your regionally relevant results. The actual formula by which all this takes place is undisclosed, in typically secretive Google fashion. The results are generally impressive, notwithstanding certain glitches that I'll get to later.

The home page for Google Local is located here:

```
local.google.com
```

Actually, you can activate Google Local from the main Google home page by including a location with your keywords, such as *austin bar* to find some of the famous musical night spots on Austin's 6th Street, or *coffee 10001* to search for coffeehouses in midtown Manhattan.

When conducting a local search from Google's home page, local results are presented above non-local Web results, as shown in Figure 8-1. Three local results are summarized briefly below a link that leads to the full page of local results at the Google Local site. Note also that Google Desktop results appear above the local results (see Chapter 13 to read about Google Desktop).

Using Google's main home page for a local search is convenient if you happen to be on the home page when a local search occurs to you. Likewise, including a town or zip code in a basic search from the Google Toolbar (see Chapter 12) is probably easier than clicking the Google Local button on the Toolbar before entering keywords. (Users of the Firefox browser enhanced with Googlebar, an emulation of the Google Toolbar, do not have a Google Local option, so using the keyword-plus-town method is essential.) But for serious local searching, the Google Local page is the place to start.

Identifying the address in Google Local

As you can see in Figure 8-2, the Google Local page contains two keyword boxes, one for the "what" and one for the "where." Put your search keywords in the What box and the location in the Where box. That location may be a town or zip code, but nothing broader (such as a state without a town name). If you do enter a state as the only geographical locator, Google whimpers and refuses to cooperate.

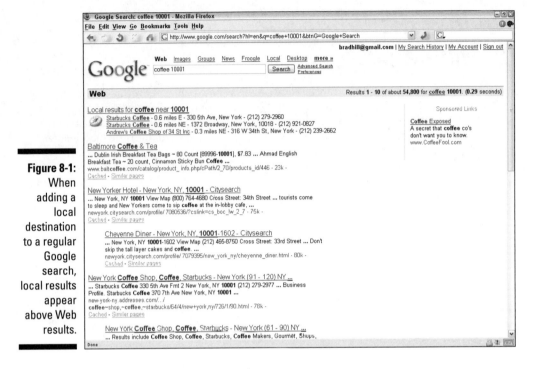

Figure 8-1:
When
adding a
local
destination
to a regular
Google
search,
local results
appear
above Web
results.

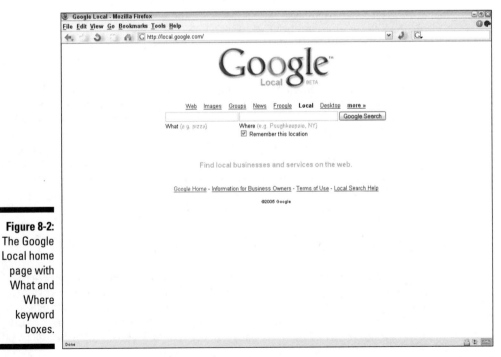

Figure 8-2:
The Google
Local home
page with
What and
Where
keyword
boxes.

Choosing keywords for a local search

Keyword choice is always important, no matter which Google index you're working with. Google Local seems especially picky and unpredictable when giving results to common-sense queries. The difficulty is reminiscent of the experience of figuring out in which category a type of store is listed in the yellow pages. You don't browse categories in Google Local as you do in a yellow pages book. But you still must sometimes play around with keywords to bring up the best results.

For example, when looking for local Starbucks outlets, I have found that searching for *coffee* gets me better results than searching for *coffee houses* or *cafes*. Both unsuccessful keywords seem more promising than *coffee*, which is what I might use if I wanted to find cans of coffee. But the most popular cafe in my town, located right in the center of the commercial neighborhood, drops out of Google Local results when I search for *coffee houses* or *cafes*.

Sometimes Google fails to recognize a local search when launched from the main Google engine or the Google Toolbar, even when a town is included. After all, entering a town as part of a keyword string is not new; people were doing that long before Google Local was introduced. In those cases, there is the risk that Google will deliver normal Web results without the Google Local results atop them. An example is *austin music clubs,* which fails to shake out local results from the Google Web engine. However, in Google Local, using *austin* as the Where and *music clubs* as the What works perfectly. Back in the Web engine, *austin music* and *austin clubs* each succeeds in triggering Google Local results atop the Web results. (All these outcomes might differ if you try the searches because of the time lag between when the book was written and when you're reading it.)

The lesson here is this: Don't give up right away if a local search delivers unsatisfying results or fails entirely, whether you launch it from Google or Google Local. Tinker with the keywords, and move from Google to Google Local to improve the results.

If you enter a town name without a zip code or state as your geographical identifier, Google will try its best to understand where you mean, but will not always succeed. When Google is forced to choose between two town names, it will often go with the larger. Such is the case if you enter Jacksonville — Google chooses the Florida town over the one in North Carolina. (In this case, Google has deemed that the Florida town is more important, based on the large number of instances of that town name in Google's Web index.) In cases of multiple small towns matching your entry (such as Anderson, which exists in South Carolina, California, and other states), Google cries out in pain: "Unable to understand anderson. Please try another address." Simply add the state or zip code, and all will be forgiven.

I know you're wondering about the "Remember this location" check box beneath the Where keyword box. Many people think that checking that box enables Google to keep a history list of your search locations, and then auto-complete saved locations when you begin typing them later. That would be a good feature, but it's not *this* feature. Check the Remember this location box when you want Google Local to default to the location currently in the Where box. It may be a street address (with town), town name (possibly with the state), or zip code. In the future, when you return to Google Local, that saved location will be waiting for you. Google saves only one location at a time.

Working with Google Local results

Within a second or two of launching a Google Local search, you see the results page. The Google Local results page (see Figure 8-3) contains four main elements:

- **Business listing:** This is the company name, phone number, and address.

- **References:** References are instances of the business name appearing in Web sites. If the listing has a dedicated Web, that site is linked as the first reference. Click the 7 more >> link (the number varies) to see all site references to the listing.

- **Distance and directions:** For the most part, Google Local lists results by proximity to your location, with closest results first. Sometimes, though, you can spot a more distant result placed higher on the page than a closer result. In those cases, Google determines, through its PageRank system, that the more distant location is more important to your search than the closer one. The Directions link is there to provide driving directions from any point to the search result listing. (Google assumes you're starting from the location you entered in the Where keyword box.)

- **Map:** Google Local positions the first ten results (lettered A through J) on an interactive map; this feature is boffo. (Sorry; I time-warped to the 1950s for a second. I'm back.) Unlike Yahoo! Local, which makes the user click away from the results page to see a map of the results, Google Local puts the map in your face. Click any lettered map point to see the name of the store or business it represents, plus the address, the phone number, and links to driving directions. (More about driving directions in the section on Google Maps later in this chapter.) Double-click any part of the map (not a lettered result point) to recenter the map at that position. Boffoest of all, click and drag the map to see past its edges.

Note: The shaded blurbs above the search results are sponsored ads generated by Google AdWords (see Chapter 17). Do not confuse them with local search results. But that's not to say that you shouldn't click them if they interest you. Many AdWords advertisers specify region-specific placement of their ads, depending on where the user is physically located (determined by IP address) and what the user is searching for locally. So, those ads might be relevant to your local search.

Figure 8-3:
Google
Local
search
results
include a
map that
can be
dragged
with the
mouse and
zoomed.

I've found it useful to conduct local searches of my hometown with various keyword combinations. You can get acquainted with Google Local's quirks when you know what the results should be. In the previous sidebar I note that *coffee* is a better keyword for finding coffeehouses than either *coffee houses* or *cafes*. I learned that by searching my town, where I know all the coffee places, and now I know the best way to search for Starbucks when I'm away from home.

The maps are zoomable. You can widen your view by zooming out or get down to street level by zooming in. Use the zoom guide (the plus and minus signs) in the upper-left corner of the map.

Clicking a search result takes you to a page dedicated to that search result, as shown in Figure 8-4. This page repeats the basic information (the company name, address, and phone number, the distance from your specified search location, and a map). Below the basic information there often appears a list of site references; these are Web pages that mention the company or store. The list of references, and links to reviews where available, are the only features that distinguish the single-listing page from the search results page.

Figure 8-4:
A listing
page in
Google
Local. Note
the display
of review
links, when
available,
and other
sites that
reference
the search
result.

A final thought about Google Local

I don't use Google Local much. You heard me. Let me explain.

Google Local was launched in March 2004, after *Google For Dummies* was published. After its launch, I was all over Google Local, using it constantly. Then Google Maps was launched in February 2005. As you can read in the next section, Google thoughtfully bundled the Google Local engine right into Google Maps. With great graphics and beautifully integrated driving directions, I now find little reason to get my local joy from Google Local. But that's just my taste.

The truth is that Google has made both sites nearly identical: Google Local is more keyword-centric; Google Maps is more map-centric. They use the same engine and deliver identical results. Use either, to your taste.

The one distinguishing feature of Google Local is the listing page containing reference sites and (sometimes) reviews. That's a significant distinction from Google Maps, but one that isn't important to me.

Other local search engines

Google is hardly the only search company delving into local search, though it does seem to be the most ambitious runner in the field, bringing three distinct tools into the mix. Two other local engines are worthy of mention: Yahoo! Local and A9 Yellow Pages. The first is operated by Yahoo!, of course, and the second is owned and operated by Amazon.com. Here are the two Web addresses:

```
local.yahoo.com
www.a9.com/optical
```

Yahoo! Local operates similarly to Google Local but makes the mistake of putting the results map on a different page from the actual results, forcing users to click to find it. (And the maps aren't nearly as cool as Google's maps.) A9 Yellow Pages is unique. A9 drove slowly through the streets of several major American cities taking photographs every few feet, and then stitched those millions of photos into an enormous, metropolis-wide slideshow. Every local query at A9 (if it lies within a covered city) yields standard search results accompanied by photos of the actual storefront and the surrounding real estate. The A9 system is intriguing, exciting, and has stimulated quite a bit of buzz. It's worth a try.

Using the Glorious Google Maps

Have you used Yahoo! Maps? Kiss it goodbye. Are you a Mapquest devotee? Break off the relationship now. Good. You're single again, and I want you to build a love affair with Google Maps. It won't be hard; I think you'll be seduced as easily as I was. Walk right up and introduce yourself:

```
maps.google.com
```

If you start poking around (which is no way to treat a new partner), you might forget to come back here and absorb the many tips in this section. But when you're ready, I'll be here with the step-by-step on how to manipulate the maps, conduct local searches, and get driving directions.

Note: Google Maps works in all recent version of Web browsers (version 5.5 or later of Internet Explorer or Netscape Navigator; version 1.0 of later of Firefox; version 5.5 or later of Opera).

Dragging, zooming, and otherwise having too much fun

As you see in Figure 8-5, Google Maps starts you off with a large U.S. map. It's important (and rather entertaining) to find out how to control the map before starting any searches.

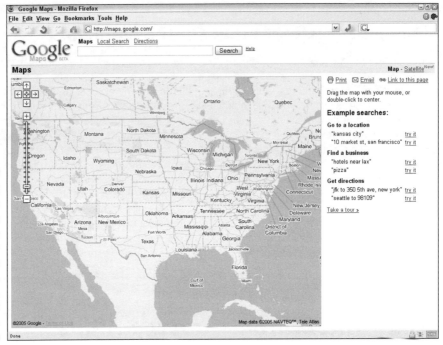

Figure 8-5:
Google
Maps starts
you off with
a highly
interactive
U.S. map.
Drag it,
zoom it, and
recenter it.

Single-clicking the map does nothing, which might make it seem unresponsive to those accustomed to one-click recentering at Yahoo! Maps. Actually, the Google Maps is interactive in several ways:

✔ Double-click anywhere to center the map around that point.

✔ Grab the map and drag it around with your mouse. (Move the mouse while holding down the left button.)

✔ Zoom in and out using the zoom guide on the left. Although it looks like a slider, the zoom guide is a 15-point incremental zoomer; you can grab it and scroll it up and down like the scroll bar of a Web page, but the map does not zoom in and out smoothly. Simply click any point along the zoom guide or the + or – sign (above and below the zoom guide, respectively) to revise the zoom perspective. Alternatively, you can zoom using the + and – keys of the keyboard.

✔ Use the arrow button above the zoom guide to move the map from side to side, or up and down, in half-screen increments. This method of moving the map around is less flexible and intuitive than dragging it with the mouse, but there it is. You may also use the arrow keys on the keyboard (press one and hold it), but they scroll the entire Web page first, and then move the map. For wider panning around the map, use the Page Up and Page Down keys (for moving up and down), and the Home and End keys (for moving left and right).

✔ Click the center button in the middle of the four arrow buttons on the zoom guide to return the map to the position of your original search result. (I'll get to searching in a bit.) This button is fantastically useful. You can drag and zoom to your heart's content without worrying about getting lost. Cruise your way from Florida to Louisiana, and then return to the original location, and zoom position, from which you started.

You may also zip to a location in Google Maps by simply typing the location in the keyword box. Try a zip code, or a town and state combination, or a street address with the town and state. (Oddly, Google Maps doesn't recognize a state name by itself, even though the map can easily zoom to a level that would display a state.)

By now you should be in love with Google Maps, and you haven't even seen the search results yet. Read on.

Local search in Google Maps

The smooth and clear graphics in Google Maps would be enough to sway me away from Yahoo! Maps and Mapquest. But then Google turned a very good service into a killer service by packing the Google Local engine into Google Maps. More than 90 percent (92.427 percent, to be imaginary) of my local searches are conducted in Google Maps, not Google Local. Superior graphics provide one reason for my loyalty; another reason is that Google Maps combines the two keyword entry boxes of Google Local into one. So instead of entering separate What and Where queries (see the preceding section), you enter single keyphrase queries such as *pet stores in annapolis* or *hotels near mco* (mco is an airport code).

On the right side of the Google Maps home page, sample searches are presented in the three service areas: Maps (see "Go to a location"), Local Search ("Find a business"), and Directions ("Get directions"). Those example search categories correspond to the links above the keyword box (Maps, Local Search, and Directions), which direct your search to one of those three services. I already covered using the map; here I focus on local searches.

After you get the hang of the type of language needed by Google Maps, using the engine is natural, and it is difficult to stump it. Following are three time-saving tips:

✔ When keying your search to an airport, the word *near* becomes important. The search string *hotels ewr* results in a zoomed-out map showing hotels all over north-central New Jersey, not just hotels closely surrounding Newark International Airport. (EWR is the code for that airport.) Changing the search string to *hotels near ewr* zooms the map in to a tight view of the airport and the hotels surrounding it (see Figure 8-6). Using *near* as a qualifier does not necessarily have this focusing effect when searching towns and cities.

✔ Save your fingers some effort by using zip codes when you know them. Typing *10010* is a lot easier than typing *new york, ny*. Beyond that simple convenience, zip codes are more precise when searching a large city that contains multiple codes. In those cases, when you enter a city name, Google simply chooses a zip code by some undisclosed formula. For example, the keyword string *coffee new york ny* brings up a map of a neighborhood in lower Manhattan and its many coffeehouses. If you were hoping to find a midtown Starbucks, that map is a couple of miles off the mark. Using the string *coffee 10001* shows you caffeine choices around Madison Square Garden, in a closely zoomed map (see Figure 8-7). To get a tight view in cities with multiple zip codes but populations not as dense as New York's, search a street address, complete with city and state.

✔ Lacking a locator of any sort, Google Maps matches your keyword(s) to the current map center. Big deal, right? Well, this feature becomes handy when you're expanding your search beyond its original locator. Let's stay in Manhattan (see the preceding bullet). Double-click anywhere in Manhattan, centering the map around that point, and then search for *coffee.* Now drag the map to recenter it, or double-click another point. Click the Search button to find coffeehouses in the newly centered neighborhood. (Your keyword remains in the keyword box for as long as you continue this exercise.) The map remains zoomed at the level you set when searching in this manner; I like to zoom out a bit to make my sequential double-clicks reasonably far from each other. For some reason, I enjoy prowling around the landscape searching for coffeehouses, pet stores, restaurants, whatever. I admit I'm easily entertained. I admit I have no life. But I bet you get hooked on neighborhood-hopping, too.

If you prefer zooming the map with the + and – keys on the keyboard, remember that you must single-click the map (anywhere on the map) after conducting a search for those keyboard commands to work. Immediately after searching, the mouse cursor remains in the keyword box. You must get it out of there (by clicking the map) before Google Maps can respond to your scroll keys.

Figure 8-6:
Using the
near
keyword
sometimes
tightens the
search
radius in
Google
Maps.

Figure 8-7:
Using zip
codes
instead of
city names
can yield
more
precise
results in
cities that
contain
multiple
zips.

Google Maps does more than dumbly pinpoint business locations. After a search, click any pointer to see details about that listing. (The right side of the screen displays the phone number for each listing.) A pop-up window (see Figure 8-8) divulges the phone number, the street address, the Web site (or the first in a list of reference sites that mention the business), and a link to driving directions. More on driving directions in the next section.

Atop the right column are three options:

- **Print:** Click this to bring up the standard printer control box used by your printer.

- **Email:** Clicking this link brings up a Compose window for your default e-mail program, with a link to the current map placed in the message body. You must enter a recipient in the To field, and (if you choose) change the default message title from Google Map to whatever you please.

- **Link to this page:** This link provides a permanent address to the current map. If you left-click the link, the map redraws with the permanent address in the browser's destination bar. You may also right-click the link and choose the Copy Link Location selection in the drop-down menu; then you're free to paste the map's permanent URL into an e-mail, blog entry, or anywhere else.

Figure 8-8:
Click any result pointer to see details of that listing.

Finding your way from here to there

Google Maps furnishes three methods for getting driving directions:

- ✔ Enter a request for directions in the keyword box.
- ✔ Click one of the Directions links (To here or From here) in the pop-up information window for any search result (refer to Figure 8-8).
- ✔ Click the Directions link above the keyword box and fill in the Start address and the End address (see Figure 8-9).

As automated search engines go, Google Maps is exceptionally intelligent when it comes to understanding a request for directions in a language that approaches normal English. Rather than making you type information into several From and To fields, as in Yahoo! Maps and Mapquest, Google Maps accepts *from . . . to* queries in the same keyword box. You can even leave out the *from* — it'll still work. Try the following keyword string:

from 141 one mile road cranbury nj to 14 witherspoon street 08542

Figure 8-9:
On the Directions page, the previous local search results remain on the map.

It brings up a splendid map with step-by-step driving directions on the side (see Figure 8-10). As with other mapping sites, you may reverse the directions (click the Reverse directions link) and print them (with the Print link).

In a typical sequence of events, you would search for a local business, and then get driving directions from your home to that business. Google Maps makes it easy:

1. **On the Google Maps home page, enter your search string and click the Search button (or press the Enter key on your keyboard).**

2. **On the search results map, click any pinpointed search result.**

   You may click on the map or on the right sidebar. An information window opens over the map.

3. **In the information window, click the To here link.**

   A different information window pops up (see Figure 8-11).

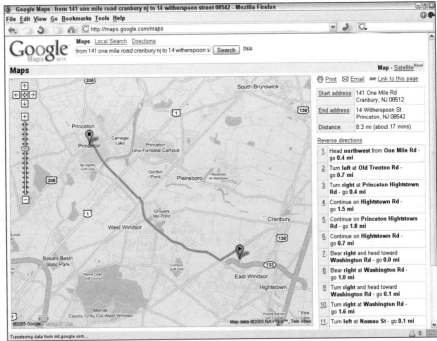

Figure 8-10: Google Maps provides driving directions and a map of the route. The route map can be zoomed and dragged.

4. In the second information window, enter your start address.

Use the same rules described in the preceding section to define your start location. Your start location may be as broad as a zip code, in which case Google determines a specific start address for you. Of course, you may enter a specific street address with town and state.

5. Click the Get Directions button.

Voilà. Notice that when getting directions by this method, Google puts your start address and destination into the Start address and End address boxes above the map. When you get directions with a long keyword string that contains both locations, Google doesn't separate the keyword form into two boxes. In the latter case, Google seems to assume that since you used only one keyword box for your query, that's all you'll ever need. But when you get directions from a search result, entering a destination separately, Google takes pity on your troubled self and provides the two keyword forms.

If you look at the right side of the page in Figure 8-10, and in any driving directions provided by Google Maps, the list of direction points is marked by linked numbers. When you click any numbered step, a pop-up box illustrates a zoomed-in view of the step.

Figure 8-11:
Enter your starting location in the pop-up box, and let Google Maps route your trip to the selected search result.

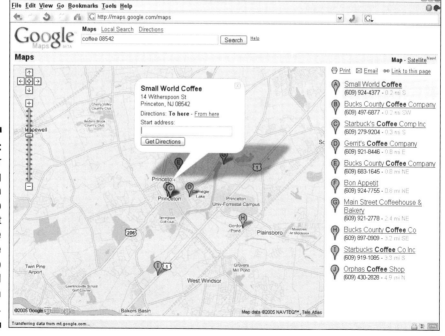

Seeing the Real Picture with Satellite Images

The maps in Google Maps are impressive, as online maps go, but you can also see a far more realistic view of your search results by using the <u>Satellite</u> link near the upper-right corner of search results pages or the Google Maps home page. Figure 8-12 shows what the opening view of North America looks like in the satellite view. The image is subject to exactly the same dragging and zooming techniques described previously for the nonsatellite maps.

Any search result displayed in map view can be redisplayed in satellite view simply by clicking the <u>Satellite</u> link. Conversely, you can switch back to the map view with the <u>Map</u> link. Back and forth you go — map, satellite, map, satellite . . . try to do something constructive today, would you?

The satellite view is more concrete than the relatively abstract map view. Figure 8-13 shows a close-up of search results for *coffee* in Princeton, N.J. Anyone familiar with the town would be able to precisely identify the locations of the pointers.

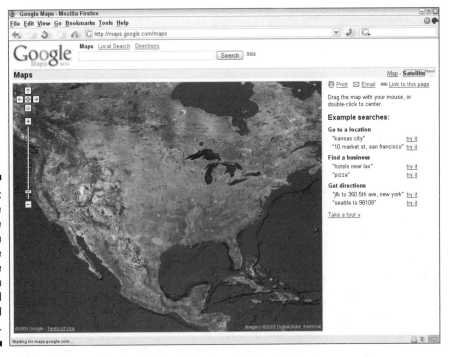

Figure 8-12:
The Google Maps home page in satellite view. The image can be dragged and zoomed.

Figure 8-13:
A close-up
image in
satellite
view,
displaying
search
result
points.

The satellite view might or might not be more useful than the map view, but it is inarguably more fun. Several Web sites have sprung up to list unusual, beautiful, and otherwise impressive satellite images turned up in Google Maps. Anyone can share a link to a great image. Just use the Link to this page link, as described earlier in this chapter, to copy the page's Web address, and then paste it into your own Web page, Weblog, e-mail, or whatever. The trick is to find great images. Success comes from exploring, and choosing likely interesting sites such as airports, stadiums, or coastlines. One excellent site, understandably called Interesting Google Satellite Maps, contains links to hundreds of outstanding images. Check it out here:

```
perljam.net/notes/interesting-google-satellite-maps/
```

Another excellent resource is Google Sightseeing, located here:

```
www.googlesightseeing.com
```

Even with satellite images, when it comes to seeing the world on your computer screen, Google Maps is just the beginning. The next section describes a Google service that lifts the information you get from Google Maps to a higher level — orbital, in fact. Your life might never be the same. Certainly, your conception of how the Internet can link with the physical world is about to change.

Local Searching from Orbit: The Wonders of Google Earth

When I first downloaded and started using Google Earth, I embarked on a lost weekend of which I have few explicit memories. Time passed in a haze of exploratory intoxication. All I know for sure is that someone stuck an intravenous line in my arm so I wouldn't expire from dehydration.

Google Earth: What it is and isn't

As I mentioned at the start of this chapter, Google Earth is a satellite-imaging and mapping service. The images and the program in which you view them come from a company called Keyhole, which Google acquired in late 2004. Google Earth is the first product to be released under Google's ownership, and the information in this section comes from a preview release given to Keyhole subscribers before the official release of Google Earth. That was then, and this is now, and as you read this Google Earth is available to everyone as an official product. As of this writing, I do not know whether a subscription fee will be charged.

According to promotions, Google Earth contains the only three-dimensional rendering of the entire planet available on the Internet. The program calls up an astonishingly smooth presentation that seems to whisk users, airborne, over the planet's terrain as they glide from one location to another.

The claim of three-dimensional rendering deserves a reality check. When viewing cities, Google Earth delivers photos, pure and simple. The program conveys a certain 3-D-ish look, as any photo does, but when you view the images from ground level (which I'll get to later), flatness prevails. Do not expect to see the canyons of Wall Street rise up around you when zooming into Manhattan. But some natural elements are rendered with a more realistic 3-D appearance, and mountains do indeed seem to rise above you when plunging into the hills southwest of Sausalito, for example.

Reality distortions notwithstanding, don't let any disappointment creep in, and don't dismiss Google Earth prematurely. The program is fabulous. I was kidding about the lost weekend, but when I first got my hands on Keyhole, and then later on Google Earth, I did do a lot of out-loud exclaiming. My wife came in to see what was wrong, and soon she started exclaiming. (Our dog was indifferent, but she has always been unimpressed by the Internet.)

This is a good time to mention that you need a fairly muscular computer and online connection to handle Google Earth's heavy graphics load. Google Earth is for Windows computers only, and minimum requirements include Windows 98, a Pentium III (or equivalent) processor, and 200 megabytes of space on the hard drive. Those are *minimum* requirements, and I think Google Earth would bog down significantly on that computer. Recommended is a machine running Windows XP, a Pentium 4 or equivalent, and 2 gigabytes on the hard drive. A high-speed connection is not listed as a requirement, but a good deal of graphics streaming takes place, and the soaring Google Earth experience would be somewhat grounded without a DSL or cable connection.

The Google Earth cockpit

Learning to use Google Earth is like learning to fly. When you first start the program, Google Earth displays a far-orbital shot of the earth and gradually zooms you toward it, stopping at a respectful distance. (See Figure 8-14.) This image of the earth's globe is called the default view. From there, the controls are in your hands. You can fly around the globe, dive down into the atmosphere, skim low and fast above the ground, hop from city to city or street to street, and lazily float above your hometown.

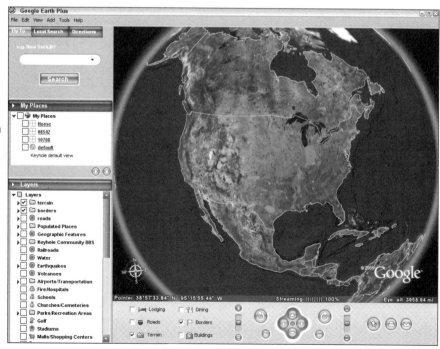

Figure 8-14:
Google Earth starts by giving you the world. Note that I have the Borders switch on, showing national boundary overlays.

Google Earth does not operate in real time. You are not viewing current images, and you are not manipulating the camera lens of an orbiting satellite. You are manipulating images stored in the Google Earth database, some of which are rather on the old side. Google Earth responds to world events to some extent; views of Fallujah, Iraq, were updated fairly frequently in late 2004 and early 2005. The views of some major cities were three years old at the time of this writing. My town started construction of a new library three years ago; Google Earth shows the old library and no sign of construction. In a test that involved flying over real estate listings, I discovered that Google Earth was not aware of some streets that were built two years ago and could not find those listed addresses.

The first things to note about Google Earth, when you can tear your eyes away from the graphics, are the control panels below and to the left of the graphic display. (See Figure 8-14 again.) The bottom panel contains image controls for panning, tilting, and swiveling the image — I'll get to these a bit later. Also on the bottom panel are check boxes that activate information overlays; that's where you can find the Borders control activated in Figure 8-14. The Roads box overlays lines and street names on the terrain, as shown in Figure 8-15. The Lodging and Dining boxes create instant search results, again overlaid.

The left panel features three panes used for multiple controls: determining flyover destinations, local searching, getting driving directions, storing book-marked locations, and activating a wide range of overlay information.

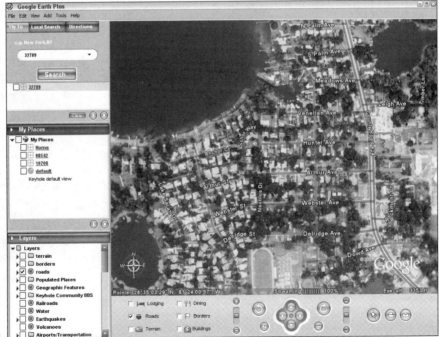

Figure 8-15: Use the Roads control to overlay a street grid and road names.

Basic flying techniques

The top pane of the left control panel contains a Fly To tab (refer to Figure 8-15), and that is where you enter a destination. Simply type your destination in the entry box (as described next), and then press the Enter key or click the Search button.

Entering destinations in Google Earth

The main navigation technique in Google Earth, aside from aimlessly floating around (which can be quite enjoyable), is entering a destination. Unlike Google Maps, unspecific queries are welcome. Google Earth accepts countries, states, cities, zip codes, street names, and numbered street addresses. Google Earth flies to the destination and zooms to a level appropriate to the specificity of your query.

Note: Google Earth always presents the first view of the destination you enter with the compass on the lower-left of the viewing screen showing north as straight up. Therefore, if you've spun the view around (more on that later), the flight to a new destination is delightfully dizzying as Google Earth smoothly recalibrates.

Anytime you zoom off to a Fly To destination, Google Earth puts the destination you entered in the space immediately below the Search button (see Figures 8-14). You can right-click that destination and select Add To My Places. The My Places pane in the left control bar stores a list of Fly To destinations (as well as Local Search and Directions searches); think of them as bookmarks. In future sessions, you can double-click any Fly To destination to revisit that view.

Zooming, panning, tilting, rotating, and possibly getting airsick

Google Earth offers four basic ways to manipulate a destination view. Each of these controls is located on the bottom control panel; hover your mouse cursor over the panel controls to see their functions. Two of the four maneuvers listed next (zooming and panning) can be controlled also with the mouse, as I describe a bit later.

- **Zoom:** The zoom control changes altitude. Zooming in, you move closer; zooming out, you move farther away. Google Earth lets you zoom out to nearly 40,000 miles, from which point the earth appears as a large marble. You can zoom in to about 35 feet, at which altitude cars and highway lane dividers are easily visible, and people are sometimes discernible. Resolution is always somewhat blurry when zoomed in all the way. I find that useful zooming bottoms out at about 250 feet. (See the alt indicator in the lower control panel, just under the image to the far right. Note that the image in Figure 8-15, which shows building and trees clearly, represents an altitude of 3355 feet.)

✔ **Pan:** Remaining at a constant altitude, you may move the view side to side, or up and down. Visually, it sometimes seems as if *you* are moving, not the image.

✔ **Tilt:** Google Earth lets you tilt the angle at which you view the ground. From a viewpoint straight above your destination and staring straight down, you may gradually tilt the distant horizon downward (more distant from your vantage point) as the foreground moves upward (closer to your vantage). The effect is remarkable (see Figure 8-16) and arguably depicts flying more naturally than the flat view.

✔ **Rotate:** Finally, you may spin the image around without affecting zoom or tilt levels. This maneuver effectively spins the compass (located in the lower-left corner of the view) so that you may see a destination from any direction. Rotating is particularly effective when combined with a tilt.

The zooming range I mentioned (down to about 35 feet) applies to screens running at the relatively high resolution of 1280 x 1024. (Right-click your desktop, select Properties, and then select the Settings tab to see and adjust your screen resolution.) Those numbers refer to the number of pixels (dots of light) displayed by your monitor. The higher the numbers, the more pixels are squeezed onto the screen and the finer the graphic resolution. Google Earth benefits from high resolution, and gives you clearer low-altitude zooms at the 1280 x 1024 setting than at a lower resolution. Because of book production requirements, the screen shots on these pages were taken at the 1024 x 768 setting, which blurs the close-up graphics somewhat. Google Earth looks a lot better at the higher resolution, which is supported by most monitors built in the last three years and some older ones.

Panning can be controlled by dragging with the mouse. Simply grab the image and drag it around. (Hold down the left button and move the mouse.) If you release the mouse while it is moving — sort of flinging the image — the panning motion continues and you can sit back while the earth moves below you. This technique is worth practicing: hard flings move the terrain at a quick pace; soft flings make it crawl.

Also worth practicing is zooming by dragging the mouse. You can use the zoom control in the lower control panel, but once you get the knack of dragging (use the right mouse button, not the left one), you'll never go back. (You can also zoom with your mouse's scroll wheel if it has one. That style of zooming is quick and incremental, as opposed to the smooth motion of dragging.) As with panning, use the fling trick to set a zoom in motion, and watch as you hurtle toward the earth or shoot upwards, away from it. Use hard or soft flings to moderate the zoom speed. Unfortunately, Google Earth doesn't allow the image to pan and zoom at the same time, perhaps fearing that the addictive giddy enjoyment would cause users to ignore all practical aspects of their lives, such as jobs and families.

Figure 8-16:
Google
Earth tilts
the image,
enhancing
the 3-D
effect in
some
locations
and making
the fly-by
effect more
realistic.

The Tilt slide in the lower control panel is an important feature. Very often, the flat default setting looks artificial and even disturbingly *wrong.* That wrongness is caused by a conflict between the flat viewpoint and the angle at which the photographs were taken by the orbiting satellite. The photographic angle can naturally produce a somewhat sideways view of tall buildings, and it's disconcerting to look straight down and see buildings pitched at an angle. Also, the lower part of the view can seem to be fading away from you in a way that induces mild vertigo. I find that a moderate tilt (the control works in only one direction: background down and foreground up, as if the earth were tilting away from you) brings beauty and order to the view. When flying low over mountain ranges, a substantial tilt is essential to get the most of the 3-D effect — the Terrain check box in the lower panel must be checked to activate that 3-D effect.

Use the Rotate left and Rotate right buttons to change the compass setting relative to your position as the viewer. Because you can't move, the rotation is accomplished by spinning the earth below you. Try it, and then enter a new destination. Google Earth rears back, arcs upward, and launches toward the new location while spinning the earth back to north pointing upward — the effect can be vertiginous, but I find it pleasing.

As Google Earth homes in on a destination, the image resolution gradually improves; this process can take a minute or so if you zoom in quickly. The images you see aren't stored in the program; they're streamed to the program over the Internet. (Google Earth doesn't work if your computer is not connected.) You can note the progress of the resolution improvement by watching the Streaming indicator in the lower control panel. When it reaches 100 percent, the image is as clear as it's going to get at that zoom level.

Global village: Local searching in Google Earth

Google Earth would just be eye candy if not for the other two tabs in the upper pane of the left control panel. Those two tabs are Local Search and Directions. This section explains how to use Google Earth to get the same results as in Google Local and Google Maps, and have those results overlaid on the Google Earth terrain.

At the basic level, there is not much to explain. Click the Local Search tab, enter a keyword or keyword string, and click the Search button. Google Earth does the rest. As in Google Maps, you may enter the entire search string (for example, *italian restaurant orlando fl*) in the top entry box or put the location in the bottom entry box.

Figure 8-17 illustrates the result of a local search for *coffee 08542* — it's an example I used several times previously in this chapter to find coffeehouses in Princeton, N.J. The Google Earth view of this search defaults to a fairly high view (more than 50,000 feet in altitude); you can zoom in to see geographical features more clearly. Note that in Figure 8-17, I turned on the Roads overlay in the bottom panel to orient the results better. Clicking any lettered result overlay on the terrain (A, B, C, and so on) pops up an information panel, just as in Google Maps and Google Local.

After you perform a local search in Google Earth, you can see how Google's three local services — Local, Maps, and Earth — are tied together. They are three different environments for displaying identical results. The displays differ, but the results come from the same index and are the same.

The results of Local Search in Google Earth can be tilted, zoomed, panned, and rotated just like any Fly To destination. Figure 8-18 illustrates a 1300-feet-up view of coffeehouses in a Manhattan neighborhood, with the view tilted and rotated.

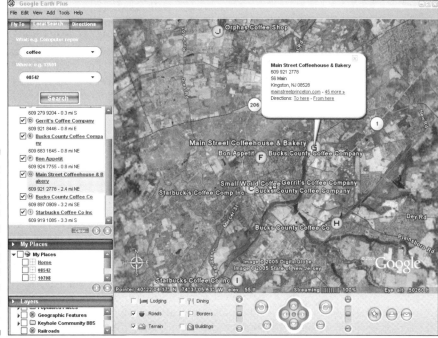

Figure 8-17:
Local Search results in Google Earth. Checking the Roads box helps orient the results.

Figure 8-18:
Zooming, tilting, and rotating local search results gives a better sense of neighborhood.

When you conduct a local search, Google Earth displays the results as a simple list below the Search button in the left panel (see Figure 8-18). Double-click any one of those results to zoom in to it in the view window; uncheck any check box to remove that result from the view window. You can also right-click the search, or any individual search result, and select Save To My Places; doing so puts that search (or individual result) in the My Places pane of the left control panel. Once there, the search can be launched afresh in the future by double-clicking it.

Plotting your course

As in Google Maps (though not in Google Local), Google Earth allows you to order up driving directions from any one address to another. In the top pane of the left control panel, click the Directions tab. You have two entry boxes here, one for the starting location and one for the destination. Fill 'em in. Click the Search button.

As with Local Search and Fly To searches, the Directions search puts its results not only in the view screen but also in the Directions pane just below the Search button. Right-click the search result (or any of the points in the directions list), and then choose Save To My Places to bookmark the search.

Most people print driving directions they get online, and Google Earth meshes nicely with Google Maps to accomplish this. When the result of your Directions search is displayed, click the Printable view link in the directions list located in the left control bar. Doing so opens a new pane below the main view showing the directions search in Google Maps (see Figure 8-19). In that pane, as in a browser window viewing Google Maps, you can use Print to make a printout of your directions. (Click the X in the upper-right corner of the new pane to close the Google Maps display.)

Now the fun begins. Look at Figure 8-19, and notice the Play button (actually called the Play Tour button) next to the Clear button below the driving directions. Clicking this button sets Google Earth in motion, driving you along your Directions route. The program moves from point to point, spinning around to position your perspective correctly, zooming up and down, tilting the image, all to convey a sense of driving along the route. Play Tour is one of the most delightful features in Google Earth.

When driving along with Play Tour, click the Roads check box and the Dining check box to get your bearings during the drive-through. Use the Pause or Stop button to . . . well, pause or stop the tour.

Figure 8-19: Google Earth shares the screen with Google Maps when you're ready to print driving directions.

Miscellaneous Google Earth features

Limited space prevents a thorough rundown of every single aspect of Google Earth. In this section I want to touch upon a few important features not covered earlier.

Printing an image

The Print button is located in the lower control panel. Clicking it brings up a small panel offering four print resolutions: Quick, Medium, High (1400 pixels), and High (2400 pixels). Higher resolutions take longer for the printer to set up. In all cases you get the view pane without the surrounding control panels.

Adding a placemark

Clicking the pushpin icon in the lower control panel starts the process of adding a placemark, which also looks like a pushpin stuck into the image window. Placemarks are automatically added to My Places, and you can visit them with a double-click in future sessions. Follow these steps:

1. **At any destination, click the Add a placemark button.**

2. **In the drop-down menu, click Placemark.**

3. **In the pop-up window, type a name for your placemark, and then click OK.**

The placemark is listed in your My Places panel. Check or uncheck the box next to that placemark to make the placemark appear or disappear from the image view when the image includes that destination. (For example, when zoomed out to view the entire North American continent, a placemark of a street address does appear when that placemark is checked.) This trick with the check boxes works for all items in My Places.

Using layers

Layers are preset overlays representing common search items such as banks, coffeehouses, ATMs, shopping malls, railroad tracks, airports, bodies of water, stadiums, grocery stores, schools, and many other community and geographic destinations. Click the check box next to any layer to overlay that feature on any image view. Figure 8-20 illustrates how crowded a view can be with many layers checked; the view is of a portion of Los Angeles. I leave most layers turned off during normal operation as I fly around the world, turning them on one or two at a time as needed.

Figure 8-20:
Layers, layers, layers! The image view can become too cluttered with them.

The Upshot of Local Search in Google

This chapter covers a lot of ground and introduces three relatively new services, all launched after the publication of *Google For Dummies*. I can imagine that anybody who has read straight through this chapter is struggling with the sudden onset of mental instability. No, that's not what I mean . . . anyone who has gotten to this point might be wondering what the final recommendation might be. Google Earth is impressive but requires an investment of time and computer resources. Google Local has received lots of publicity but seems less advanced than Google Maps. Where should a person turn first and last for high-quality, fast local searching?

I say, go to Google Maps. It stands between the high-tech glitz of Google Earth and the basic search-and-map functionality of Google Local. The maps might seem drab after soaring around in Google Earth, but they are, in fact, unusually clear and usable. Search results and integrated driving directions could hardly be more intuitive and friendly. Google Earth is for special occasions, and Google Local has, in my mind, been mostly supplanted. Google Maps is the centerpiece of local searching in Google.

Chapter 9

Shining the Search Spotlight on Specialty Categories

In This Chapter

▶ Finding your way to Google specialty searches

▶ Limiting searches to government sites

▶ Searching the Linux and BSD worlds

▶ Using the Apple Macintosh and Microsoft search engines

▶ Schooling yourself in university searching

*T*ake Google's hand and let it lead you into a specialized universe or two. Or three, or four, or five. Google has created alternate search engines whose results are limited to certain subject areas. Google accomplishes this topical restriction by choosing the source sites that can contribute to the search results. Google pulls these sites out of the main Web index, and then pools them into specialized indexes.

On the technical side, Google has isolated the worlds of Linux and BSD (both computer operating systems), Apple Macintosh, and Microsoft. Each of these areas enjoys a dedicated engine that searches sites provided by these organizations or related to them. On the nontechnical side, Google invites searching for government sites, including the related fields of military, local government, and global government. (Google playfully refers to this search engine as UncleSam.)

Rounding out the specialty categories is a large group of university-specific search engines, each of which prowls through a single college or university Web site. This mission is less limiting than you might think, because students and professors stash all kinds of documents on their school's computer. This engine is also less innovative than the other specialty engines because the searches are accomplished by simply adding the *site* operator (see Chapter 2) to your queries. You could do that yourself if you knew the domain name of the school you wanted to search.

This chapter is mostly recreational, unless you have a professional interest in one of these subjects. The sites are Google experiments that you get to play with. Having said that, though, I find myself returning to the UncleSam engine over and over for truly productive specialty searches.

Finding the Specialty Searches

Following its quiet tradition of refusing to promote its fringe features, Google buries its specialty services, perhaps discouraging regular use. You can get to the search engines described in this chapter through the main Google home page, but you have to know where to click, and the procedure is tiresome. Your online lifestyle is too busy for excessive mouse clicks. You have virtual places to go and ephemeral people to meet. Chips to devour and soda to drink. This section provides some tips for quickly reaching the government, BSD, Linux, Mac, Microsoft, and university search pages.

First, the URLs of the specialty search pages. The direct Web addresses are so easy to remember (with the exception of the university page) that your preferred method might be to simply type the URL in your browser's address bar. Here are the addresses, which point self-evidently to their respective search pages:

```
www.google.com/bsd
www.google.com/linux
www.google.com/unclesam
www.google.com/mac
www.google.com/microsoft
```

The university page is perplexingly more obscure, but if you have a good memory it doesn't pose much of a problem:

```
www.google.com/options/universities.html
```

Yes, you *do* need to type the `.html` at the end. Another option is to leap directly to the search page for a specific university by constructing a URL like this:

```
www.google.com/univ/princeton
www.google.com/univ/nyu
```

Notice that some universities are abbreviated, requiring some guesswork on your part. But most names are fairly obvious. Frustratingly, this address

```
www.google.com/univ
```

does not deliver the main university search page, though it is the basis of specific university pages.

U.S. Government Searches

Arguably, the most useful of Google's specialty search areas is that devoted to the U.S. government. Actually, this distinct search engine is both larger and smaller than the name implies. This engine is global in reach. At the same time, it reaches below federal government sites to the state and municipal level.

You might think that this entire search engine merely replaces the *site:.gov* operator:keyword combination described in Chapter 2. Not so. In fact, *site:.gov* remains quite useful in the UncleSam search because the results pages dish up a hearty mix of *gov*, *mil* (for military), and *com* sites that bear some relation to government, public policy, law, defense, and other fields of administration, the judiciary, and the legislature. All domain extensions are represented here.

The best way to get a feel for the blend of results you get in the U.S. government search is to throw in some keywords and let it rip. Don't think too hard about it — any keywords will do. Try generic, common words that you'd use in a general Web search, such as *internet* or *music* or *paris vacation.* Or choose newsy words such as *bush* or *terrorism* or *treaty.*

Use the results of your search to find Web sites that you can later search with the *site* operator. You can perform such a search in a general or UncleSam Web search. In fact, some of these discovered sites might make it to your bookmark list for regular visitation. The following are some examples of interesting sites that turn up in UncleSam searches:

```
speaker.house.gov
freedom.house.gov
democraticleader.house.gov
memory.loc.gov
gop.gov
```

Many related domains are too numerous and related to list, such as state government sites and the sites of individual House members.

Searching on issues and hot phrases can reveal who in the government (individuals, agencies, committees) is involved in that issue. Some examples include:

```
pledge of allegiance
fcc deregulation
abortion legislation
```

These searches display sites of agencies and members of Congress, in addition to more general information pages. See Figure 9-1 for an interesting search.

Figure 9-1:
Searching
the Uncle-
Sam search
engine for
current
events
offers a
dynamic
enhance-
ment of
Google
News.

All the specialty search engines recognize the same search operators you use in a normal Web search (see Chapter 2). I often use the *filetype* operator to search for PDF files in the U.S. government area, plumbing a rich trove of Congressional hearing transcriptions, court judgments, and other official documents that are customarily posted online in PDF format. Using *filetype:pdf* transforms any search; try adding it after any keyword string. For example:

```
music hearings filetype:pdf
housing starts filetype:pdf
testimony military filetype:pdf
consumer confidence filetype:pdf
```

The *intitle* and *allintitle* operators also work well in UncleSam searches. In fact, combining the power of those operators with the *filetype:pdf* combination is particularly fruitful because PDF files are usually titled so carefully — far more carefully than Web pages. Get specific with the title words. These examples have worked well to sharply narrow results:

```
allintitle:bush social security filetype:pdf
allintitle:social security future filetype:pdf
allintitle:iraq reconstruction filetype:pdf
```

The preceding examples also work nicely — and quite differently — without the *filetype:pdf* addition.

Think about using keywords that are applicable to different fields of inquiry, such as *testimony* or *"congressional hearing"* or *policy.* Putting almost anything after one of those yields fertile results; try *music, movies, abortion, taxes, airlines* paired with one of them.

Linux and BSD Searches

Linux is the open-source operating system that has been making waves for the past few years. Linux is much older than that, but only in recent years have developers created ready-for-primetime versions of Linux that have been loaded into computers selling in mainstream stores. Linux loyalists regard their operating system as a dynamic competitor of Microsoft Windows. Nobody owns Linux, though several companies own their respective operating system products based on Linux. Accordingly, Linux really refers to a family of operating systems, all built on the same foundation and with similar features.

BSD is also an open-source family of operating systems based on Unix. BSD got its start at Berkeley, and the acronym stands for Berkeley Software Distribution. BSD has less prominence in the consumer marketplace than Linux does, but BSD servers (operating systems for Internet and intranet computers) are in fairly wide use.

The term *open source* refers to any software authoring project operating in the public domain. Anyone may grab the code of such a project and alter it. Normally, open-source projects are organized to some extent by volunteer programmers who work on the program either as a hobby or as a potential profession. By definition, open-source software code is not owned. But in most cases, an individual or company is free to make a commercial product from a tailored version of open-source software.

If you have no interest in Linux, BSD, operating systems, or the open-source movement, the Linux and BSD specialty search areas might not be of much interest. If you want to take an interest, either search site is a good place to find out about the history and current state of Linux or BSD. As with the U.S. government search site, the BSD and Linux engines both forage in a restricted universe of relevant Web sources.

One fun experiment, even for those with merely a passing interest in these subjects, is to search for *microsoft windows* in the Linux engine. One recent search turned up, as the first result, a source site for obtaining Windows refunds. (No bashing intended — I run a Windows-only household. I'm just easily amused.)

Mac and Microsoft Searches

Apple Macintosh and Microsoft Windows: two operating system behemoths representing a fundamental polarity in the computer world. Nobody can claim that the Mac is a behemoth in terms of market share, because Apple sells less than 5 percent of all new computers. But when it comes to ferocious loyalty and PR stamina, Apple has world-class clout. Google has assembled a trove of Web sources relating to each system and segregated them into distinct search engines.

A favorite game of mine (I am *very* easily amused) is to open two browser tabs (or two windows in Internet Explorer), one for the Mac search engine and one for the Microsoft search engine. Then I search both for the same terms. Try *internet explorer, ipod, "steve jobs",* and *"bill gates".* Compare results for mind-twisting alternative perspectives. Good times!

Because Apple and Microsoft both maintain substantial Web domains, the pages of those domains tend to appear disproportionately. Get around this by using a minus sign, which is the symbol for the *NOT* operator (see Chapter 2). When searching the Mac engine, blot out *microsoft.com,* and when searching the Mac site, eradicate *apple.com.* Here are two example search strings:

```
itunes specifications -site:apple.com
windows xp networking -site:microsoft.com
```

You can override the limitations of the Mac and Microsoft search engines by using the *site* operator, pointing it to any site. This is a marginally useful tip, granted, but there might be a time when you want to break out of Macland or Microsoftville by searching another site without tracking your way back to the Google home page. Of course, this point is superfluous if you use Google Toolbar. Are you using the Google Toolbar? You should be. See Chapter 12 for more tiresome exhortations.

University Searches

High-school seniors take note: Google has your search engine. The university specialty searches let you rummage through a single university's Web site with the power of Google's search algorithms and operators.

University search operates differently than the other specialty searches described in this chapter. Google does not aggregate many university sites for searching. And this is not a search engine for getting information *about* universities in general. Instead, Google has actually created dozens of small search engines, each dedicated to a single university Web domain.

Useful? Well . . . this specialized search helps if you repeatedly search in a certain college site. Or, if you learn the URL syntax I divulge in the first section of this chapter, you can seamlessly surf from one specialty university engine to another.

You can avoid the inconvenient trip to Google's university search pages by using the *site* operator, assuming you know the university's URL. Virtually all university site domains end with the *.edu* extension, so you need to know the primary domain name, which is often easy to guess. Let's say you want to search for keywords matching inside Princeton's site. A simple (and correct) guess of Princeton's domain is *princeton.edu.* So this keyword string

```
admissions policies site:princeton.edu
```

gets you the links you want from the Google home page or the Google Toolbar.

Remember, also, that you can conduct a search across all educational domains by using the *edu* extension with the *site* operator, like this:

```
undergraduate stress site:edu
```

But let's not diverge too far from the straight and narrow. You can always approach the university specialty search sites the way Google intended:

1. **Go to the following page:**

   ```
   www.google.com/options/universities.html
   ```

2. **Click the university link you want to search.**

   All university links are contained on this single, long page. Scroll down or click an alphabet link to leap ahead.

3. **On the resulting search page, launch your search in the regular fashion.**

   All results point to pages in that university's Web site.

Not all colleges and universities are represented in these search engines, by a long stretch. I sometimes visit Rollins College in Winter Park, Florida, and am disappointed that it's missing from Google's college list. But this is when using the *site* operator is handy. Because I know the Rollins domain is `rollins.edu`, I can search it from Google's home page or the Google Toolbar at any time.

The university search engines are not affiliated with the universities. Go directly to the university Web site for a glossier presentation of the school.

Chapter 10

The Professional Rescue Team at Google Answers

*I*n the background, behind your screen, next to the heaving mass that is the living Google index, resides a freelance staff of human researchers approved by Google to track down answers to specific queries. Whereas keyword search queries display automated search results — basically page after page of links — Google Answers queries result in conversations and expert answers.

Google rigorously screens this staff of researchers for informational agility and communicativeness. They are paid 75 percent of the fees assigned by users to their posted questions. Google gets the other 25 percent. Researchers are not assigned to certain questions; they claim them, based on their areas of expertise and their willingness to tackle the query's needs.

The only Google-branded consumer service that isn't free, Google Answers lets you set the price for expert advice, facts, and linkage. No other portion of Google lives up to this book's title — *Search and Rescue* — more than Google Answers, which can be an informational lifesaver when your search is too exotic or academic for the free engines.

This chapter covers every aspect of Google Answers — from creating an account to posting a question, from setting a price to rating the answers. Don't blow off this chapter, no matter how against the Google grain it might seem. Even if you're a veteran Googler who never needs research assistance, knowing your way around Google Answers (if only its directory archive of previously posted queries) can be invaluable. And if you're a budding researcher with no interest in paying someone else, this chapter shows you how you can sharpen your skills by observing Google Answers in action.

Creating an Account and Logging In

This section establishes how you create a Google Answers account. Creating an account allows you to participate in one free aspect of Google Answers: posting comments to questions. (Later in the chapter, I offer guidelines for this type of participation.) Creating the account does not obligate you to pay a research fee or post a question. In fact, there's no need to provide credit card information until you post your first question, at which point you're prompted for it.

A Google Answers account is different from a Gmail account, but if you have Gmail, your username and password can be used for Google Answers. (Gmail is Google's Webmail service; check out Chapter 14.) However, it doesn't work the other way around: having a Google Answers account does not open a Gmail account. Google's account system is a little confusing — or more than a little. But the need for multiple accounts is understandable when you consider that payment information is required in some but not others. Hence, Gmail (which is free) uses a different account structure from Google Answers, AdWords, and AdSense, all of which involve financial transactions.

Anyway, if you want to ask a question in Google Answers, you need a Google Answers account. You don't need an account to browse the Answers database. The account ID enables you to post a comment to somebody's question and be recognized by the system. Then, when you're ready, you can add payment information to your account and post your own question.

If you have Gmail, just go to the Google Answers home page (see Figure 10-1) and click the <u>Create a Google Account</u> link. Google Answers is located here:

```
answers.google.com
```

Depending on your computer's cookies, Google might recognize you and place your Gmail address on the screen; if so, simply enter your password and click the Sign In button. On the next page you select your account nickname (which identifies you whenever you post a contribution or question), and select whether you want e-mailed notifications of responses to your questions. You also must agree to a Terms of Service document. The statement includes warranty information, details on how your account is billed, the refund policy, a lot of disclaimers about the nonprofessional nature of the service's financial and medical information, and a declaration that, should you become stupider by using Google Answers, Google will not supply you with smart drugs.

Figure 10-1:
The Google Answers home page.

Note: You may use a non-Gmail e-mail address to establish a Google Answers account, even if you have a Gmail address. If Google recognizes your Gmail address and puts it in the sign-in box, click the If you are not you@gmailaddress.com, click here link to start fresh.

If you don't have a Gmail account, create a Google Answers account by going to this page address:

```
https://www.google.com/accounts
```

On the Google Accounts page, click the Create an account now link, and follow the instructions.

Creating a Google Answers account does not authorize Google to collect fees from you. Google does not require your credit card information to establish the account. However, you can't post a question (see the following section) without providing payment information.

Note: Whenever your Google Answers nickname appears on the screen, the following hyphenated suffix is attached to it: -ga. So if your chosen nickname is mynickname, your onscreen nickname is mynickname-ga. This alteration identifies you in the Google Answers portion of your Google Account, which covers a few different services.

Posting and Canceling Questions

Posting a question to Google Answers is simple enough, but never free. For putting a question in play, the minimum charges are

- ✔ A $0.50 listing fee
- ✔ A fee between $2.00 and $200.00, determined by you and paid to the researcher

So the least you can pay to get a question on the board is $2.50. The listing fee is credited to Google at the time of posting. The researcher's fee is charged when an expert answers your question — no answer, no payment.

Your credit card is charged on a schedule determined by your balance and the time of month. If you run up listing fees and researchers' fees come due of $25.00 or more, your credit card is hit for the full amount. If your due balance stays under $25.00, Google collects the dough once a month. Remember, researchers' fees come due not when you ask a question, but when you get an answer.

When you created your Google Answers account you did not provide credit card information or any other way for Google to bill you. Google Answers fees are always paid by credit card. You can't post a question without providing that information. There's no point in providing it *before* you want to ask a question, so the following steps assume that you've sat down at the computer, opened up your browser, and want to post your first question to Google Answers.

1. **Go to the main Google Answers page at** `answers.google.com`**.**

2. **Click the <u>Log in or Create a Google Account</u> link.**

   This step is not necessary if you're already logged in to your Google account (for example, if you used Gmail during the current browser sessions and didn't sign out).

3. **Log in to your Google account with your e-mail address and password.**

4. **On your account page, click the <u>Ask a Question</u> link, located at the top right.**

   You can also begin setting up your payment information by clicking the <u>My Profile</u> link. But proceeding directly to Ask a Question takes you through the credit card process, too.

5. **On the Ask a Question page (see Figure 10-2), fill in the Subject, Question, and Price fields, and select a Category.**

This seems a lot like work, doesn't it? It's worth it. For more about how to fill in these fields and maximize your chances of getting the answer you need at the price you want to pay, see the next section of this chapter.

6. **Click the Continue to payment information button.**

   You might be asked to enter your Google Account password again. No need to include the -ga suffix.

7. **On the Google Answers: Enter Payment page, fill in your credit card and billing information.**

8. **Click the Pay listing fee and post question button.**

   If you click this button, the listing fee of 50 cents immediately becomes collectible by Google. You may also use the Go back and edit question button to reword your query or set a different price. The preview posting of your question as currently worded and priced is displayed below the buttons.

That's it — your question is immediately posted. Click the View your question link on the confirmation page to see what you did. Figure 10-3 shows a posted question. Note that the time of posting and the expiration date are both listed. Questions remain posted, unanswered, for one month. Answered questions remain in the Google Answers directory permanently.

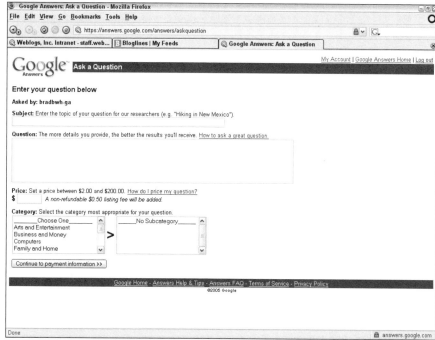

Figure 10-2:
Ask your question, title it, set a price, and choose a category all on this page.

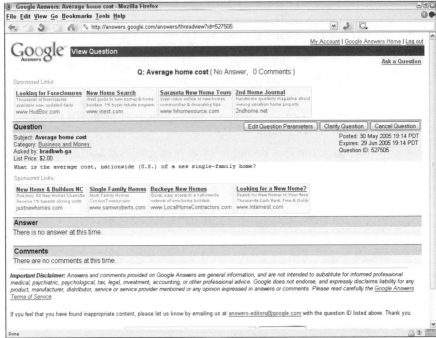

Figure 10-3:
A question
posted to
Google
Answers,
viewed on
the poster's
View
Question
page.

The View Question page contains enough features to warrant a closer look:

- ✔ You might see sponsored links on your View Question page (see Figure 10-3). Other Googlers see them, too. Google's AdWords program (see Chapter 17) positions these paid links throughout the service, not just on the search results page, where they are prevalent.

- ✔ Use the Edit Question Parameters button to adjust the wording of your question or the price you're offering for an answer. You may continue to tweak your words and price until the moment a Google researcher claims the question. Once claimed, the question is locked in place, and you may not make changes to it.

- ✔ Use the Clarify Question button to add information to your question that would help a researcher better answer it. You can do so at any time.

- ✔ Use the Close Question button if you change your mind and no longer want to receive a paid-for answer. On the following page, simply click the Yes, Close Question button. Or if you're truly indecisive and now want to keep your question alive, click the No, Keep Question button. If you close the question, it remains posted, but researchers can't claim it. And although you don't have to pay for an answer, you do still owe Google 50 cents for posting the question in the first place.

✔ Below your posted question is space for the answer (which, when it comes in, is as publicly viewable as your question) and space below that for comments from other Googlers. You don't pay for comments from the peanut gallery.

You may post as many questions as you like. Manage your questions, billing profile, and invoice information on your Google Answers account page, which is available through the <u>My Account</u> link on every Google Answers page.

A fair amount of dialogue can ensue between the person who posted a question and the researcher(s). In some cases, a second researcher joins the party. Researchers may seek to clarify questions, just as users may seek to clarify answers, so more than one researcher might be attempting to clarify a question before one of them finally claims and answers it.

Figure 10-4 illustrates a posted question with a researcher's request for clarification, followed by the questioner's clarification.

Farther down the page (see Figure 10-5), the expert asks for further clarification, and answers the question while doing so. The questioner acknowledges that the expert has "nailed it."

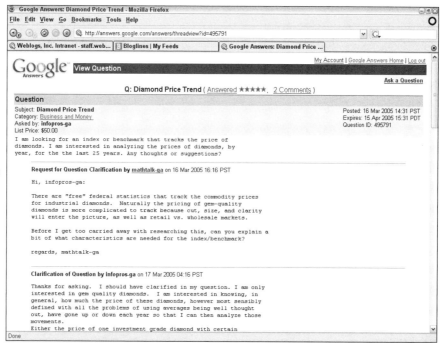

Figure 10-4:
An exchange begins with a posted question and a researcher's request for clarification.

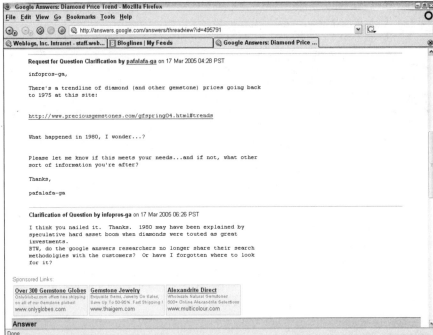

Figure 10-5:
More
clarification
results in
the question
being
answered.

Still farther down the page (see Figure 10-6), the researcher repeats the answer in the proper space and includes an explanation of the research. The questioner rewards the high-quality work with a substantial tip. Tips are encouraged and frequently seen, but they are not required.

Note: Questions with relatively high monetary bids ($20 and over) are likely to generate the most interest among researchers, naturally enough. I have notices also that those high payers tend to be generous with tips, also. You can see all bid prices listed with questions in the Google Answers directory, as shown in Figure 10-7.

Locked questions

A posted question is *locked* when a researcher has claimed it and is working on the answer. The lock remains in place for two hours, during which time a small padlock icon appears next to the question in the Answers directory. If the researcher doesn't post an answer after two hours, the question reverts to open status.

Locked questions do not prohibit comments, though, so if you have something worthwhile to contribute to a posted and locked question, go for it. Just click the question, and then click the Add a Comment button to display a form in which you type your comment. More on this later in the chapter.

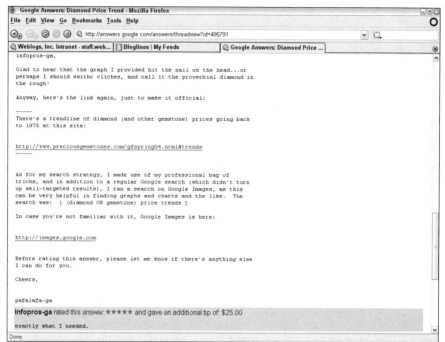

Figure 10-6:
Finally, an
answer is
posted.

Figure 10-7:
Directory
pages show
question
headers and
the prices
bid for
answers.

If only this tip were about tips. That would be so clever and hilarious. Never mind. What I do want to recommend is this: Browse Google Answers for research techniques. Most experts divulge their research paths when answering questions, and reading through the answers is like taking a crash course in online research. To be sure, these experts sometimes use specialized tools that aren't easily available to most people. But much of their work takes place right within Google's various engines.

Comments and Conversations

A lot of clarifying goes on in Google Answers, both before and after a researcher gets hold of your question. The system is devised to encourage conversation and cooperation between user and researcher. It's not *Jeopardy!* Flexibility is built in to the system to increase the chance of satisfaction on both sides. Because of the conversational nature of the Google Answers system, combined with the eagerness to share knowledge shown by Google researchers and other users browsing posted questions, you can often find the information you want (or some of it) without getting a formal answer to your posted question.

Anybody can add a comment to a posted question, and the authors of added comments are not identified as researchers or regular users. The result is an information milieu in which everyone is sharing what they know. The trick is to distinguish between good information and bad information — an issue that can be universally applied to the Internet. Many Google Answers comments, and nearly all official answers, are documented with links to research sites, which helps establish their authenticity.

Figure 10-8 shows an open question followed by two comments that effectively answer the question. The figure isn't large enough to reveal that, in fact, four comments were posted to the question, which still doesn't have an official answer. The question is a scientific one and apparently easy to answer. The offered payment was low, discouraging any researcher from claiming it before others jumped in. The comments appear to answer the question; it is often the case that interesting questions get answered quickly, and free of charge, before experts become involved.

Your question might be answered by comments, without an official researcher's answer. This development is somewhat rare in the case of specific, data-oriented questions, which researchers jump on with dizzying speed. But it's not so uncommon when a question requires deep research, has multiple answers, or is priced low.

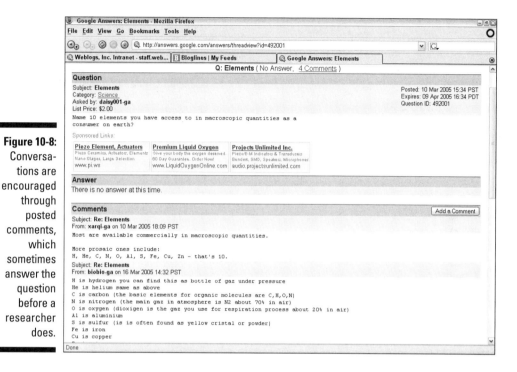

Figure 10-8:
Conversa-
tions are
encouraged
through
posted
comments,
which
sometimes
answer the
question
before a
researcher
does.

If you're satisfied with the posted comments your question has attracted and no longer need an official answer, feel free to close the question by following these steps:

1. **Click the <u>My Account</u> link on any Google Answers page.**

2. **Click the link to your question.**

   You might have more than one posted question. Use the drop-down menu to narrow your list, if necessary, by choosing Questions Awaiting Answers.

3. **On your question's page, click the Close Question button.**

   The page reloads with a confirmation notice at the top, asking whether you're sure that you want to close the question.

4. **Click the Yes, Close Question button.**

   After closing a question, that question appears on your Google Answers account page, with CLOSED in the Status column (see Figure 10-9).

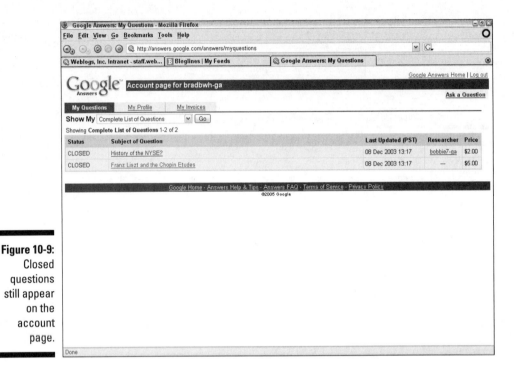

Figure 10-9:
Closed
questions
still appear
on the
account
page.

All the back-and-forth discussion following a posted question can make Google Answers seem almost like a message board. Almost. The conversations are not *threaded* as a message board is, meaning you can't see at a glance who is responding to whom in Google Answers. However, the similarity to message boards brings up an interesting point: If you can get good information from informal comments in Google Answers, maybe you can likewise get questions answered on message boards elsewhere. That, in fact, is partly what Usenet newsgroups are all about, and Google provides a Web interface to Usenet newsgroups. Chapter 6 dives in to Google Groups in excruciating detail. The point here is that, in general, informal knowledge sharing on the Internet can be as good as paid expertise and can be found in many venues.

The great values of Google Answers are these:

✓ **Speed:** Google staffs the Answers section with hundreds of researchers, each waiting to pounce on a question and claim its payment. Most questions, unless they are hopelessly obscure, start drawing information within hours — sometimes minutes.

✓ **Accuracy:** Google Answers pops into my mind when I have an extremely detailed question. Surfing the Answers directory, you can see that such questions receive hard work and good results from researchers, who seem to enjoy sinking their teeth into a sharply defined information challenge.

Newsgroups can also be fast and accurate, but they yield a more slapdash experience, replete with conversational sideshows and a generally impatient and grumpy attitude. Google Answers is a cleaned-up, more polite, and far more literate arena for extracting information than Usenet newsgroups. You get what you pay for, I suppose, with the bonus that sometimes Google Answers does its best work for nothing more than the 50-cent listing fee.

Clarifying Questions and Evaluating Answers

You can interact with the Google Answers service on three levels:

- ✔ **Waiting for an answer:** You've posted a question and await a researcher's answer.

- ✔ **Received an answer:** You've posted a question, and a researcher answered it.

- ✔ **No question:** You're browsing questions posted by others.

Each level offers options, covered in this section.

Clarifying and modifying a question

Previously in this chapter, I described how to formulate and post a question. Doing so is the first of four options available to the Answers user requesting expertise:

- ✔ **Ask:** Posting a question is always the first step.

- ✔ **Modify:** You may change the title, category, or pricing of your question while it's still in open status. Click the question title on your account page, and then use the Edit Question Parameters button.

- ✔ **Clarify:** You may adjust your question while it's still in open status. Click the question title on your account page, and then use the Clarify Question button.

- ✔ **Comment:** You may respond to comments posted to your question, as long as the question's status remains open. Click the question title on your account page, and then click the Add a Comment button. This button appears only after somebody comments on your question.

Refunds and repostings

In the rare event that a Google Answers expert lets you down completely, your recourse is to apply for a price refund. You have two options, actually:

- ✔ Apply for a refund. Getting a refund closes the question to all further activity, including comments.

- ✔ Apply for a credit for the amount of your expert payment, plus a reposting of the question. Getting the credit automatically reposts the question for research by a different expert. The second 50-cent listing fee is waived.

Both options are included in one online form. You must go to this page:

```
http://answers.google.com/
    answers/main?cmd=
    refundrequest
```

If you don't want to copy that long URL, find the link by clicking the <u>Answers FAQ</u> link, which is listed at the bottom of every Answers page.

Choose the Repost My Question or Request a Refund radio button, and explain why you think either option should happen. You need to include the question ID, which is located on the question's page, not on your account page. (Figure 10-8 shows a question ID, in the upper-right corner.)

Fine-tuning and rating answers

When you receive an answer to a posted question, your have four options:

- ✔ **Request clarification:** If an answer isn't satisfactory, you may request further work from the researcher. Use this option with great discretion! Its purpose is not to squeeze out more information than you originally asked for. If your question was unclear, you can acknowledge such and ask for a bit more writing from your expert. Likewise, if the answer is unclear, you have every right to ask for a clarification. Click the question title on your account page, and then use the Request Answer Clarification button.

- ✔ **Rate the answer:** Usually, the final step in the conversation between you and the researcher is to rate the answer. For some reason, most people don't feel motivated to assign a rating other than five stars. If you're unsatisfied with the answer, the best approach is to request clarification. But no matter how you feel at the end, you're free to rate the experience you paid for. Click the question title on your account page, and then click the Rate Answer button.

- ✔ **Tip your expert:** You might feel that an exceptional answer deserves more than you originally agreed to pay. A tipping system is built in to Google Answers. Tip amounts can be between $1 and $100. The money is charged to the same credit card you have on file in your Answers account. Click the question title on your account page, click the Rate Answer button, and then fill in the amount of your optional tip. Click the Submit Rating button to post your rating and authorize your tip. Both the rating and the tip amount are publicly viewable.

✔ **Request reposting or a refund:** For the truly disgruntled user, requesting a refund is the last resort. You may issue the complaint and be finished with it, or you may ask for a price credit and also for your question to be reposted as a new, open question.

The tip is optional. Even though it's bundled onto the rating page, do not feel pressured to issue a tip with your rating — they are different, independent options.

Adding a comment

When cruising through Google Answers as an interested observer, with no open questions of your own, you may participate by posting comments to the queries of others. You can join the conversation on both open and closed questions, whether they have been answered by a researcher or not. Everyone in Google Answers is of equal status when it comes to posting comments. Simply click the title of any question, and then click the Add a Comment button.

It might sound obvious, but don't add a comment unless you have something worthwhile — and germane — to say. This isn't a message board in the Net-culture sense, so don't indulge in "Me too!" posts or in merely expressing your interest in the question at hand. Contribute information that helps answer the question, clarifies the subject, or somehow increases knowledge for everyone reading, especially the person who posted the question.

Good Questions at the Right Prices

The best way to maximize your Google Answers experience is to ask the right question, at the right price. Asking a difficult, multipart question and offering $2 for its answer might not attract the best — or any — researchers. Offering $30 for the answer to a simple question will create a researcher feeding frenzy but leave you feeling ripped off. Additionally, posting an unclear question (even though it can be corrected with the Clarify feature) is liable to generate timewasting clarifying conversations, perhaps leading to the researcher feeling ripped off or you feeling obligated to tip heavily.

Good questions = good answers

First off, certain types of question head straight into a dead end because of Google's legal restrictions. In some cases Google will even delete the question from public view. So keep in mind the following:

- ✔ **Don't place any personal contact information in your question.** Don't ask researchers to phone you or e-mail you privately. Google Answers is an open forum. While you're at it, avoid putting up anyone else's contact information, too. I have seen researchers answer questions in part by providing phone numbers or addresses. But for regular users, the only contact information permissible is the Google Answers user ID name.

- ✔ **Don't ask for help doing something questionably legal or outright illegal.** For example, requesting assistance in making unauthorized music downloads would probably get your question removed or at least incite warning comments from researchers.

- ✔ **Don't spam.** If you try to use the Google Answers space to promote your Internet business or sell products, you'll get bumped off for sure.

- ✔ **Don't get X-rated.** References to porn, and especially links to it, are over the line.

- ✔ **Don't cheat on your tests.** Google Answers encourages student use while doing homework, but getting a researcher to answer a test question is against the rules. The two uses are separated by a fine line, to be sure, and questions stay or go at Google's discretion.

Questions spawn related questions all too easily. Asking multipart questions isn't against the rules, but you should know what you're doing. Don't ramble on with every query that enters your head. Be aware, too, that you're essentially bidding for a researcher's time, and the more complex your questions, the more money you should offer. Researchers are generous, and chances are good that you'll get a bit more than you asked for in a simple query.

If you want to hit several points of a query subject, try breaking the subject apart and posting a few low-priced queries. This clarifies your needs to the researchers, and gives them a chance to focus on specific questions rather than grapple with a bundle of them. It doesn't hurt, too, to spell out explicitly the parameters of the answer you need. Include what you already know, and explain what you need to know.

The Google Answers directory is a virtual laboratory of questions, comments, and answers, in which you can discover what works and what doesn't. Surf the directory by following these steps:

1. **Go to the Google Answers home page.**

   To do so, click the Google Answers Home link on any Answers page or use the Google Toolbar (see Chapter 9).

2. **Scroll down the page to see the Answers directory topics.**

3. **Click any subject category.**

   You can also click a link under Recently answered questions.

4. **On the category page (see Figure 10-10), click a subcategory, and then click a question.**

   The right columns show the date and price of each question.

You can discover a lot just by glancing down a main category page. Many question titles are explanatory; the price is right there in the far-right column, and you can see the Comment and Answer traffic each question has attracted. Click a few questions, too, to see how researchers handle various types of questions. You might be amazed at the detail and depth of the answers. Notice the star-rated answers — most ratings are five stars, signifying an extremely successful transaction between seeker and expert (and also signifying a customer who took the time to apply a rating). Asking a good question is half that equation.

Figure 10-10:
A category
directory
page.

Creating a descriptive heading for your question and placing the query in an appropriate category are both as important as the phrasing of the question. As I write this, an open query requests information about activity in Saudi Arabia immediately following the 9/11 terrorist attacks and is vaguely titled "current events." After a day, no answers or comments were attached to the question. When creating the query title, don't worry about crafting a good sentence. You can even word the title as if it were a Google search string. (While you're at it, you might want to try Googling your query in the Web index before posting to Google Answers.) Do whatever it takes to convey the subject of your query precisely.

Putting your money where your query is

Setting your own price for the Google Answers service might seem awkward, and it's best to avoid the temptation to bottom-line your every query. Likewise, don't pay too much for simple questions because you're reluctant to appear cheap. Google recommends estimating how long it will take to research your question and then pricing it accordingly. This advice, although relevant to the researchers, is nearly pointless to regular users who aren't information experts and can't anticipate the type of research needed. A better bet is to gauge, roughly, how demanding your question is based on two factors:

- ✔ **Speed:** Do you have a deadline or are you just impatient? Then attracting a quick answer has more value to you.

- ✔ **Complexity:** If your query contains more than one part or more than three sentences, chances are you're requesting more than $2 of expertise.

If you have plenty of time, one pricing strategy is to start at the bottom and work your way up. Post a $2 question and see what it brings in. Interested users post comments regardless of price, because they're not getting paid. If your $2 post doesn't get the attention you want, raise the stakes to $5, and so on.

The overwhelming majority of questions are priced at $20 or less. Browse through the directory (see the preceding section, "Good questions = good answers") to get a feel for the type of questions being answered at certain price points.

Chapter 11

Experimenting in Google Labs

Google is a brainy company, and its many Ph.D. employees are always conceiving new ideas. Google itself — the main Web index and search algorithms — was a college experiment turned corporate, in the finest tradition of Internet entrepreneurism. Many of Google's now-standard features began as tentative experiments that survived testing and arrived on the home page. At this writing, Google News — one of Google's anchor services — is still a *beta* product, meaning that it's still officially in the testing phase. Same with Froogle. (Both seem to work pretty darn well to me.)

Some of Google's newest brainstorms get piled into Google Labs, an open testing area that any user can play with. You enter this area at your own risk, but honestly, the risk is minimal. In most cases, all that can really go wrong is that something you try won't work as advertised, and even that is rare. All the Google variants described in this chapter except one (Google Compute) operate on Google's computers, not yours. You interface with them through your browser, just like regular Googling.

When I wrote *Google For Dummies,* Google did not promote Google Labs experiments, and the entire Labs area lurked in the shadows. More recently, Google has been forthcoming about its Labs projects, and new Labs launches often receive lots of publicity. Because of the attention now shone on all Google projects, Labs experiments cross less of a dividing line when "graduating" from Google Labs. I mention this because some of the major features of this book — such as Google Maps, My Search History, and Site-Flavored Google Search — are still (as of this writing) Google Labs experiments. Yet I treat them as if they were fully mature products, and indeed, they operate as such. This chapter covers Labs projects that have not found a place elsewhere in the book.

Be sure to check the Google Labs page at the following URL from time to time to see if anything's new:

```
labs.google.com
```

Keyword Suggestions

Many considerations go into determining the perfect keyword string. Frequently, tapping into the greatest number of results is not the goal — and, in fact, can be detrimental to finding the best results. But when searching a topic with which you are not familiar, suggestions based on a large set of results can be useful. That's the idea behind Google Suggest, an interactive keyword suggestion tool that responds to every character you type in the keyword box.

Google Suggest is easy to try and requires no setup. Just go to the Google Suggest site here:

```
www.google.com/webhp?complete=1&hl=en
```

That URL is a drag to copy; you can also go to Google Labs and click Google Suggest.

Figure 11-1 shows Google Suggest in action. Each letter that you type alters the drop-down list of ten suggestions. Use the up and down arrow keys to select one of the suggestions. That's really all there is to it. Useful? I haven't found many reasons to return to Google Suggest. But I'd like to see this tool bundled into Google Local (see Chapter 8), where it could come in handy completing names of businesses. Until then, Google Suggest is a mere novelty.

Google Suggest works with recent browsers only — they include Internet Explorer 6 or later, Netscape 7.1 or later, and Firefox 0.8 or later.

Figure 11-1:
Google
Suggest
offers
possible
keyword
strings
based on
what you
type.

Standing on the Shoulders of Giants

Isaac Newton's famous admonition to "Stand on the shoulders of giants" is the catchphrase of Google Scholar, a search engine that purports to uncover scholarly resources off the commercial Web. Google Scholar is Google's first stab into the hidden Web — the enormous untapped virtual library of books and academic resources that remains untouched by the Web. Google Print, which seeks to digitize books in major institutional libraries, is another effort in a similar direction. But whereas Google Print is a digitizing project whose results will eventually be incorporated into the main Google index, Google Scholar crawls resources that are already digitized and gathers them in a separate index. That index is located here:

```
scholar.google.com
```

Searching for previously unavailable material sounds more exciting than it actually is. The unfortunate fly in the ointment is that academic and scholarly resources are still mostly unavailable, hidden behind subscription services, academic firewalls, and password protections. Google Scholar reveals locations but often cannot reveal actual documents. This is one Google Labs project that is mostly theoretical.

But all is not lost. For one thing, searching in Google Scholar does sometimes bring up entire documents, especially when using the *filetype* operator (see Chapter 2) to find PDF files. Using *filetype:pdf* yields different — but not necessarily better — results in Google Scholar than in the Web index.

Google Scholar works best for those who have access to the type of electronic resources available through a university library, such as JSTOR (a database of academic journals), or access to the physical shelves of a university library. In that case, Google Scholar can help identify and locate authors and titles relevant to a research project. In particular, the lists of citations provided by Google are convenient. Figure 11-2 shows a Scholar results page. Note that each result contains a <u>Cited by</u> link, which leads to a list of books and papers that refer to the search result. Each citation contains its own list of citations. Following these leads reveals, in typical Google fashion, a living network of scholarly resources surrounding a topic.

Google Scholar rewards persistence. Try many searches and click through many search results. I have found wonderful, full-text results amidst the many protected abstracts that typically populate the search results.

Figure 11-2:
Google
Scholar
search
results. Use
the citation
links to dive
deeper into
a topic.

Video without the Video

Google Video is one of the most curious Labs projects. Launched as a beta-testing feature in January 2005, it was perceived by many (including myself) to be a response to Yahoo! Video. Yahoo! Video searches for video files stored on the Internet. Google Video, inexplicably, does not have any videos in its index. This dedicated engine searches for closed-caption transcripts of TV shows.

Why, you might ask, is a TV-transcript search engine called Google Video? If only I had the answer. The service is not without its uses, but it is definitely misnamed. However, it might eventually live up to its name. At this writing, Google is soliciting homemade videos from all comers. Google is attempting to assemble a massive index of authorized video content, which would remove the service from the danger of copyright infringement, a danger that Yahoo! courts with its video engine. I don't see where TV transcripts fit in, but I can envision a fun and useful index of uploaded video from amateurs, semi-pros, and professionals.

Google's video uploading page is here:

```
https://upload.video.google.com
```

Anyway, let's get to Google Video as it currently operates. The feature is located here:

```
video.google.com
```

Enter a keyword, and off you go. Figure 11-3 shows search results for the keyword *letterman*. Each result is a TV show on a certain date; the match is of your keyword to some portion of a show's transcript. Click any result to see a detailed log of those mentions, as shown in Figure 11-4. Each reference is given in context, surrounded by about a paragraph of closed-caption transcript. Although still shots are provided, there is no video in the search results as of this writing.

You can't be blamed if you think this is pretty lame. The real problem, as mentioned before, is the feature's name: Google Video. I admit that Google Closed-Caption Transcripts doesn't have a ring to it, but nobody forced Google to come up with this strange service. As a research tool, however, Google Video isn't all that strange. Students who want to cite television news programs, for example, can find their quotes more easily and accurately in Google Video than by any other means.

Figure 11-3:
Search
results in
Google
Video,
which
crawls
transcripts
of TV
shows.

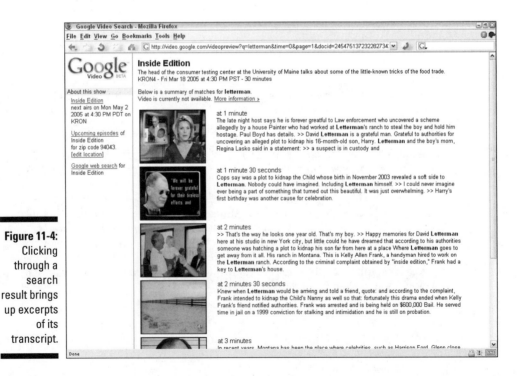

Figure 11-4:
Clicking
through a
search
result brings
up excerpts
of its
transcript.

A new twist to Google Video was introduced in April 2005, a few months after the closed-caption site was launched. Switching direction, the added service invites video producers of all stripes — amateur, professional, and everything in between — to upload their videos to Google Video for inclusion in a big, searchable index. There is even a mechanism in place for assigning a price for your video, if you think somebody would be willing to pay for a shaky look at your cat playing with string. Or perhaps you have a more refined product. Whatever; it is come one, come all. The upload page with instructions is located here:

```
hupload.video.google.com
```

Real-Time Rides

After viciously dissing Google Video in the preceding section, I'm glad to bubble with enthusiasm over Google Ride Finder, which uses Google Maps to help you find a nearby taxi. Working with taxi companies in selected cities, Google tracks the movements of individual cabs in eleven cities (at this writing; more cities on the way) and places their locations on Google Maps. (See Chapter 8 for more on the wonderful Google Maps.)

Google Ride Finder is easy to use; get started here:

```
labs.google.com/ridefinder
```

On the front page (see Figure 11-5) you see a map of the entire country with a few pins stuck in it. Don't do anything on this map — those pins aren't useful. Either click a city to the right of the map or enter a street address (in one of the selected cities) in the keyword box.

Clicking Houston, TX, brings up the map shown in Figure 11-6. That zoomed-out map doesn't help much in locating cabs, so use the map slider to zoom in. Figure 11-7 shows a detailed view of a Houston neighborhood; each colored pin represents a taxi on the move. You cannot immediately see that they are on the move; use the Update Vehicle Locations button below the map to track the movement of taxi.

So, here's the question about Google Ride Finder: Is it useful or merely cool? I can imagine a brainy Google engineer developing this thing after some difficulty getting a ride. But knowing where a cab is driving doesn't necessarily get you into that cab. Listing the phone numbers of taxi companies might be the most useful part of Ride Finder. But there is something undeniably fun, in a geekish way, in peering down into the taxi traffic of a city.

Figure 11-5:
The home
page of
Google Ride
Finder.

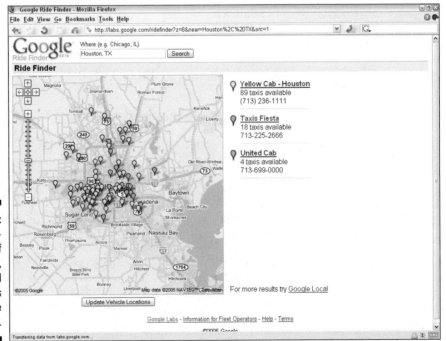

Figure 11-6:
A zoomed-
out view of
Houston,
Texas, and
some of its
in-service
taxi cabs.

Figure 11-7:
A Houston
neighbor-
hood and its
taxi cabs.

When you want to update a map to see cab movement, do *not* use your browser's Refresh (or Reload) button. Doing so reloads the entire Google Ride Finder site, and throws you back to the zoomed-out view of the United StatesInstead, use the Update Vehicle Locations button below the map.

Building Google Sets

A peculiar experiment in creating related keywords, Google Sets is marginally fun and occasionally useful. I can imagine the appeal of this idea to Google researchers because it turns the tables on most search enhancements. Usually, Google Labs is occupied with improving search results. Google Sets concentrates on using the Google index to enhance keyword selection.

Google Sets is easier to try than to describe. You can try it here:

```
labs.google.com/sets
```

Figure 11-8 shows the Google Sets page, which contains five keyword boxes. Type a word or a phrase into at least one box. Then press Enter, or click the Large Set and Small Set button. The results (see Figure 11-9) consist of other, related keywords. Click any keyword result to conduct a Google Web search on that keyword.

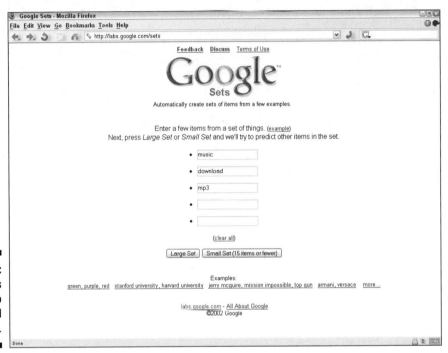

Figure 11-8:
Google Sets
attempts to
find related
keywords.

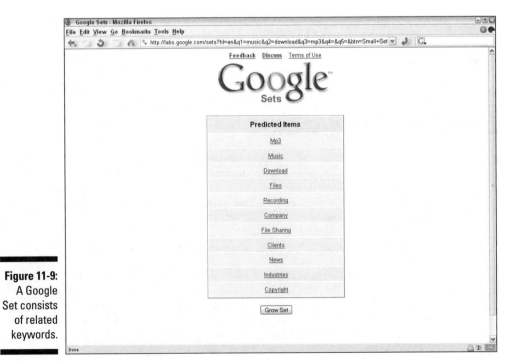

Figure 11-9:
A Google
Set consists
of related
keywords.

Frankly, Google Sets has limited appeal to most daily Google addicts. I know a few writers and journalists who use Sets as a sort of research tool to increase their awareness of key concepts related to an assignment topic. In that way, Sets could be a homework helper, too. But honestly, it's a stretch to imagine Google Sets fitting into most people's lives. As one bewildered user posted to the Google Sets bulletin board, "Who is using Google Sets?"

Actually, there are uses for Google Sets. For one, you can use Sets as a rough sort of thesaurus: Type a word, select Large Set, and see what synonyms pop up. Anyone who has a limited English vocabulary might find this use especially rewarding. Google Sets also works well with brand names — type one car manufacturer, for example, and get a list of others.

You might also try Google Sets as a sort of esoteric recommendation engine with a mind of its own. Because Sets accepts phrases, try typing one or two movie titles and see whether it recommends others. The results lead to exercises in six degrees of separation, as you try to figure out how Google connected the disparate titles in the resulting set. A request for a set built on *Remains of the Day* and *Silence of the Lambs,* two Anthony Hopkins films, returned *Fargo, Reservoir Dogs, Pulp Fiction, Goodfellas,* and *The Shawshank Redemption.* (By the way, if you haven't seen *Shawshank*, rent it soon.) It might be difficult to connect the dots between all those movies, but what's not fun about lists of movies? Try the same thing with books and music.

The Mythical Internet Library Comes to Life

Way back in Chapter 1, I discuss the fabled idea of the Internet Library, which was often suggested as a rationale for the very young World Wide Web. It was thought that in time, the Internet would make libraries obsolete. The truth is that online academic resources have changed the function of university libraries in some ways, to the great troublement of those campus administrators. But to regular folks — consumers — the Internet has not begun to replace libraries and has certainly not become an alternative venue for reading books.

Just now, that state of affairs is starting to change, and Google Print is behind the change. Google Print is an ambitious initiative to digitize enormous libraries of books, both scholarly and not-so-scholarly. Google is aiming to scan every book in the New York Public Library, the libraries of Harvard University and Oxford University, and many others. Google Print has two branches: Google Print for Publishers (which approaches publishers individually to gain licensing rights to scan their books) and Google Print for Libraries (which takes a broader approach and gives publishers a way to opt out of the whole-library scan).

Google Print is still in its nascent stages; the enormous project will take a long time to complete, if it is ever completed. But partial as it is, a dedicated Google Print engine exists to service your book-oriented queries, and it is located here:

```
print.google.com
```

Enter any keyword or keyword string and click the Search Print button. Your search results probably look a lot like Figure 11-10 but with different books appearing on the left side of the page. Click any book title or thumbnail cover image to see results for that individual book.

Figure 11-11 shows the results page for an individual book after I searched for a phrase within that book: *key signatures.* I entered that phrase in the Search within this book keyword box. The result of that search is a list of pages, by page number, that contain those keywords.

There's one more step before you actually read within the book, and that is to click a page number. Doing so displays a page of the book, with your "Search within the book" keywords highlighted in yellow on the page. (See Figure 11-12.) Note the arrows above the page; clicking them allows you to browse two pages in either direction from your search results page.

Figure 11-10: Search results in Google Print. Clicking any book brings up a page for searching within that book.

Figure 11-11:
Searching within the book brings up a list of pages containing your keywords.

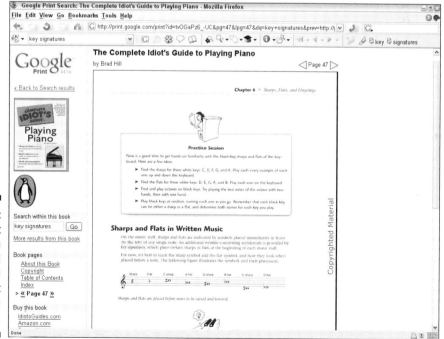

Figure 11-12:
Google Print allows you to read selected pages but not the entire book.

You can continue searching within the book and clicking other search results pages in the book, but two things happen eventually:

✔ Google requests that you sign in to your Google account if you are not signed in already. After signing in, you can continue searching and browsing book pages. (If you don't have a Google account, go to www.google.com/accounts.)

✔ Google prevents you from viewing any more pages in the currently displayed book. How many pages you get varies; Google has different copyright agreements with different publishers. I have read as many as fifty pages before being shut down. When Google lowers the boom, you are free to conduct another search and browse through another book.

Google Print is fun to use and a valuable research tool, small though the available library is at present. The catalog of available books is growing all the time, and the service promises to get better and more useful.

Horrors! A New Home Page!

In May 2005, the unfathomable happened: Google changed its home page. But the change is optional, and you get to decide whether to see a new home page or the traditional one. The new home page can be personalized to your taste. If you ignore this new feature, nothing changes; Google does not force any screen clutter upon you.

This new feature doesn't have a name, oddly. The personalization of the home page is part of an initiative called Fusion. Presumably, other products will come into the Fusion portfolio; the personalized home page is the first.

The idea behind Fusion is to tie together Google's many disparate services. Comparisons to Yahoo!'s personalization feature, called My Yahoo!, are inevitable — and unflattering to Google so far. (Google suffers by comparison at this writing, but perhaps will have made the features more robust by the time you read this.) My Yahoo! benefits not only from Yahoo!'s much larger platform of features and services, but also from Yahoo!'s more flexible and up-to-date customization of news from a huge number of sources. Google News allows personalization, as I describe in Chapter 5, but very few news sources are available in the home-page personalization as of this writing. That will change — probably at about the time this book is published.

Start at the beginning: right on Google's home page. Figure 11-13 shows the home page as somebody with a Google account sees it when signed in to that account. For the remainder of this section, I will call this view Classic Home, as Google does. If you don't have a free Google account, go here to start one:

www.google.com/accounts

Figure 11-13:
The Google
home page
as it
appears
when
signed in to
a Google
account.

Note the Personalized Home link in the upper-right corner of Figure 11-13. (Also note the My Search History link, referring to a service covered in the next section.) If you click Personalized Home, a similar home page is displayed, with a big Further personalize your home page link on it. Click *that* link to see Figure 11-14. At the time of this writing, twelve blocks of information were offered; clicking any check box assigns that information block to your Personalized Home and, as shown in the figure, offers a bit of additional customization in some cases. Your information options are limited. This page will doubtless change as the service evolves.

After checking boxes, click the Save Personalization button. Doing so returns you to your Personalized Home view, as shown in Figure 11-15. Quite a change from the chaste classic view, isn't it? It's almost shocking to see Google's home page in this state, but I must say that Google does a good job keeping everything looking clean and fairly uncluttered. No advertisements pollute the Googly goodness of the page.

Want to make changes to your Personalized Home view? Scroll the page down to the Further personalize your home page link and edit away. When you're finished, click the Save Personalization button.

Figure 11-14:
The simple
and friendly
personaliza-
tion page
is not over-
whelmed
with
options.

Figure 11-15:
Your new
personal
home page
view.

After personalizing your home page, you can toggle between Classic Home and Personalized Home using the links in the upper-right corner of the page.

Keeping a Record of Your Searches

Google's relatively new service, My Search History, was introduced in May 2005, partly in response to search-history tools offered at some other search engines. My Search History works behind the scenes, often without you being aware of it. You need a Google account to use this feature. If you don't have an account, go here to create one:

```
www.google.com/accounts
```

When you have an account and have signed in with that account to a Google service (for example Gmail, Google Groups, the personalized home page, or Google Print), My Search History keeps track of your queries and your click-throughs to result pages. Google does this without you needing to turn it on. Being signed in to your account is the only on switch.

It is important to understand the meaning of Google's automatic tracking of searches. I have placed a rare Warning icon next to this paragraph to drive home its importance. If you use a shared computer, you might not want to publicize the content of your searches. Many people couldn't care less; for them, searching is utilitarian and not especially personal. But it's easy to imagine many innocent scenarios in which a person wouldn't want his or her searches divulged to another. Imagine a husband searching Google for an anniversary present for his wife. My Search History makes it uncomfortably easy for his wife to view those searches and the results her husband clicked.

Because of the preceding warning, I want to explain how to turn off My Search History, before showing what it looks like. You can avoid having your searches tracked in four ways:

- ✔ Do not create a Google account if you don't have one already. This solution is drastic and prevents you from posting in Google Groups, personalizing the home page, browsing at length in Google Print, and using Gmail.

- ✔ Make sure you are signed out of your Google account when you conduct private searches. (Use the <u>Sign out</u> link on the home page.) This solution is inconvenient and prone to failure. Most Google users have become accustomed to searching quickly, without fussing over settings. The speed bump caused by this extra step, and the likelihood of forgetting to do it, is chiefly what recommends the next solution.

- ✔ If you have an account, click the <u>My Account</u> link on the home page when you are signed in, and then click the <u>Delete My Search History</u> link. The irreversible nature of this action recommends the final solution.

✔ You can pause My Search History by clicking the <u>My Search History</u> link on the home page, and then clicking the <u>Pause</u> link. The feature remains inactive until you choose the <u>Resume</u> link that takes the place of the <u>Pause</u> link.

When you use My Search History, Google keeps track of your queries and clickthroughs, and organizes the list by date. Figure 11-16 illustrates the historical list of searches; note the calendar on the right that invites you to click a day to see that day's searches.

Clicking the <u>Remove items</u> link puts check boxes next to each item on the list so you can select which to delete from view.

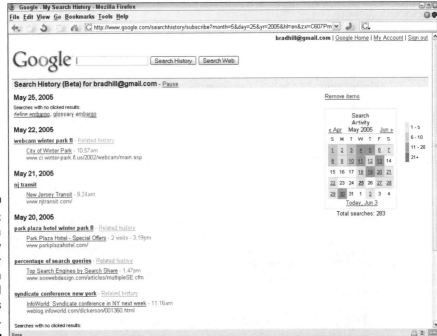

Figure 11-16:
My Search History tracks your search queries and the results you clicked.

Part IV
Putting Google to Work

The 5th Wave   By Rich Tennant

"Look, I've already launched a search for 'reanimated babe cadavers' _three times_ and nothing came up!"

In this part . . .

Like a supportive parent, Google is there when you need it but wants you to soar on your own.

You might think of Google as the ultimate search engine. You go to it, you humbly feed it your keywords, you heed its magisterial declamations, and you surf where it bids you. We live online lives guided, influenced, even determined by Google. All this is true and good. Yet Google stands ready to serve no less than it commands. The Google Toolbar is a loyal information butler that never strays from our side. Likewise, the Deskbar and Google Browser buttons. These hand servants are explained in Chapter 12.

Chapter 13 introduces Google Desktop Search, a relatively new service that allows you to apply Google's powerful indexing and retrieving technology to your computer's hard drive. Desktop Search is local search with a new meaning, and Google Desktop can solve the shambles into which your computing life has disintegrated. (No offense.)

Chapter 14 exposes Gmail as the landmark e-mail system that it is. You have to think a little differently about how mail is organized and presented to feel comfortable in Gmail, but the slight effort is worth it. Chapter 15 is all about putting Google on your site, if you have one.

The chapters in this part encourage you to build a deeper relationship with Google. It is almost a marriage, really: constant companionship, cooperative prosperity, and a partnered relationship with the larger community.

Prepare to have your horizons widened and your worldview expanded. You're going far afield in this part, from e-mail to your own hard drive. The atmosphere is heady with innovation, and you are a pioneer in the Googlesphere. [Editors' note: The good news is that Brad's caffeine saturation is wearing off. The bad news is that he's headed to the espresso maker for another jolt.]

Chapter 12

Lifelines: Googling from Anywhere

- -

In This Chapter

▶ Installing and using Google Toolbar version 2.0

▶ Understanding the new features of Google Toolbar version 3.0

▶ Getting a toolbar for the Firefox browser

▶ Downloading and using Google Deskbar

- -

*I*f Google is your most important online destination, launching your searches from the Google.com home page can be a nuisance. Even if Google isn't the most frequently visited page in your Internet life, it would be convenient to have a gateway to Google lurking by your side at all times. There are two such gateways:

✔ Google Toolbar

✔ Google Deskbar

Google Toolbar clamps onto your browser with an always-ready search box and many other features. It's a fairly complete Google bag of tricks that follows you around the Web.

Google Deskbar is even more independent, attaching itself to the Windows taskbar with a search box and easy gateways to many of Google's distinct engines. Deskbar doesn't need a browser, even to display search results — it uses its own pop-up window to furnish a complete search experience, including clicking through to target sites.

I can hardly overstate the importance of these two free products. They streamline the Google lifestyle tremendously. Of the two, I prefer the Toolbar for its range of features and seamless performance. The Deskbar operates a little sluggishly, even on my fastest computer. But I do like its browser-independent nature. The upshot? I run them both constantly. In so doing, I've noticed that I use the Toolbar for deep searches that are likely to result in lots of mouse clicks. I incline toward the Deskbar when I think the search will be a hit-and-run affair, perhaps using Google Q&A features that don't require any clicks to get the information I want. (See Chapter 3 for a rundown of Google Q&A.)

Note: This chapter covers the Google Deskbar as an independent product, and it is. But the Deskbar is also bundled into Google Desktop, a separate product that indexes and searches your computer's hard drive (see Chapter 13). It doesn't matter how you acquire Deskbar; the two packages (independent and bundled with Desktop) are identical.

Installing the Google Toolbar

If you're not (yet) using Google Toolbar, you must begin immediately. I mean it. I'm not cutting any slack on this point. It will change your life. It will consolidate awesome information power that's only a click away at all times. It will both deepen and streamline your relationship to Google.

Google Toolbar is built for the Internet Explorer browser, versions 5.0 and later. If you use the Firefox browser, Google has no toolbar product for you, but don't be discouraged — I cover your options later.

Figure 12-1 shows the Google Toolbar installed, ready for action. The keyword box is evident, over to the left. There's much more to the Toolbar than a portable keyword box, though. This following section describes installing the Toolbar; the section after that explains its many options.

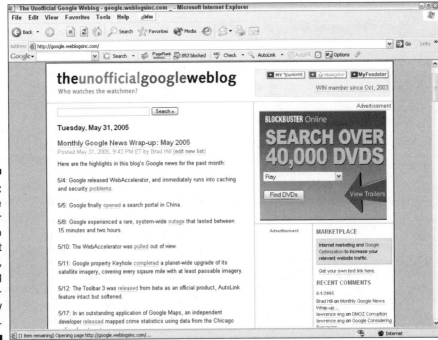

Figure 12-1:
The Google
Toolbar
bolts onto
Internet
Explorer,
providing
always-
ready
searching.

The Toolbar installation process is almost completely automated. You just click your way through a few buttons before Google takes over. Follow these steps:

1. **Go to this page:**

   ```
   toolbar.google.com
   ```

2. **From the drop-down menu, scroll down and select a language.**

3. **Click the Download Google Toolbar button.**

   A dialog box pops up, enabling you to choose a location for the file you're about to download.

4. **Select a location on your hard drive, and then click the Save button.**

   The Toolbar installer downloads to your computer and is stored in your selected location. You need to double-click the file after it downloads, so don't forget where you put it.

5. **Double-click the downloaded file (probably called GoogleToolbarInstaller.exe).**

   The installer pops open a new window on your screen.

6. **Click the Agree & Continue button.**

   You are agreeing to a Terms and Conditions document presented at the bottom of the window. The legalese specifies that Google owns the Toolbar, that Google is not responsible if it blows up your computer (it won't), and that you can't try to make money from the Toolbar (for example, by charging admission to watch you Google with it, which sounds a little disgusting). Other options can be set in this window before clicking the button. Select a national version of Google as your default engine if you are not in America, or if you prefer a non-English language. The check box to make Google the default search engine in Internet Explorer does not affect Toolbar functions; it enables you to launch a Google search from the browser's Address bar. It doesn't really matter whether or not you uncheck this box; the purpose of the Toolbar is to initiate a Google search. Finally, the installer asks to close Explorer windows as part of the installation but gives you the choice of closing them yourself. I always let the installer do it.

7. **Use the radio buttons to choose whether or not you accept the Toolbar features that require sending your surfing information to Google, and then.**

   The information sent to Google is anonymous; it is not connected to you personally. I enable these features, but many people prefer to not communicate their surfing destinations to Google, even anonymously, and choose Disable advanced features. You will not see the PageRank indicator if you disable the features at this point.

8. **Click the Finish button.**

   Google Toolbar bolts onto your browser, and Internet Explorer opens. Figure 12-1 shows the Toolbar with the advanced features, which refer to the PageRank display and its corresponding tracking of the browser's movements on the Web. All browsers using this feature of the Google Toolbar contribute to PageRank by telling Google what sites are visited.

You're ready to go. Try a search immediately by typing a keyword in the keyword box of the toolbar and pressing Enter. It's that easy. At first, search results appear in the current browser window, even if your Google Preferences are set to open a new window, as I suggest in Chapter 2. The following section shows you how to make that same setting for the Toolbar.

The appearance of your Google Toolbar might not correspond to Figure 12-1, depending on your settings, browser, and screen resolution. The next section reviews your configurable options.

Choosing Toolbar Options

Google offers a great deal of configurability in the Toolbar. To see your choices, click the Google logo at the left side of the Toolbar, and then click the Options selection. The Toolbar Options dialog box pops up on the screen, as shown in Figure 12-2. Note that this dialog box provides three tabs — Browsing, Search, and More — each filled with choices.

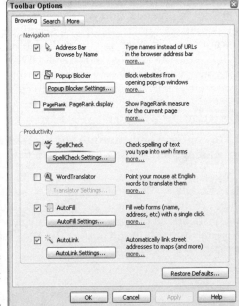

Figure 12-2: The Google Toolbar Options dialog box provides three tabs full of personalization choices.

Navigation and productivity options

The first tab in the Toolbar Options dialog box, called Browsing, presents two groups of personalization features. The first group relates to navigation:

- ✔ **Address bar browse by name:** This navigation feature encourages you to type company names, brand names, or Web site names into the browser's Address bar. If Google divines where it is you want to go, it takes you directly there. If something about what you type is ambiguous, Google runs a search.

- ✔ **Popup blocker:** The pop-up blocker prevents free-floating ads from sprouting atop and behind your browser. In certain conditions, this blocker doesn't touch the ads streamed directly to the desktop in Windows XP, as I explain more fully later. The feature does block ads associated with Web sites.

- ✔ **PageRank display:** For those interested in the ranking of Web sites in the Google index, the PageRank display is essential. In fact, the Toolbar provides the only glimpse of PageRank offered by Google — and it is only a glimpse. A glimpsed approximation, actually. PageRank is a complex measurement, and the simple PageRank display is (as they say in car ads) for comparative purposes only.

The next group of options in the Browsing tab relates to productivity:

- ✔ **SpellCheck:** Now, this is handy. The built-in spell-checker (it's the ABC check button) corrects typing mistakes in Web site forms. This feature might not help if you mistype your address, but it has great application in Weblog comment forms.

- ✔ **WordTranslator:** You point to English words on a Web page with your mouse and receive a translation to the language of your choice. The feature was not enabled in Google Toolbar at the time of this writing.

- ✔ **AutoFill:** This feature works identically in Toolbar 3.0 as in Toolbar 2.0 (see the preceding section).

- ✔ **AutoLink:** This is a controversial one. Google uses AutoLink to change certain text on Web sites into links. For example, if the toolbar detects an address on a Web page, AutoLink turns that address into a link to Google Maps, which, if the new link were clicked, would display a map of the address. Many Google pundits were up in arms when AutoLink was introduced because it dared to change the content of a Web site (turning unlinked text into linked text). Google doesn't own the Web sites you visit, so this feature can easily be deemed intrusive. AutoLink must be enabled manually; the button appears on the Toolbar by default, but you must click it to activate the feature on any Web page. At the time of this writing, Google was under pressure to remove AutoLink.

Search options

Under the Search tab of the Options panel, you can select half-dozen toolbar behavior characteristics when searching, and also select which search buttons appear on the toolbar:

- ✔ **Open a new window to display results each time you search:** I always keep this option checked. It leaves my original browser window anchored at its current site, while displaying Google search results in a fresh window.

- ✔ **Drop-down search history:** Select this option to see previous searches beginning with the same letters you type in the search box. Clicking the downward-pointing arrow next to the search box drops down a list of all previous searches. Normally, this search history is erased when you shut down the browser. But the next option saves your searches even if the browser is shut down or crashes.

- ✔ **Save the search history across browser sessions:** Check this box to prevent your search history, described above, from being erased when you close Internet Explorer. (You can always clear the search history manually by selecting Clear Search History under the toolbar's Google button.)

- ✔ **Automatically search when you select from the search history:** This option is great for recurring searches. Selecting this option forces Google into action when you select a previous search from the drop-down search history list, without the need to press Enter or click the Search Web button.

- ✔ **Remember last search type:** Select this option to make your search choices persist from one search to the next. Select which Google engine to search using the drop-down Search menu to the right of the keyword box. If you use the Toolbar to run an Images search, for example, the Toolbar will default to the Images index in future searches until you make a new choice.

- ✔ **Use Google as my default search engine in Internet Explorer:** Didn't you deal with this selection during installation? Yes, you did. The option persists now. Checking this box enables you to launch a Google Web search from the browser's Address bar.

The remaining options in the Search tab offer five search buttons that can be placed on the Toolbar. Three of the buttons correspond to Google engines: Images, Groups, and Froogle. Another is the famous I'm Feeling Lucky button, which takes your browser directly to the top search results before displaying the results. The Search Site button is extremely useful: It matches your keyword against the contents of the site currently displayed in your browser.

More options

The final tab in the Options panel is the More tab. Most of these options place buttons on the toolbar:

- **Highlight button:** This dynamic and extremely helpful button highlights your keywords, each in a different color, on any Web page displayed since your last Toolbar search.

- **Word-find buttons:** This feature places a button on the Toolbar for each of your keywords. (The buttons appear after you launch the search, not as you type the words.) If you have your options set to deliver search results in a new window, the word-find buttons follow you to the new window. Furthermore, they stay with you when you click search results, *even* if your Google Preferences cause yet another window to be opened. It's when you're at a search results site (not the search results page) that the word-find buttons become useful. Click any one of them to make a highlight bar jump from one instance of that keyword on the page to the next. These buttons should be used with the Highlight button, which accents all instances of all keywords. (Honestly, the Highlight button is the more useful of the two. But word-find buttons are great, too, if only to remind you what your keywords are.)

- **BlogThis!:** This button is for users of Blogger.com, Google's recently acquired Weblog service. Clicking the BlogThis! button enables users to post an entry to their Weblog that automatically refers to the Web page currently displayed.

- **News button:** Simple and indispensable, the News button surfs you directly to Google News, the essential current events portal of today's Internet.

- **Up button:** Cryptically named, this button keeps track of the layers you travel through a Web site and stands ready to jettison you back up to the home page or to an intermediary page. Click the small triangle next to the Up button to display a list of higher levels in the site. Click one of the list items to begin moving toward the surface.

- **Next and previous buttons:** These arrow-shaped buttons swing into action when you leave the search results page to visit a result page. After poking around a bit, you can click the next button to surf directly to the next hit on the search results list, without backtracking to the search results page. Of course, if your Google Preferences are set to open a new window when clicking a search result, you always leave one browser window anchored on the search results page, making the next and previous buttons superfluous.

✔ **Voting buttons:** when these buttons are on the toolbar, click the smiling or frowning face to vote for or against a page — even a Google search results page. Google compiles these votes and . . . does something with them. At this writing, nobody outside the company knows what. Call me cynical, but I'm waiting to see what votes get me before exercising my Googly democratic right.

✔ **Options:** This selection places the Options button on the toolbar, making it easy to invoke the Options panel.

✔ **Page Info button:** The Page Info menu button offers the cached (stored) version of the current page, similar pages, backward links to the current page, and a translation of the current page into your default language. These same options are in the right-click menu.

The final options allow you to select whether the toolbar buttons are identified with full text labels, shorter text labels, or remain unidentified by text labels.

Using AutoFill

If you register at as many sites and shop online as much as I do, filling out online forms is a tedious hassle. The AutoFill function in Toolbar 3.0 invites you to fill in your crucial information just once, and then let the Toolbar handle any forms you encounter.

Use the AutoFill Settings button in the Browsing tab of the Options panel to enter your information, as shown in Figure 12-3. You may add your name, e-mail address, phone number, two mailing addresses, and one credit card. (AutoFill would become much more useful if it accepted multiple credit cards.) Credit card information is protected by a password — and remember, all Toolbar information, including AutoFill, is stored on your computer, not on an Internet computer.

Conveniently, the Toolbar highlights the portions of an online form that it's capable of filling in. You may proceed to fill them in manually if you choose or just click the AutoFill button on the Toolbar to complete those fields all at once. AutoFill never fills in username and password fields, which can change from site to site. Not so conveniently, AutoFill takes the extra step of telling you what it's about to do, instead of just doing it. That confirmation window gives you a chance to review your information in a concise format, but it also gets annoying after a while.

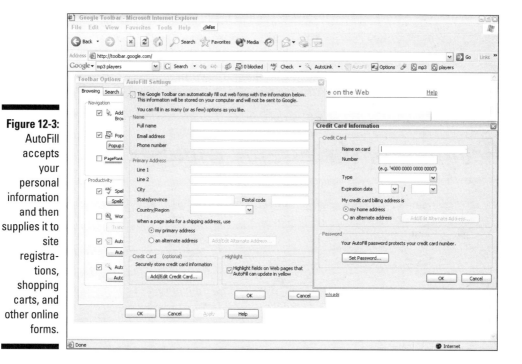

Figure 12-3:
AutoFill
accepts
your
personal
information
and then
supplies it to
site
registra-
tions,
shopping
carts, and
other online
forms.

The toolbar pop-up blocker

Like many toolbars these days, Google's includes a pop-up ad blocker that
creates a less commercial Web site experience. After you add the pop-up
blocker to the Toolbar (you can remove and add it at will through the
Toolbar Options dialog box), the blocker destroys pop-up browser advertisements before they hit your screen, makes a proud little noise for each
blocked ad, and keeps track of the total number of killed pop-ups.

If you want to allow pop-ups from a certain site, simply click the Pop-up
Blocker button after you arrive at that site. Google reloads the page, this time
allowing the ads to pop up. The button changes appearance to notify you
that pop-ups are enabled for that site and keeps track of your selection. Any
time you return to that site, pop-ups are allowed, and the button tells you so.
The liberation of pop-ups pertains to the entire site. When you surf away
from the liberated site, the button reverts to its original appearance, and ads
are blocked as normal.

Note: Google's pop-up blocker does not block pop-up browser windows
launched by any spyware and adware that might be infecting your computer.
It can be difficult to distinguish pop-ups launched by the Web site you're

visiting from pop-ups launched by hidden software buried deep in your computer. If you're tormented by pop-ups while running Google Toolbar with the Pop-up Blocker, it's a good indication that your machine is hosting spyware that tracks your movements around the Web and flashes ads based on your site visits. Run a Google search for spyware solutions and adware solutions; several free and inexpensive programs help clean infected computers.

Googling in the Firefox Browser

Firefox users are shut out of the pure Google Toolbar experience. But the Mozilla Foundation, which develops Firefox, has built a Google toolbar called the Googlebar. The Googlebar is sanctioned by Google and can be downloaded here:

```
googlebar.mozdev.org
```

The Googlebar (shown in Figure 12-4) contains most of the basic features of the Google Toolbar, plus some original ones. For example, a direct link to Gmail is incorporated in the Firefox toolbar.

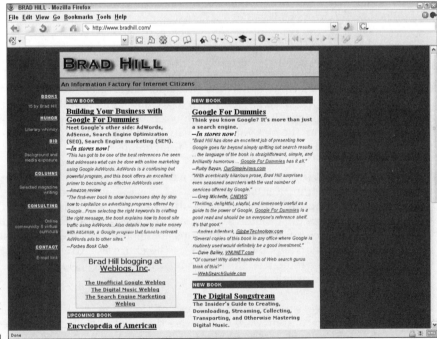

Figure 12-4: The Googlebar, a Google-sanctioned alternate toolbar for the Firefox browser.

Firefox users have much more control than IE users over certain features such as highlight colors and keyboard control of the Googlebar's functions. However, the PageRank display, one of the most important features to some users of the IE toolbar, is missing. Some Webmasters say that the PageRank display is the only feature of the Internet Explorer experience that keeps them tied to that browser.

Searching from the Desktop with the Deskbar

The Google Deskbar offers a scaled-down version of the Google Toolbar that is free of the browser. The Deskbar does not contain the toolbar's more exotic features such as PageRank display, pop-up blocking, spell checking, AutoFill, and AutoLink. But the Deskbar does accomplish basic searching and display of search results without opening a browser (if it's closed) or disturbing its current display (if it's open).

Go here to get the free Google Deskbar:

```
deskbar.google.com
```

Figure 12-5 shows the Deskbar quietly lurking in the Windows taskbar, where it lives. The Deskbar sits to the right of your program tabs and to the left of the system tray. Using the Deskbar is simple enough; type a keyword into the search box and press Enter. The Deskbar mini-viewer pops up to display search results (see Figure 12-6). The mini-viewer operates similarly to a browser window, but it's not Internet Explorer, Firefox, Netscape, or any other browser.

Clicking a search result in the mini-viewer displays the target page in the mini-viewer, unless you determine in the Toolbar Options that a browser window should be opened to display target pages. To see the Toolbar Options dialog box, click the small arrow next to the Deskbar, and then click the Options selection.

Alt+Shift+G puts your mouse cursor in the Deskbar search box. Pressing that combination and then typing a search query is an unbeatable, streamlined, quick way to launch a Google search.

Figure 12-5:
The Google
Deskbar
lives quietly
in the
Windows
taskbar.

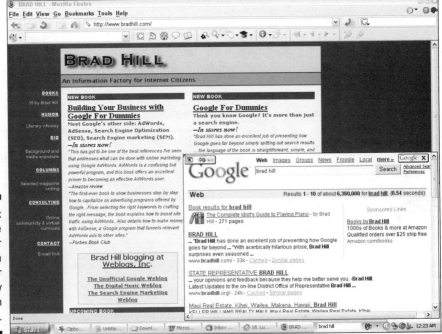

Figure 12-6:
The
Deskbar
opens a
mini-viewer
to display
search
results.

Chapter 13

Reclaiming Your Lost Stuff: Google Desktop to the Rescue

*I*n 2004 momentum was building in the search industry for a push into two frontiers: local search and desktop search. Google's impressive innovations in the former are covered in Chapter 8. The desktop searching frontier presented unexplored territory for Google, but it was no less urgent that the company release a product enabling users to Google their own hard drives. Microsoft was planning such a thing for its next version of Windows. Smaller search companies had already launched impressive desktop products. In October 2004, Google announced the availability of Google Desktop Search.

Google Desktop is deliberately integrated with Google Web searches, but it can also be used independently. This chapter explains the dual nature of the product and steps you through downloading and installing it. You might notice that many of the screen illustrations in this book showing Google search results reveal Google Desktop Search results from my computer above the Web results. Those results come from the Google Desktop program installed on my computer, which places relevant results from my hard drive atop relevant search results from the Internet.

That slick integration is one of the selling points of Google Desktop, but it also points to the ever-present nature of the program. When Google Desktop is installed and running, it is always lurking and working, indexing the contents of your computer and waiting for opportunities to contribute to your Web searches. This constant vigilance and participation in your online searches makes Google Desktop an awkward program for use on shared computers. It should *never* be used on public computers; do not download it at a library, for example. (Most public computers do not allow installations of new software.) At home, use Google Desktop only on computers that harbor no secrets.

The In(dex) and Out(put) of Desktop Searching

Do not confuse Google Desktop with Google Deskbar. The Deskbar (described in Chapter 12) conducts *online* searches from the desktop. Google Desktop conducts *computer* searches from the desktop. Both programs reside in the Windows taskbar. The search term *desktop,* referring to finding content on the computer's hard drive, is an odd one. Application programs of all types operate on the computer desktop. Understand that Google Desktop doesn't search the desktop; it searches the entire hard drive.

There are five stages in the operation of Google Desktop:

1. Download and install the program.

2. Allow the program to index the contents of your hard drive.

3. Run the program while you go about your normal computing life.

4. Activate the Google Desktop window when you want to launch a search of your hard drive.

5. Allow the program to contribute computer content to your Google Web searches.

The only speed bump in your use of Google Desktop occurs when the program indexes your hard drive. The process is not unlike Google's index-building crawl of the Web (see Chapter 16). If you have a large hard drive with plenty of files, Google crunches through the process in bits and pieces during idle computer time. The indexing does not interfere with your work or play on the computer, but it might be several hours before you can effectively use Google Desktop. The program becomes fully functional when the indexing is complete. You can conduct a search before the indexing is complete; Google Desktop provides results from its partial index.

The ideal use of Google Desktop allows it to run continuously, all the time. (However, it's easy to pause its operation at any time.) Desktop watches the computer hard drive and incorporates new files into the index. Those files could be things that you create, such a business letter written in a word-processing program, or things that you download, such as e-mail stored on the computer through programs like Outlook Express. Those files could also be online material that you access and that are placed in your computer invisibly, such as Web pages cached by your browser. Google Desktop's ambition (though it is not fully realized) is to match your search keyword to any piece of digital content captured by your computer.

Searching with Desktop involves clicking its icon, which opens a window that looks rather like Google's home page. This gets a little confusing — are you online or offline? That's exactly the boundary that Desktop hopes to erase.

Google wants you to think of the online and offline realms of your computer as an undivided landscape of content. Google will help you find anything in that landscape.

Anyway, when starting a search in that activated Desktop window, the program explicitly searches your hard drive and returns results only from the hard drive. It is when you search the Web (using the Google site, the Google Toolbar, or the Google Deskbar) that hard-drive results get mixed with Web results.

What Google Can and Can't Find in Your Computer

Most likely, Google Desktop can't index every single file on your hard drive. At the time of this writing, the Desktop's original (and fairly limited) functions had been expanded to include the recognition of many basic, common types of computer content. These file types include the following:

- ✓ Text files
- ✓ E-mail accessed with Microsoft Outlook, Microsoft Outlook Express, Netscape Mail, and Mozilla Thunderbird
- ✓ Cached browser pages viewed in Microsoft Internet Explorer, Netscape, and Firefox
- ✓ Microsoft Office files created in Word, Excel, and PowerPoint
- ✓ IM chat transcripts recorded in AOL Instant Messenger
- ✓ Adobe Acrobat files (PDF files)
- ✓ Standard music-file formats, including MP3, WAV, OGG, and WMA
- ✓ Standard image formats, including JPG and GIF
- ✓ Standard video formats, including MPG and AVI

In addition to file recognitions built in to Desktop by Google, independent developers are permitted and encouraged to create plug-ins that add functionality to the program. Many Desktop plug-ins add obscure features that the developers personally need; they create the enhancement mostly for themselves and then give it to Google as an afterthought. But others are excellent additions with broad appeal. One such plug-in adds several graphic file formats omitted in the original Desktop. Another replaces the entire Desktop interface with a more flexible one. The universe of plug-ins is growing quickly and getting more impressive; the development in this area reminds me of the alternate Google interfaces I describe in Chapters 19 and 20.

After you install Google Desktop (which I cover in the next section), you can survey the available plug-ins here:

```
desktop.google.com/plugins.html
```

Downloading and Installing Google Desktop

Google Desktop is free and is easy to download and install. Start by going to the Desktop page:

```
desktop.google.com
```

Then follow these steps:

1. **Click the Agree and Download button.**

   If you're one in a million, you will first read the Terms and Conditions document. This legal harangue is much like the terms and conditions attached to the Google Toolbar. The most important point to most people relates to privacy. Google Desktop has the ability to collect non-personal information about your computer use and give that information to Google. You can opt out of this function during installation.

2. **Download the setup file, which is probably named GoogleDesktopSetup.exe or something similar.**

3. **Double-click the downloaded file.**

   The installation procedure begins automatically. In most cases, the installation program requests permission to shut down some applications. Save any work in progress before agreeing. After Google Desktop is installed, the program opens your default browser to an Initial Preferences page.

4. **On the Initial Preferences page, choose your options.**

   At the time of this writing, four initial options were presented:

   • Searching AOL Instant Messenger chat transcripts

   • Searching secure pages viewed in your browser

   • Displaying a Google Desktop search box on the taskbar or floating on the desktop

   • Sending usage data to Google

When setting initial preferences, think over the first two. Allowing Google Desktop to index AOL chat transcripts and secure Web pages could reveal personal information (such as online bank statements) to anyone using your installation of Google Desktop. That person wouldn't have to search for *online bank statements* or *compromising chats;* a search keyword would merely have to match any word in a bank statement or chat transcript.

Note that in the third preference, the search box (on the taskbar or floating on the desktop) is distinct from the Google Deskbar; if you run Deskbar already, you'll end up with two search boxes (see Figure 13-1). That last preference is the controversial feature I mentioned earlier; now is your first chance to opt out if it makes you uncomfortable.

5. **Click the Set Preferences and Continue button.**

   Initial indexing of your computer begins now.

6. **Click the Go to the Desktop Search homepage button.**

   This is the page that opens whenever you double-click the Desktop icon. Right now, it indicates the progress of the initial indexing, which could take hours in big, file-laden computers. Figure 13-1 shows this page.

Figure 13-1:
The taskbar holds a Google Desktop search box and a Google Deskbar.

Once installed, Google Desktop reveals its presence with a swirly icon in the system tray of the Windows taskbar (shown in Figure 13-1). If you selected a search box on the Initial Preferences page, that too announces the presence of Google Desktop.

The Google Desktop search box (on the taskbar or floating on the desktop) conducts both Web searches and hard-drive searches. For many people, that makes the Google Deskbar irrelevant. However, the Deskbar can launch a Google search into the Images index, Froogle, Google News, Google Groups, and other autonomous Google engines. The Deskbar is more of an online-search agent than Google Desktop. I run them both. I also run the Google Toolbar.

Daily Use of Google Desktop

Google Desktop Search is thoroughly integrated with the Google experience. You can initiate a hard-drive search in three ways. Each is no more than one click away from extending that search to the Web:

- ✔ Type keywords into the Google Desktop search bar (on the taskbar or floating on the desktop, if you enabled it), and then press Enter. Doing so takes your browser to Google, where the results of a Web search are displayed with Desktop results above them. (You must be online.) You can also configure the Desktop search box to search only your hard drive; click the small arrow next to the search box and select Search Desktop.

- ✔ Double-click the Google Desktop icon in the system tray of the taskbar. Doing so displays a Google Desktop search page that looks pretty much like the Google.com home page, except for the slightly different Desktop logo (see Figure 13-2). However, you're not viewing an online page at this point; the page is manufactured by Google Desktop, not taken from Google servers. Note that your keywords can be applied to a Web search, or Images, or Froogle, or any of the main Google indexes.

- ✔ Go to the Google.com home page, type your keywords, and click the Desktop link. This might be the coolest integration of all. Google knows that you're a Desktop user and serves up a different version of the Google home page that accommodates your potential need to search your hard drive.

The result of this integration is confusion over whether you're online or offline: exactly what Google wants. Increasingly, residential computers stay online all the time, connected to high-speed Internet links. To *Google,* which once meant to search the Internet, now means to search an unbounded realm that encompasses the Internet and your personal computer.

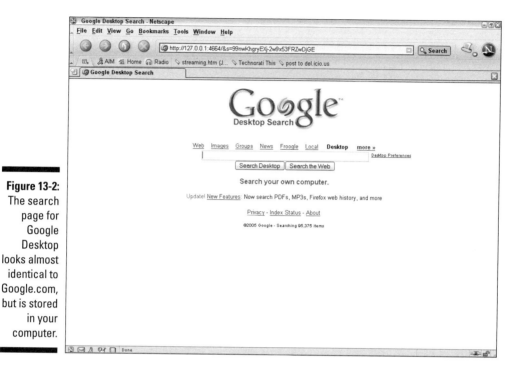

Figure 13-2:
The search
page for
Google
Desktop
looks almost
identical to
Google.com,
but is stored
in your
computer.

Personalizing Google Desktop

To change your Google Desktop preferences, right-click the Desktop icon in the system tray and choose Preferences. A page like the one in Figure 13-3 opens in your browser (the page is actually stored on your computer). On this page, you can select and unselect file types to be indexed.

One of the most interesting options is the Don't Search These Items box, where you type local file paths and Internet domains, the content of which will be avoided by Google Desktop. You can set up a folder on your hard drive for storing files that you don't want appearing in Desktop search results; then type the path to the folder in the Preferences page. Click the Save Preferences button when you're finished.

Also on this page, you can decouple the tight integration of Desktop results and Google Web results. To do so, uncheck the box next to Google Integration.

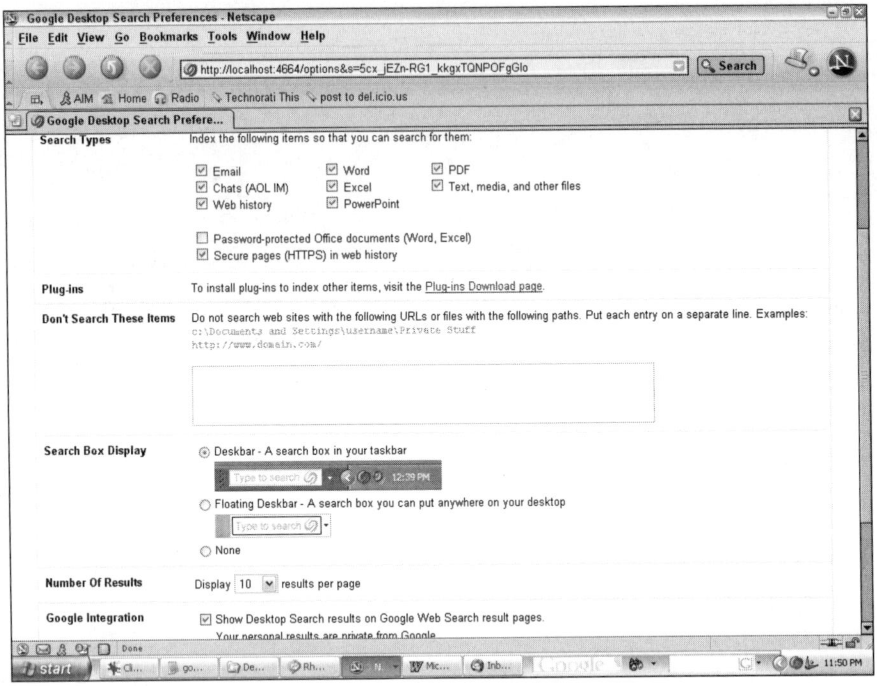

Figure 13-3:
Setting
Google
Desktop
preferences.

Giving it a rest

At any time while running Google Desktop, you can pause its relentless indexing. If you're going to encounter online material that you don't want indexed, or you know you're getting mail that you don't want crawled, simply pause Desktop. Right-click the system tray icon and choose Pause Indexing. Doing so creates a fifteen-minute rest period. You can repeat the process (choosing Pause for fifteen more minutes). When you're ready to resume indexing, right-click and choose Resume Indexing.

Chapter 14

Saved by a Thread: Reinventing E-mail with Gmail

Google introduced Gmail on April 1, 2004, and at first many people thought it was a joke. The service was difficult to verify because it wasn't opened to a public beta-testing period as most other new Google services are. Gmail was (and remains, at this writing) an invitation-only service. But it was for real, and it was immediately apparent on April 1, 2004, that Google had accomplished a significant reinvention of Web-based e-mail.

It's important to be clear on the distinction between Web-based e-mail (often called *Webmail*) and e-mail viewed through a non-browser program such as Outlook Express. Webmail is presented within a Web browser, and you must be online to read the mail. By contrast, you can read mail in Outlook Express while offline — though you have to go online to get the mail. That last point illustrates another key difference. Outlook Express (and other stand-alone e-mail readers) downloads the mail from its temporary storage location on a Web server. Webmail keeps the mail permanently on the server, allowing you access to that server for reading, sorting, and replying.

Why Webmail, and Why Gmail?

Two other popular Webmail services are Yahoo! Mail and Hotmail. (AOL users have something similar to Webmail inside the AOL program.) The three pillars of the Webmail movement — Gmail, Yahoo! Mail, and Hotmail — make the case for using a Web-based service instead of (or in addition to) using a stand-alone mail program to access your ISP's e-mail service. The main advantages of using Webmail are these:

- ✔ You can access your account and read your mail from any Internet-connected computer in the world.
- ✔ Webmail offers a single, consolidated e-mail location for people who routinely use multiple computers.
- ✔ Your mail is immune to crashes or breakdowns of your computer.

Countering those advantages are the disadvantages of Webmail:

- ✔ The display of Webmail messages is slower than in stand-alone programs accessing downloaded mail that resides in your computer.
- ✔ Webmail features are generally not as powerful as features in stand-alone programs.
- ✔ Webmail does not offer as much storage as a typical computer hard drive.
- ✔ Webmail services put advertisements on your e-mail pages.

That's a lot of disadvantages. Yet, Webmail is extraordinarily popular. One reason, besides the compelling nature of its advantages, is that you don't need an Internet account to use Webmail. Basic Webmail is free. You must be willing to do your computing in public places such as libraries, and that might explain why so many library screens display Webmail in progress. (Walk around with an eagle eye at any large library to see what I mean.)

Google has introduced innovations that make Gmail especially attractive. I've dabbled in many Webmail systems, but Gmail is the only one that has earned any degree of loyalty in my Internet life. My Gmail account is not my primary e-mail location, but it's a strong secondary inbox. I move some types of mail into the Gmail environment exclusively. In particular, I find e-mail discussion lists work especially well in Gmail's conversational format. (More on that conversational format later.) Also, the easy searchability of stored e-mail (this is Google, after all) convinced me to move much of my business correspondence to Gmail as well.

Elbow room for your e-mail

When Gmail was introduced, its most startling aspect was the amount of available mail storage. Each Gmail account came with 1 gigabyte (1000 megabytes) of storage. Typical Webmail services at that time furnished somewhere between 5 and 100 megabytes. Google's proposition was unprecedented, and it rattled the industry. Other services, notably Yahoo! Mail and Microsoft's Hotmail, scrambled to catch up — not only to provide comparable storage but to emulate Gmail's fast page displays and generally slick performance. But massive upgrades can't be accomplished overnight, and Yahoo! and Microsoft fell behind their own promises. When they finally began to draw close to Gmail's features, Google threw in another gigabyte.

That second gigabyte demolished any notion of parity in the Webmail business, at least in the storage department. Google didn't stop with the second gigabtye; it announced that every Gmail account's capacity would gradually increase over time like a rising thermometer. Indeed, as I write this, my Gmail capacity stands at 2174 megabytes, and it inches up every day. I have 187 megabytes of stored mail, equaling 9 percent of today's capacity. Google's intent is clear: to make storage issues irrelevant. Neither of the other major Webmail providers have dared match this pioneering value. Google is proposing that you adopt Gmail for life, and is seems to promise that you'll never run out of room.

Of course, 2-plus gigabytes of storage is a small chunk of digital real estate by the standards of modern computers, with hard drives holding hundreds of gigabytes. But 2 gigs is huge in the context of Webmail, which is both free and immune to hard-drive crashes and other home-computing problems. Indeed, people use Gmail as an archive location, forwarding files not related to e-mail simply to protect them. Such strategies were unthinkable when Webmail could barely hold all of one's mail.

The three broad, compelling features of Gmail are storage (there's a lot of it), display (the conversational format I keep promising to describe), and searching. Combine these features with the inherent advantages of Webmail, and Gmail becomes a service that hard-core Internet lifestylers *must* take seriously as a long-term e-mail solution.

Gmail Availability

I've written this chapter with the assumption that by the time you read it, or soon thereafter, or at *some* point before humanity is destroyed by rampaging turtles, Gmail will be an open service available to all comers. At this writing, Gmail exists as an invitation-only Webmail platform while the service is undergoing testing.

Most Gmail account holders are given some number of invitations to distribute as they choose. At the beginning, five invitations, at most, were given to any single account. Believe it or not, an underground trading movement began, with people all over the Internet offering to pay or trade for a Gmail invitation. The number of invitations per account grew to fifty, and the frenzy to get on the inside died down. While it lasted, that intense seller's market (actually selling a Gmail invitation is forbidden by Google) was great publicity for the service. In fact, the entire method by which Gmail was launched — encouraging the April 1 hoax rumors and frantic efforts to acquire accounts — seems brilliantly sly in retrospect.

Most people who want to try Gmail have been able to locate an invitation by this point, so I proceeded with this chapter with the thought that most readers are already in or can find their way in — or, as I mentioned before, that Gmail will be entirely public by the time this book gets into your quivering hands. And if your hands are really quivering, dial back your coffee consumption.

One handy clearinghouse for free Gmail invitations is the isnoop Web site, at this location:

```
www.isnoop.net/gmail
```

Volunteer donors have given away many thousands of invitations.

It's All About Conversations

Although Gmail's capacious storage received most of the launch publicity, in my opinion that's not really Gmail's strongest feature. Gmail's most original innovation is the manner in which it strings together related e-mails. This feature lends a conversational feel to reading e-mail. Unlike other Webmail systems and typical mail interfaces, which throw each incoming letter into a queue, one after another, Gmail keeps intact the natural connections between responses. The result is that an incoming message, even if a month has passed since you wrote the letter to which it responds, is tied to your original outgoing letter and displayed with it. This display logic overcomes time, making it seem as if the response arrived moments after your letter was sent.

Figure 14-1 illustrates the conversational display style at work. In this particular view, the conversation is collapsed: Each message preceding the last of the string is compressed to a single line showing the sender and the first line of the message. The dates show the time span during which this conversation transpired. The entire conversation takes on the appearance of a series of folders in a file cabinet — to me, at least. My editor disagrees. Who are you

The advertising issue

On the right side of the page in Figure 14-1, note the presence of advertisements (under Sponsored Links) and other stuff (under Related Pages). Those ads, just like the ones on search results pages, come from the Google AdWords program. Nearly all Webmail services place ads on the page, so why did Google's ads cause a storm of controversy when Gmail was introduced, and why are they still despised by some people? The perceived problems result from the way in which Google selects the ads, which is identical to the way Google selects ads that appear on the Web pages of AdSense publishers. (See Chapter 17 and 18 for more on AdWords and AdSense.)

When you call up an e-mail to read, Google crawls that e-mail, determines its context, and places relevant ads (and related page links, which are not sponsored) in the margin. To some people, opening your mail to a Google crawl is little different from allowing strangers to read your mail. This attitude is fallacious on two counts. First, humans at Google do not read your mail. Second, there is no such thing as ironclad privacy with any e-mail service,

especially Webmail, in which all mail is stored on the service company's computers.

Another issue that troubles people, especially people in business, is that Google places relevant (and perhaps competing) content on mail. Imagine you're a lawyer writing to a client, and that client uses Gmail. When the client reads the lawyer's letter, advertisements appear in the margin — including, perhaps, an ad from a competing law firm. Google is so adept at determining context and regionality that such a thing is eminently possible. Fearing and resenting such possibilities, a few people and firms refuse to send mail to Gmail addresses. The Boycott Gmail movement took on some steam in the early days, but fizzled.

As for appearances, Google's advertising style is much easier on the eyes than flashing banners (look at Yahoo! Mail sometime). Unlike the ads on Google search pages, which I often read and click, I find that Gmail ads seem invisible to me. That's not good news for advertisers, but it makes the Gmail experience feel decidedly noncommercial.

going to believe, her or me? Well, it doesn't matter what they look like, the point is that collapsed messages concisely illustrate who has participated in the conversation, and the message snippets sometimes effectively summarize the discussion.

Click any collapsed message to expand it and read it. Gmail keeps track of your reading history and presents read messages in collapsed mode and unread messages in expanded mode. (The exception is the final message of any conversation, which is always shown in full.) You can collapse any expanded message and expand any collapsed message. Moreover, the Expand all link — look to the right of the page — lets you expand the entire conversation or, in reverse, collapse every message in the conversation.

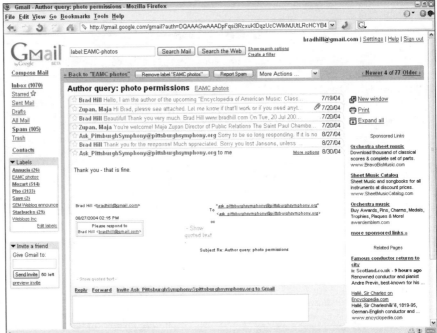

Figure 14-1:
Gmail
displays
connected
e-mails as
a single
conver-
sation.

Gmail's inbox display is shown in Figure 14-2. (Actually, the figure shows the contents of the inbox as sorted by a label. More on labels in a bit.) The conversational format is established in the inbox, before opening any conversations. This format is quite different from many other e-mail systems, which list every message as a distinct entity, unrelated to other messages. In Figure 14-2, the number in parentheses in some of the headers indicates the number of messages in that conversation. Dark shading indicates that all messages in that conversation have been viewed; if a new response comes in, the shading is removed from that conversation, and it is moved to the top of the inbox. The stars are activated with a single click, and make an easy way to highlight conversations (or single messages) that you want to find quickly again later. (Use the Starred link to view all your starred messages.)

The check box next to each message, when checked, signals that you want to take some action on that message (or conversation). Use the More Actions pull-down menu to see what actions are available. They include moving the message to another part of Gmail, marking a read message as unread (removing the shading), applying a label (I *promise* to cover labels soon), or moving the message to the trash. Google discourages throwing out any mail. With so much storage at

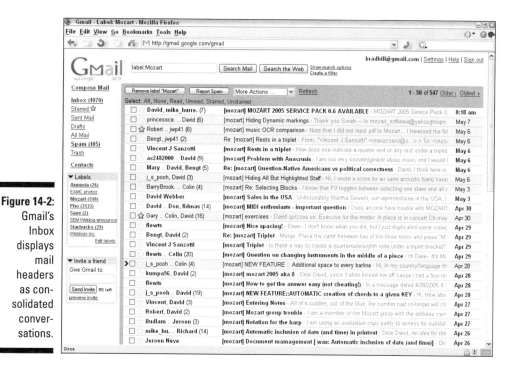

your disposal (so to speak), there is little reason to trash anything. I occasionally do discard items, though, if I'm certain I'll never want to look at them again.
Do not throw out spam, though; check the check box next to any piece of spam
that finds its way into your inbox and click the Report Spam button. Gmail files
away the information on that e-mail and removes it from your account.

Writing Mail

Enough about reading mail; put down your chips and write somebody a
letter. Click the Compose Mail link to see the page shown in Figure 14-3. As
you type a recipient's address in the To field, Gmail searches your address
book and suggests possible recipients; use the arrow keys to scroll down that
suggested list. Gmail automatically adds the recipient's address to your contacts list (that's what Gmail calls the address book) when you write somebody. If you're new to Gmail, you don't have any contacts stored, and Gmail
will not suggest names as you type.

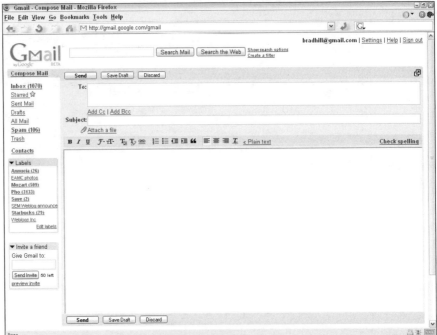

Figure 14-3:
Use this page to compose an e-mail.

The quickest way to build up your contacts list in Gmail is to import your address book from another e-mail program you've been using for a while. There are too many e-mail programs floating around, each with its own methods, to attempt a step-by-step explanation of how to do this. The main thing to know is that Gmail accepts imported address books in the CSV format — that's the Comma Separated Values format. CSV is a database format that separates each entry with a comma. In your e-mail program, find the export feature, and choose CSV as the export format. The program will allow you to save the address book in that format. Having saved it, follow these steps in Gmail:

1. **Click the <u>Contacts</u> link.**

2. **Click the <u>Import Contact</u> link.**

   The Import Contacts window pops open.

3. **Click the Browse button.**

4. **Find and select your saved CSV file, and then click the Open button.**

5. **Click the Import Contacts button.**

In the Compose Mail window, you may use *rich formatting* to add color, alternate typefaces, boldface, italics, underlines, bullets, and other style elements to your outgoing mail. Keep in mind that not all e-mail programs interpret rich formatting conventions in the same manner. This inconsistency has long been a problem, especially with mail systems (such as AOL) that encourage their users to gunk up . . . I mean, enhance their mail with extra formatting. These systems are meant to work well when members mail each other, but don't always look pretty when mail leaves the system. So, have fun ruining . . . I mean, distinguishing your mail with nontext formatting but be aware that others could see a different result. (My bias against formatting comes from nearly fifteen years as a text-only e-mail writer. E-mail historically is a text medium, and incompatible platforms make nontext formatting problematic. Now leave me alone and let me be a curmudgeon in peace.)

If you don't have time to finish an e-mail, click the Save Draft button. Your work-in-progress is stored in the Drafts folder. You can return to it later and undo the horrible rich formatting. All right, that was uncalled for.

Sorting with Labels

In this section I finally discuss labels. Gmail labels are the primary sorting device, and one of Gmail's great innovations. Developed just as the *tagging* frenzy of sites such as Flickr and Del.icio.us was gaining momentum, Gmail labels work by tagging messages and conversations as a grouping mechanism. Labels take some getting used to. Most people reach a point when a light goes off (not literally; I'm being metaphorical), they yell "Eureka!" (no they don't; I'm exaggerating for effect), and then they kiss their monitors (nobody does that; I'm just going for cheap laughs now).

Labels in Gmail take the place of folders in traditional e-mail and Webmail programs. In Gmail, instead of dragging a message to a labeled folder, you tag it with a label. Importantly, any message or conversation can be tagged with multiple labels. Multifaceted tagging is what gives tagging sites their great appeal; each tagged item is important in different ways and shows up on different lists depending on which tag is activated. In Gmail, your list of created tags is displayed on every page. Click any label to see all message and conversations tagged with that label.

Another part of Gmail's label system is that you can filter incoming mail by label, if you can predict common elements of that incoming mail. This is one reason discussion lists work so beautifully in Gmail. I belong to one high-volume list called Pho, and although I read it every day, I don't want its steady stream of e-mail cluttering the main (which is to say, unlabeled) display of my inbox. Since I know that every e-mail from that list contains the word *Pho* in the subject line, I can tell Gmail to tag all such mail with the Pho label and immediately archive it. That way, I don't see any of it unless I click the Pho label.

Filtering incoming mail by label is so important a feature that I want to walk through it in detail. It's not hard! Follow these steps:

1. Click the <u>Create a filter</u> link next to the keyword search box.

2. Fill in the criterion or criteria that will identify incoming messages to be labeled.

   You can specify a sender or a recipient. If the recipient is you, all mail will be filtered, which is probably not your goal. Perhaps you frequently receive mail copied to your partner and want to label it; identify that incoming mail by typing your partner's name or e-mail address. In this example, I am using the Subject field to identify the Pho discussion list, as shown in Figure 14-4.

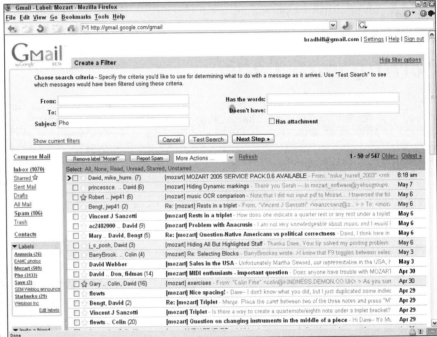

Figure 14-4: When creating a filter, first establish the criteria that will identify incoming mail.

3. Click the Next Step button.

4. On the next page, choose what should be done with identified incoming mail.

   I'm labeling identified mail and archiving it, as you can see in Figure 14-5. You may also choose to automatically forward such mail, mark it with a star, or throw it out.

5. Click the Create Filter button.

   Now, identified mail will be immediately labeled and archived, and will not appear in the unlabeled inbox.

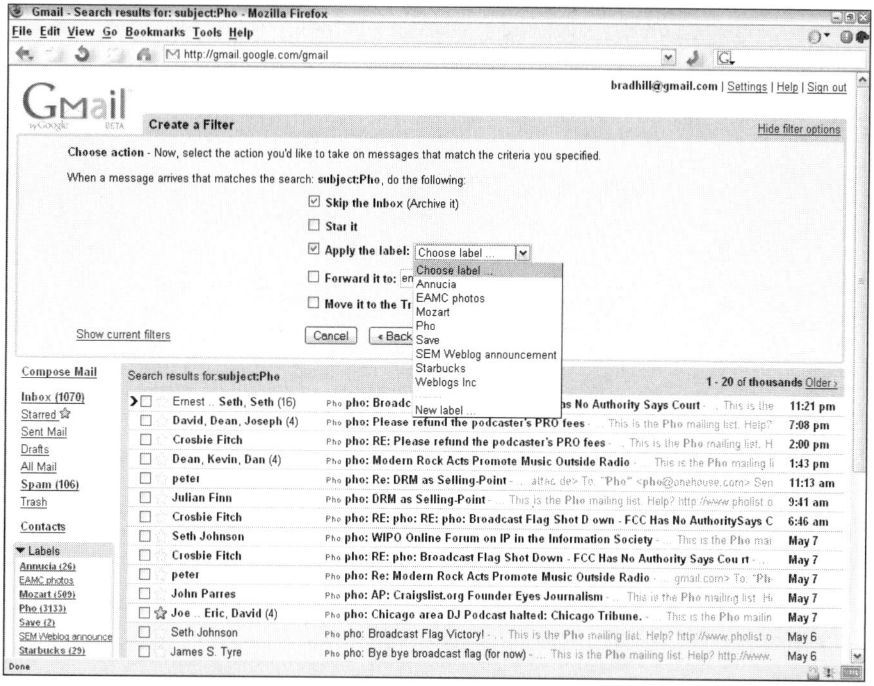

Figure 14-5:
Use this
screen to
choose
what
happens to
filtered mail.
Here, it's
labeled and
archived.

Customizing Gmail

Gmail is not as powerful or flexible as desktop e-mail programs. That observation is not a criticism; the same is true of all Webmail. However, Gmail does offer a few personalization features. Click the Settings link to see your options. Figure 14-6 shows the general settings.

All the settings in the General tab are self-explanatory, but the keyboard shortcuts deserve special mention. Google experimented with keyboard shortcuts as a Web search feature but discontinued that particular Google Labs experiment. Only a small band of loyal users developed around the search shortcuts, but Gmail might tell a different story. People are in their e-mail accounts so often, and for such long periods, that keyboard shortcuts make life easier for those who dislike mouse movements. When you turn on the shortcuts, you have a choice of using the mouse or the keyboard to navigate Gmail.

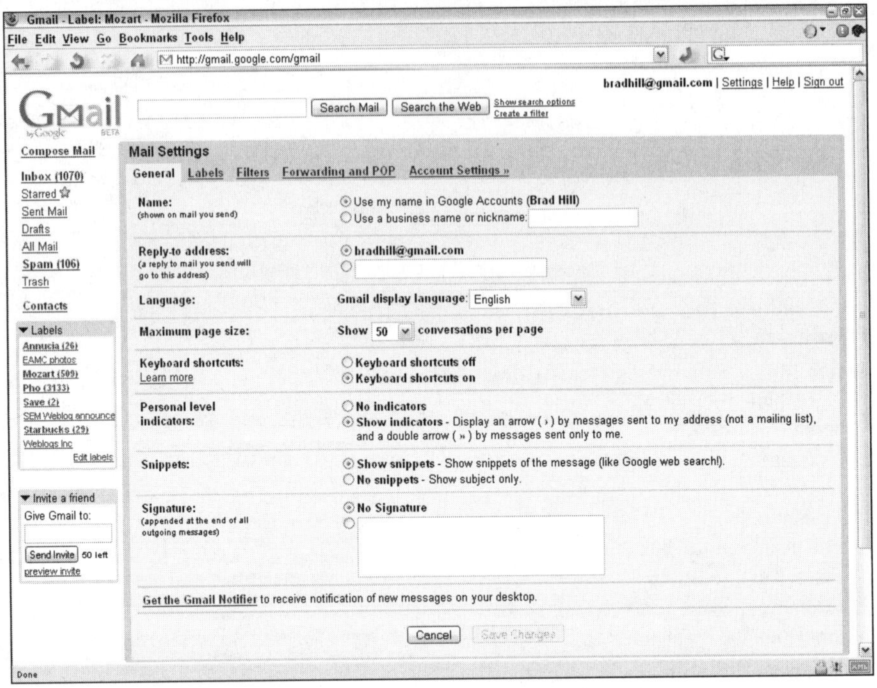

Figure 14-6:
The General
tab is where
you choose
basic Gmail
display
options.

One more feature to point out: POP access to your Gmail. POP, an acronym for Post Office Protocol, is the technology that allows mail delivered to one e-mail system to be accessed and read in another e-mail system. If you want to download and read your Gmail in a desktop program such as Outlook Express, you need to enable POP downloading in the forwarding and POP tab of the Mail Settings page. Then you need to configure your e-mail program to go get your Gmail. Each mail program differs in this process; you might need to check the Help files of other documentation. Click the <u>Configuration instructions</u> link for help with three popular e-mail programs.

If you've been using Gmail for a while and are storing a lot of mail, be certain to choose Enable POP only for *mail that arrives from now on.* If you select the other option (Enable POP for all mail), your mail program will reach into Gmail and download *everything.*

You have another decision to make regarding POP access of Gmail, and that is what to do with the mail after you download it. You download copies of the mail; it's not like physical mail which is either here or there. Use the pull-down menu in the Mail Settings under Forwarding and POP to choose whether Gmail leaves downloaded mail in the Inbox, archives it (removes it from the Inbox but preserves a copy), or deletes it.

Chapter 15

Giving Your Visitors a Leg Up: Google on Your Site

In This Chapter

▶ Getting Google Free on your site

▶ Customizing Google Free

▶ Tailoring Google searches

Generously, Google allows site owners to put Google search boxes on their sites, and many thousands of Webmasters do it. This gift of Google is not sheer generosity, though; it results in greater traffic for the search engine and more exposure to its advertising. Google doesn't really care where a search originates from: the Google home page, the Google Toolbar, the Deskbar, or your site.

When you offer your visitors a Google search box for general Web searching, you are inviting them to leave your site — that's one drawback for some people. However, that Google search box can be configured to search your own site, not the Web at large. That way, even though Google gets your visitors briefly when they view the search results page, you get them back if they click through to a destination on your site.

You can place Google on your site in three ways:

▶ **Google Free:** Actually, all three methods are free; this plan is the original one. It places a keyword box on your page(s), with the option of making results specific to your site. That option is in the hands of your visitors. You can't make the search box exclusively about your site.

▶ **Customizable Google Free:** This option provides the same service as basic Google Free but with tools to make the search results look more like your pages. Google still serves the results; you can place your logo at the top of the page and determine the page's color scheme. You cannot, however, place navigation items such as sidebars of JavaScript on the search results page.

✔ **Site-flavored Google search:** This Labs experiment builds a general profile of your page, and then delivers results influenced by that profile. Your visitors get results that might be aligned with their interests, assuming they're interested in the topic of your site. If they're not interested in your site, you're lucky that they visited. Or perhaps you're unlucky; maybe they're sending you hate mail. Let's not think about that now.

Using any of these three services is fairly easy, and they're all similar. For all three services, you need to know how to cut and paste HTML into your page's source document.

Your site must conform to typical Terms of Service guidelines — the same sort of content restrictions as those for AdSense (see Chapter 18). Nothing illegal, nothing immoral, no hate content, no copyright infringement. The complete Terms of Service document is linked on the Google Free site. No application procedure is required to use Google Free or its spinoffs. It's generally unknown how much Google polices the many sites using Google search boxes. Violating the Terms of Service and getting caught will result in a letter from Google demanding that you remove its branded search box from the site.

Free Google on Your Site

The first step in obtaining a Google search box is to visit the Google Free page:

```
www.google.com/searchcode.html
```

On that page, you have three choices represented by three snippets of HTML code:

✔ **Google Free Web search:** This option provides the basic search box; your users Google the Web index.

✔ **Google Free SafeSearch:** This option is the same as the basic option but with SafeSearch protection built in to all searches originating at your site.

✔ **Google Free Web search with site search:** This option gives your users a choice of searching the Web or just your site.

Figure 15-1 shows the Google Free page with one of its blocks of HTML code. Each code snippet is followed by an illustration of the resulting search box.

Figure 15-1:
The Google
Free page
provides
HTML code
for placing a
search box
on your
Web page.

Proceed like this:

1. **Decide which type of Google Free you want by scrolling down the page and looking at the examples.**

2. **Scroll down the page to see the corresponding HTML code.**

3. **Press Ctrl+A to highlight and select the entire code block.**

4. **Press Ctrl+C to copy the code.**

5. **Go to your Web page's source document, position the cursor where you want the search box to appear, and press Ctrl+V to paste the code into your Web page's source document.**

Customizing Your Free Google

Google acknowledges how jarring it could be for visitors who search from your site, and are then yanked away from it to a Google results page. If you have lovingly designed your pages and labored over perfect color combinations, tossing your users into the stark black-blue-white world of Google seems almost cruel. Doing so breaks the continuity of your site experience and is especially galling if your users are using the Google keyword box to search for content within your site.

Google makes up for this discontinuity, at least partly, by allowing you to determine the color scheme of result pages generated from your search box and allowing you to place a graphic logo at the top of the page. The result rarely looks exactly like a site page, but it does look distinctive and reminds the user of where he or she came from (your site).

Start customizing by going here:

```
www.google.com/services/free.html
```

Starting on that page, follow these steps:

1. **Click the <u>Start here to customize Google for your site</u> link.**

2. **Under Step 1 of 4, click which Google Free service you're customizing, and then click the Continue button.**

   For simplicity, I chose the second choice, simple Google Free.

3. **Under Step 2 of 4, fill in any box corresponding to a page element you want to customize.**

   Figure 15-2 shows this page. Notice that Google offers a choice of site search, even though you clicked simple Google Free. Whatever. Ignore it or fill in a site domain. All boxes below that field are optional. If you have a page logo, enter the location and filename (on your Web server) of the graphic file. When choosing colors, use names or hex numbers. (You can find the hex numbers of your background color, links color, and other element colors in your page's HTML source document.) If you use a background image instead of a solid color, put the exact Web address of the background image in the Background URL box.

4. **Click the Preview button to see the results of your choices.**

   Figure 15-3 shows one result. Unfortunately, Google does not allow you to precisely change the background color of the huge Google logo, so that always stands out. In this case, as on many pages, the logo has its own background color, which doesn't look very good. I subsequently changed the page's background to match that color. It then became necessary to change the text and link colors. The better result is in Figure 15-4. These multiple changes demonstrate how easy it is to tweak the color scheme before moving away from the Step 2 of 4 page; simply close the Preview window, make changes to the customization fields, and click the Preview button again.

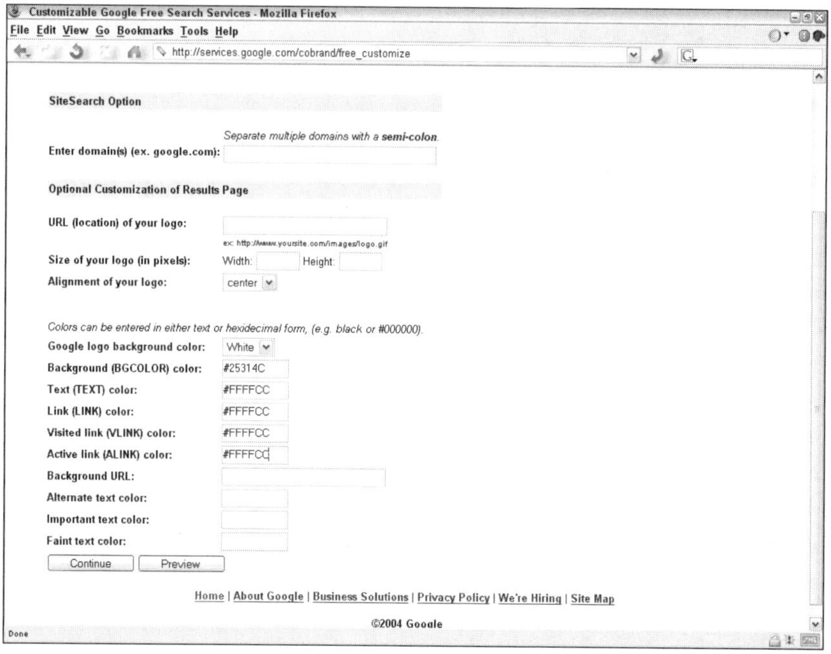

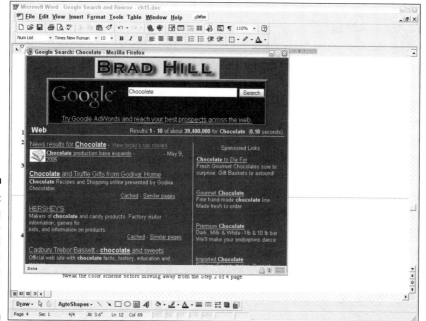

Figure 15-2:
Customizing the color scheme of search result pages.

Figure 15-3:
Previewing a customized search results page. Kind of ugly.

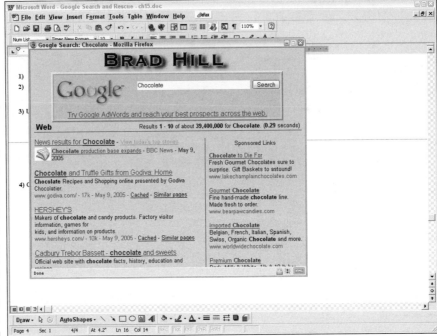

5. **Click the Continue button.**

6. **On the Step 3 of 4 page, fill in the registration boxes, and then click the Continue button.**

7. **On the Step 4 of 4 page, place your mouse cursor anywhere in the HTML code.**

8. **Highlight and select the entire block of code, copy it, and paste it into your page's source document.**

The resulting search box looks like a simple Google Free search box and returns customized results. Remember that the content of the results is not customized; only the page upon which the results are displayed. For customized results content, read the next section.

Site-Flavored Google Search

The third option for Google on your site slants search results toward the content of your page. If you operate a Web site about the local music scene, for example, Google can skew search results to favor music-related sites and sites about your region. To accomplish this tailoring of results, Google crawls your site and attempts to determine its subject matter. Whether it is successful or not, you have a chance to alter the profile of your site.

To start with site-flavored search, go here:

```
www.google.com/services/siteflavored.html
```

From that page, follow these steps:

1. **Click the <u>Start here to customize Google for your site</u> link.**

2. **On the next page, enter the URL of your site.**

   Actually, you can use any URL; no matter what you enter, chances are good Google will fail to build a profile. I recently tried the address for the *New York Times* site, and Google could not figure out what it was about (understandably, as a major news site is about everything).

3. **Use the directory links to build your site's profile.**

   This is fun. Click a broad category, and then select a subcategory. The second choice shows up under your profile, as shown in Figure 15-5. Repeat with as many profile entries as you like. Some subcategories are further divided, but for the most part your profile is broadly defined.

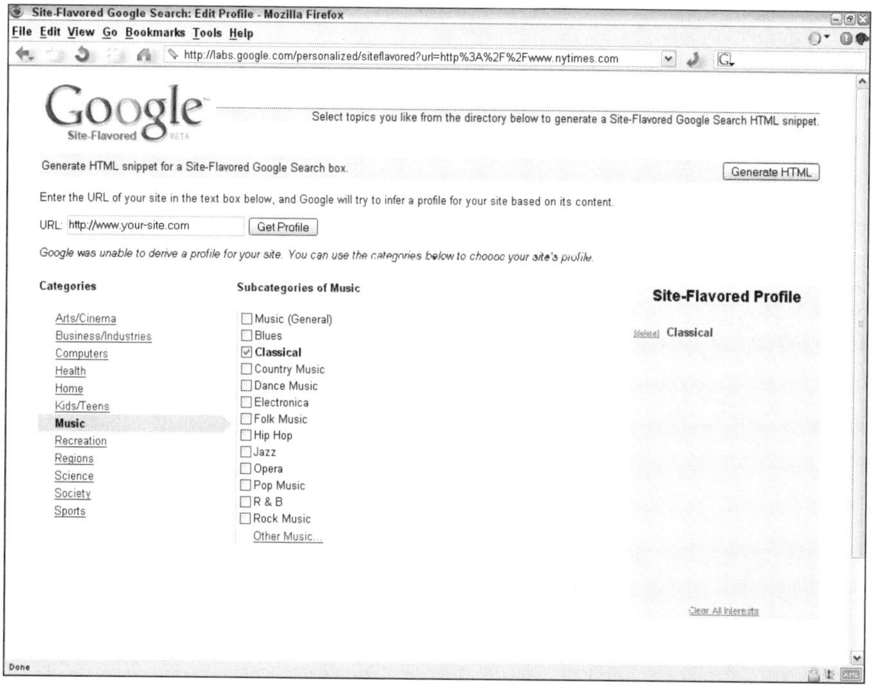

Figure 15-5:
Building a site profile for site-flavored searches.

4. Click the Generate HTML button.

5. Select, copy, and paste the resulting HTML into your Web page's source document.

You can test the results of your site-flavored search box by starting a search in the keyword box on your page. Search results indicate which target sites were moved higher on the list as a result of site flavoring.

Figure 15-6 shows a site-flavored search results page. Note the three-ball logo next to the top three entries. They are prominent because of site flavoring.

Figure 15-6: Site-flavored search results include customized results pushed high on the page.

Part V
The Business of Google

"He saw your laptop and wants to know
if he can run a quick Google search."

In this part . . .

Most of this book deals with the consumer side of Google — the search engines we know, love, and use daily. Increasingly, regular folks are becoming aware of, and interested in, Google's other side, the business services. That's where this part comes in.

Google's business side is mostly about advertising. You can participate in two main ways: by advertising your business and by running other people's ads on your Web site as a business in itself. Chapters 17 and 18 cover these adventurous possibilities. As a great populist force, Google has singly brought targeted, high-powered Internet advertising to amateur and semipro Webmasters the world over.

Chapter 16, the first chapter in this part, is a general tutorial for Webmasters (which means anyone with a Web page) about getting into the Google index and staying there, so people searching for your subjects can find you in Google. You meet the Google spider, understand when and how it crawls, and find out how to create pages that attract the spider and make it like you.

The business of Google contributes an extra dimension to the Googling experience, like the unearthly theoretical dimensions of cosmic string theory. (Note: It's not really like that at all. I just wanted to mention string theory in this book.) You might not think advertising has any relevance to your life, but even nonadvertisers should understand how Google displays ads, why it does, and how to distinguish the ads from search results. [Editors' note: Brad seems reasonably lucid for the first time in this book. We have no explanation and only hope that he finishes the manuscript before undertaking his next mochaccino binge.]

Chapter 16

Bringing Google and Its Users to Your Site

*F*rom the inception of the Web, it has been the goal of every person with even a modest Web page to attract visitors. Advertising, reciprocal linking, word of mouth, getting listed in directories — all have been tools in the mad scramble for traffic. In the Google era, getting into the index has become the single most important task of Webmasters large and small.

Search engine listing has always been crucial. Page owners have spent hours submitting requests to innumerable directories and engines. Coding a page in a way that attracts a search engine crawler and puts the page high on the search results list became a crafty art form in the late 1990s. Google has become so dominant in the search field that if your page can't be Googled, it might as well not exist — that's today's presumption.

Some people resent Google's power as the main determining factor of a site's visibility. The complaint that Google rewards popular sites, making them even more popular at the expense of worthy competitors, has some legitimacy. But there is good news. Google's index is so huge (over eight billion Web pages at this writing) and its indexing computations are so precise that Google can create niches of visibility that didn't exist before. If your site does one small thing well, and you take the necessary steps to make it Google friendly, you can be rewarded with a top-ranked site in your niche. It's probably not important to be visible to everyone; it *is* important to be highly visible to the people who match your site's mission.

All about PageRank

Google's secret sauce is PageRank, a mathematical formula that grades every Web page in Google's gigantic Web index. When you search in Google, the results are listed first by relevance to your keyword(s), and then according to PageRank, with the higher-ranked pages placed above lower-ranked pages of equal relevance. PageRank is responsible for the usefulness of Google searches; it is the intelligence of the engine. PageRank is also of ferocious interest to Webmasters, many of whom are fanatically concerned with raising the PageRank of their sites and pages. The higher the ranking, the more visible is the site on relevant search results pages.

Changes in PageRank, up or down, mean sudden prosperity or disaster for commercial Web sites.

The PageRank formula is a closely held secret and one of Google's most valuable corporate assets. Nobody outside the company knows exactly how it works, but Google has divulged certain core values in a Web site that lead to high PageRank. These values — high-quality incoming links, user-friendly page optimization, and avoiding violations dictated by Google — are what this chapter is all about.

Getting your site into the Google index requires patience and networking skill, but it's not hard. Improving your *position* in the index — how high your site places on search results lists — can be trickier, but success likewise depends on fairly simple steps. Old coding tricks don't work in Google, which means bad news and good news. The bad news is that there are no shortcuts to prominence in Google. The good news is that the index is utterly democratic, affording any Web site, large or small, a chance to gain good positioning based on merit.

This chapter covers how Google crawls the Web, how a new page can get into the index, and how a new or established site can improve its position in Google's search results.

The Google Crawl

As with most search engines, Google's work has two parts: searching the Web and building an index. When you enter a search request, Google doesn't really go onto the Web to find matching sites. Instead, it searches its index for matches. Google is special at both ends of its work spectrum: first in the scope of its Web searching (and therefore the size of its index) and second in the method by which it matches keywords to Web pages stored in the index.

Most search engine indexes start with an automatic, wide-flung search of the Web, conducted by automated software fancifully called a *spider* or *crawler.* Google's crawl is farther-flung than most, resulting in an index that includes over eight billion Web pages, as of this writing. (The current total is specified in small print on Google's home page.)

Google performs two levels of Web crawl. The main survey, often referred to as Google's *deep crawl,* is conducted roughly once a month. Google's spider takes slightly more than a week to accomplish its profound examination of the Web. Then, as a bonus, Google launches a fresh crawl much more frequently. The *fresh crawl* is an update to Google's index that runs every day, or several times a day, or not quite every day, depending on the site and at the company's discretion. Don't think of the fresh crawl as a scheduled event; it is a term that denotes Google's determination to pick up new material from sites that change often. Material gleaned from the fresh crawl is added to the main Google index.

Webmasters can see the fresh crawl in action by searching for their new content in the main Google index. The continual index shifting is sometimes called *everflux,* and the big index shift that happens after a deep crawl is called the *Google dance.* Eager Webmasters should never forget that the everflux is unpredictable, and that they should never pin their hopes on the Google dance. The Google index has no guarantees, including one saying that any particular site must be included in any crawl. Hold fast to persistence and patience. The daily crawl is by no means designed to provide the Google index with a daily comprehensive update of the Web. Its purpose is to freshen the index with targeted updates.

Getting into Google

You can get your site into the Google index in two ways:

- ✔ Submit the site manually
- ✔ Let the crawl find it

Both methods lead to unpredictable results. Google offers no assurance that submitted sites will be added to the index. Google does not respond to submissions, and it does not promise to add or discard the site within a certain time frame. You may submit and wait, or you may just wait for the crawl. You may submit *and* wait for the crawl. Submitting does not direct the crawl toward you, and it does not deflect it. Google is impassive and promises nothing. But Google *does* sometimes add sites that would probably not be found by the crawl.

If you have added a new page to a site already in the Google index, you do not need to submit the new page. Under most circumstances, Google will find it the next time your site is crawled. But you might as well submit an entirely new site, even if it consists of a single page. Do so at this URL:

```
www.google.com/addurl.html
```

The submission form could hardly be simpler. Enter your URL address, and make whatever descriptive comments you feel might help your cause. Then click the Add URL button — which is a bit misleading. Submitting a site is not the same as adding it to the index! Only the Google crawler or a human Google staffer can make additions to the index.

Luring the spider

The key to attracting Google's spider is getting linked on other sites. Google finds your content by following links to your pages. Links that lead from other pages to your site are called *incoming links* (they are incoming from your viewpoint). With no incoming links, you're an unreachable island as far as the Google crawl is concerned. Of course, anybody can reach you directly by entering the URL, but you won't pluck the spider's web until you get other sites to link to you.

Checking your status

How do you know whether your site is in the Google index? Don't try searching for it with general keywords — that method is hit-and-miss. You could search for an exact phrase located in your site's text, but if it's not a unique phrase you could get tons of other matches.

The best bet is to simply search for the URL. Make it exact, and include the *www* prefix. If you're searching for an inner page of the site, precision is likewise necessary, and remember to include the *htm* or *html* file extension if it exists.

The *link* operator (see Chapter 2) is invaluable for checking the status of your incoming links

and, by extension, the health of your PageRank. Use the operator followed immediately by the URL, like this: `link: www.bradhill.com`. The search results show pages containing a link to your URL. When you try this operator with an inner page of your site, remember that you most likely link to your own pages with menus or navigation bars, and Google regards those links as incoming links, artificially inflating your incoming link count. Incoming links within a domain do not contribute to PageRank. You need to get other sites linking to you.

Index or directory?

Most of this chapter is devoted to getting a foothold in Google's Web search index, which should not be confused with Google Directory. Although the search index is largely automated, Google Directory consists of hand-picked sites selected by a large volunteer staff. Chapter 7 describes Open Directory Project, which Google uses and upon which Google imposes its PageRank formula.

Getting into the directory is more direct than getting into the search index but not necessarily quicker. You must go to the Open Directory Project, not to Google, at this URL:

```
www.dmoz.org/add.html
```

Follow the instructions there. See also the "Submitting a Web Page to the Directory" section in Chapter 7.

In theory, any single page currently crawled by Google (that is, in the index) that links to your page or site is enough to send Google's spider crawling toward you. In practice, you want as many incoming links as possible, both to increase your chance of being crawled (sounds a little uncomfortable, doesn't it?) and to improve your PageRank after your site is in the index.

Keep your pipes clean. Don't make life difficult for Google's spider. That is to say (how many different ways can I say this before I finally make myself clear?), host your site with a reliable Web host, and keep your pages in good working order. The Google crawl attempts to break through connection problems, but it doesn't keep trying forever. If it can't get through in the monthly deep crawl and your site isn't included in the fresh crawl, you could suffer a longish, unnecessary delay before getting into the index.

Don't expect instant recognition in Google when you add a page to your site. If your site is part of the fresh crawl, new page(s) show up fairly quickly in search results, but there's no firm formula for the frequency of the fresh crawl or the implementation of its results. If the spider hits your site during the deep crawl, the wait for fresh pages to appear in the index is considerably longer. The same factors apply if you move your site from one URL address to another (but not if you merely change hosts, keeping the same URL). Complicating that situation is that your site at the old address might remain cached (stored) in Google's index, even while search results are matching keywords to your site at the new address. This confusion is one reason some Webmasters don't like the Google cache — when they make a change to a site or its address, they don't want the old information living on in the world's most popular search index.

On your own

Creating the Google index is an automated procedure. The Google spider crawls through more than eight billion pages in its surveys of the Web. Some sites (small ones in particular) might be tossed around by the Google dance, even to the extent of dropping out of the index for a month at a time and then reappearing. PageRank can fluctuate, influencing a site's position in search results. Some sites have trouble breaking into the index in the first place.

Although Google receives and attends to URL submissions, as described in this chapter, the company does not provide customer service in the traditional sense. There is no customer contact for indexing issues. The positive aspect of this corporate distance is that the index is pure — nobody, regardless of corporate size or online clout, can obtain favorable tweaking in the index. The downside is that you're on your own when navigating the surging tides of this massive index. Patience and diligent networking are your best allies.

Keeping Google Out

Your priority might run contrary to this chapter, in that you want to *prevent* Google from crawling your site and putting it in the Web search index. It does seem pushy, when you think about it, for any search engine to invade your Web space, suck up all your text, and make it available to anyone with a matching keyword. Some people feel that Google's cache is more than just pushy and infringes copyright regulations by caching an unauthorized copy of a site.

If you want to keep the Google crawl out of your site, get familiar with the robots.txt file, also known as the Robots Exclusion Protocol. Google's spider understands and obeys this protocol.

The robots.txt file is a short, simple text file that you place in the top-level directory (root directory) of your domain server. (If you use server space provided by a utility ISP, such as AOL, you probably need administrative help in placing the robots.txt file.) The file contains two instructions:

- ✔ **User-agent:** This instruction specifies which search engine crawler must follow the robots.txt instructions.

- ✔ **Disallow:** This line specifies which directories (Web page folders) or specific pages at your site are off-limits to the search engine. You must include a separate `Disallow` line for each excluded directory.

A sample robots.txt file looks like this:

```
User-agent: *
Disallow: /
```

This example is the most common and simplest robots.txt file. The asterisk after `User-agent` means *all* spiders are excluded. The forward slash after `Disallow` means that *all* site directories are off-limits.

The name of Google's spider is Googlebot. ("Here, Googlebot! Come to Daddy! Sit. Good Googlebot! Who's a good boy?") If you want to exclude only Google and no other search engines, use this robots.txt file:

```
User-agent: Googlebot
Disallow: /
```

You may identify certain directories as impervious to the crawl, either from Google or all spiders:

```
User-agent: *
Disallow: /cgi-bin/
Disallow: /family/
Disallow: /photos/
```

Notice the forward slash at each end of the directory string in the preceding examples. Google understands that the first slash implies your domain address before it. So, if the first `Disallow` line were found at the `bradhill.com` site, the line would be shorthand for `http://www.bradhill.com/cgi-bin/`, and Google would know to exclude that directory from the crawl. The second forward slash is the indicator that you are excluding an entire directory.

To exclude individual pages, type the page address following the first forward slash, and leave off the ending forward slash, like this:

```
User-agent: *
Disallow: /family/reunion-notes.htm
Disallow: /blog/archive00082.htm
```

Each excluded directory and page must be listed on its own `Disallow` line. Do not group multiple items on one line.

You may adjust the robots.txt file as often as you like. It's a good tool when building fresh pages that you don't want indexed while still under construction. When they're finished, take them out of the robots.txt file.

Building Your PageRank Through Networking

Earlier in this chapter, I explain that getting into Google is best accomplished by incoming links from other sites. Google regularly crawls every site in its index, and when links from one (or more) of those sites are added to their pages, Google automatically sniffs you out. There is more to the story of incoming links than merely getting your foot in the door. It turns out that Google depends on the quantity and quality of those links to help it determine your site's PageRank. That means that the effort you put into networking your site among other Webmasters affects how visible you are in Google.

There are two aspects of your site's exposure in Google: appearing under the correct keywords and appearing high up in the listings. This section deals with the latter — improving your PageRank so that you get the best possible positioning wherever you appear. (Actually, these two topics are not completely divided. Achieving a good PageRank is partly the result of proper keyword positioning.) The first aspect of Google exposure — making your site appear on relevant search results pages — is covered later in this chapter in the site optimization section.

Incoming links and PageRank

Google is secretive about the details of PageRank. Most people wouldn't understand the equations if they were divulged, but other search engine operators would, so you can't blame Google for protecting a major corporate asset.

One aspect of PageRank that Google has always been forthcoming about is incoming links. The number and quality of incoming links plays the largest part in a site's PageRank. So, to gain greater visibility in Google, you need to increase and upgrade those incoming links, or *backlinks*.

Webmasters seeking to drive traffic to their sites through Google spend immense portions of their time networking to develop their backlink network. (The backlink network is simply the surrounding sites that link to the Webmaster's site.) This networking is often accomplished the old-fashioned way, by introducing oneself and talking to other site owners.

Human networking

Building a vibrant backlink network involves contacting other sites, introducing yourself, and asking to be linked — it's as simple as that. Offering to link to *that* site in return smoothes the way to a reciprocal agreement in many cases.

When networking, it's important to keep things relevant. That means approaching sites that overlap your site's topicality to some extent. Believe it or not, Google's algorithm does know when backlinks are irrelevant, and they carry little weight in the PageRank equation. In fact, by accumulating many irrelevant incoming links, a site can be punished with a lower PageRank. So approaching high-profile sites merely because you want your PageRank boosted by their powerful ranking can be a waste of time, and even dangerous.

For the most part, you want incoming links to point to your top page or home page, sometimes called the index page. Whatever page offers the broadest introduction to your entire site is the best landing destination for visitors coming across on incoming links. The risk of developing a backlink network that points to all sort of inner pages is that you could end up with an unfocused assortment of incoming links scattering visitors all over your site. From a PageRank perspective, such a disorganized backlink network does you little good. The goal is to get your main page — the page with all your navigation links — as high in Google as possible. Like a rising tide, it will lift your other pages.

Blog backlinks

Weblogs (also called blogs) are popular online journals; at this writing some forty million of them exist. Blogs add a new twist to acquiring incoming links, and Google has had to work hard to master the blogging trend in its index. Blogs are rich in both outgoing and incoming links, thanks to their link-intensive style of writing and their *blogrolls* — traditional sidebar lists of selected Weblogs. Google does not deny blogs their space in the Web index, and running a blog is a good way to network. However, the advantages of intensive linking come with a price, which is hard, relentless work. The best and most-linked blogs are updated daily at least; sometimes many times each day. You must have a lot to say about a subject to devote a Weblog to it, and this is not a casual way to build content or backlink networks.

But once you are up and running with a blog, networking is easier than with a collection of static Web pages. Inserting yourself in the blogosphere generates backlinks as a matter of course, simply by being part of the wide conversation in your topic. Leaving comments on other blogs usually includes leaving a backlink. If you become fairly well known, other bloggers will put your site in their blogrolls, which get replicated on each page of the Weblog. The result is that good, authentic Weblogs can zoom up the PageRank ladder faster than traditional Web sites.

The key word is *authentic*. It's pointless to try fooling Google or other bloggers. If you're in the blogging game just to build PageRank, and you start littering the blogosphere with unsubstantial or meaningless comments (most of which will be removed), you will be scorned by other bloggers and get nowhere in Google.

Certain sites are set up to automatically facilitate backlinking. Called *link farms,* these clearinghouses have attained reasonably (sometimes very) high PageRanks, and placing an incoming link on one of them presumably lifts your own site's PageRank. Google dislikes automated link farms and claims to have the ability to distinguish links that come from them. These places often pay no heed to the relevance of links. Google would rather reward sites with substantial human-placed linkage that reflects true value on both ends. Most conscientious and successful Webmasters avoid using link farms.

Trading content

Trading links with relevant sites is fine; even better is trading content. Every site needs relevant content. Article exchanges make participating sites better destinations, with the secondary PageRank-building effect of placing links in both directions. In fact, three types of link are possible with each article you place on another site:

- ✔ A byline link
- ✔ An attribution link, which might come immediately after the byline or at the article's end
- ✔ Embedded links to your site in the article text

Just as you should avoid link farms (see preceding section), you should also sidestep *article farms,* which are automated upload sites where anybody may place content stuffed with backlinks. Beware: Google either knows or will soon know. The company is continually working to keep its index clean and its PageRank honest.

Optimizing Your Site for Google

The field of search engine optimization (commonly shortened to *SEO*), is pretty old by Internet standards and can be as simple or as complex as you want it to be. The purpose of SEO is to get placed accurately on search engine results pages. High ranking is also a goal, but the core emphasis of SEO is identifying your site with certain keywords, so that when people search Google (or another search engine) with those keywords, your pages appear in the results.

SEO doesn't enjoy an entirely positive reputation, thanks to unscrupulous consultants who have attempted, and sometimes succeeded, to game the system by cheating. Cheating implies rules, and indeed, Google has them.

Violation of those rules can result in the worst punishment possible for a Web site in search of traffic: expulsion from the Google index. Don't think of this as an abstract threat; it happens all the time.

But basic site optimization, which on many points is just good design and common sense, helps everyone. A well-optimized site helps Google categorize it properly; helps visitors make the most of the site; and helps the Webmaster gain the type and amount of traffic desired.

This section covers the basic points of ethical SEO.

It's all about keywords

When building a highly optimized site, you should always be thinking about keywords. Keywords are the kernels of your site's content. The process ideally begins before you build pages and put content into them, but any time is a good time to get aware of the *what* and *where* of each page's keywords.

Imagine that you're searching for your own site. You are your site's ideal visitor — perfectly interested in, and attuned to, its mission and content. How would you search? What keywords would you use? Those are the keywords around which your content should hang. Those essential words and phrases should be embedded in your page's text in a few crucial ways:

- ✔ In headers
- ✔ In the page title
- ✔ In the page's meta tags
- ✔ In the page's text, but not so much that your readers feel hit over the head with them

(See your page design software for information about filling in the *keyword* meta tag.)

Keywords are the battleground in the fight for Google exposure. If your site is not appearing on the correct result pages but similar sites are, or if your site is not appearing high enough to attract traffic, your keyword optimization probably needs work. Remember, also, that certain keyword have greater value and more daunting competition than others. If you're fighting for space around the keywords *music downloading,* you're more likely to get clobbered than if you find a niche of your own, such as *icelandic electronica.* Deciding on your site's keywords is, essentially, deciding on your site's position in the universe — at least, in the Google universe. You're not optimizing for the whole world; you're optimizing for a certain type of visitor with certain defined interests.

Effective site design

An important element of search engine optimization is using design elements that don't confuse, frustrate, delay, or anger the Google spider. The following SEO principles are widely known to get a site smoothly integrated into the Google index:

- **Place important content outside dynamically generated pages:** A dynamic page is one created on-the-fly based on choices made by the site visitor. This method of page generation works fine when the visitor is a thinking human. (Or even a relatively thoughtless human.) But when an index robot hits such a site, it can generate huge numbers of pages unintentionally (assuming robots ever have intentions), sometimes crashing the site or its server. The Google spider picks up some dynamically generated pages, but generally backs off when it encounters dynamic content. Weblog pages do not fall into this category — they are dynamically generated by *you,* the Webmaster, not by your visitors.

- **Don't use splash pages:** Splash pages (which Google calls doorway pages) are content-empty entry pages to Web sites. You've probably seen them. Some splash pages employ cool multimedia introductions to the content within. Others are static welcome mats that force users to click again before getting into the site. Google does not like pointing its searchers to splash pages. In fact, these tedious welcome mats are bad site design by any standard, even if you don't care about Google indexing, and I recommend getting rid of them. Give your visitors, and Google, meaningful content from the first click, and you'll be rewarded with happier visitors and better placement in Google's index.

- **Use frames sparingly:** Frames have been generally loathed since their introduction into the HTML specification early in the Web's history. They wreak havoc with the Back button, and they confuse the fundamental format of Web addresses (one page per address) by including independent page functions within one Web page. However, frames do have legitimate uses. Google itself uses frames to display threads in Google Groups (see Chapter 6). But the Google crawler turns up its nose when it encounters frames. That's not to say that framed pages necessarily remain out of the Web index. But errors can ensue, hurting both the index and your visitors — either your framed pages won't be included, or searchers are sent to the wrong page because of address confusion. If you do use frames, make your site Google friendly (and human friendly) by providing links to unframed versions of the same content. These links give Google's diligent spider another route to your valuable content and give us (Google's users) better addresses with which to find your stuff. And your visitors get a choice of viewing modes — everybody wins.

✔ **Divide content topically:** How long should a Web page be? The answer differs depending on the nature of the page, the type of visitor it attracts, how heavy (with graphics and other modem-choking material) it is, and how on-topic the entire page is. Long pages are sometimes the result of lazy site building, because it takes effort to spin off a new page, address it, link to it, and integrate it into the overall site design. From Google's perspective, and in the context of securing better representation in the index, breaking up content is good, as long as it makes topical sense. If you operate a fan page for a local music group, and the site contains bios, music clips, concert schedules, and lyrics, Google could make more sense of it all if you devote a separate page to each of those content groups. Google also likes to see page titles relating closely to page content. Keeping your information bites mouth-sized helps Google index your stuff better.

✔ **Keep your link structure tidy:** Google's spider is efficient, but it's not a mind reader. Nor does it make up URL variations, hoping to find hidden content. The Google crawler is a slave to the link. If you want all your pages represented in the index, make sure each one has a link leading to it from within your site. Many site-building programs contain link-checking routines and administrative checks to diagnose linkage problems. Simple sites might not warrant such firepower; in that case, check your navigation sidebars and section headers to make sure you're not leaving out anything.

The folly of fooling Google

For as long as search engines have crawled the Web, site owners have engineered tricks to get the best possible position on search results pages. Traditionally, these tricks include the following:

✔ Cloaking, in which important, crawl-attracting keywords are hidden from the view of site visitors but remain visible to spiders

✔ Keyword loading, related to cloaking, in which topical words are loaded into the page's code, especially in page titles and text headers

✔ Link loading, through which large numbers of incoming links are fabricated

Spider-manipulating tricks have worked to some extent in the past thanks to the automated nature of search crawling. Google is highly automated, too, but more sophisticated than most other spiders. And as a company policy, Webmaster chicanery is dealt with harshly. Obviously, you're not breaking any laws by coding your pages in a certain way, even if your motive is to fool

Google. But Google doesn't hesitate to banish a site from the index entirely if it determines that its PageRank is being artificially jiggered. No published policy states when or if a banished site is reinstated. Google is serious about the integrity of PageRank.

The best rule is this: Create a site for people, not for spiders. Generally, the interests of people and Google's spider coincide. A coherent, organized site that's a pleasure to surf is also a site that's easy to crawl. Keeping your priorities aligned with your visitors is the best way to keep your PageRank as high as it can get.

Chapter 17

Stimulating Your Business with AdWords

· ·

· ·

*H*ow do you define Google — as a search engine? Fair enough, but that's just half the story, and perhaps the lesser half. The hidden side of Google is its advertising business. Since the company's initial public offering, that hidden half has come into the light, but normal Google users going about their online lifestyles do not necessarily understand everything that transpires on the advertising side.

Google doesn't make money by simply fulfilling your search requests. (Have you sent in a check lately?) Google makes almost all its money from advertisers who place ads on Google's result pages and on other sites that partner with Google in running those ads. This advertising is not the traditional sort of advertising you see in a magazine, or on TV, or even as flashing banners on a Web site. Google advertising is mostly connected to the search requests processed by Google and is designed to connect people searching with companies providing goods and services, at the very moment that the need is greatest.

Companies still pay good money for banner placement and for the development of new interactive features within banners. But the effectiveness of banners has been devalued in many marketing scenarios and in the Web's amateur, semi-pro, and small-business space. A new way of reaching individuals with targeted, relevant links is what's needed. The natural placement of a highly relevant promotional link is on a search results page because the person viewing that page is obviously looking for something and is ready to click through to another online destination.

Purchasing placement on a search results pages is not new, and the history of this business strategy is rife with disrepute. Many a pre-Google search engine ruined its reputation by polluting its search results with advertisements that were difficult to distinguish from the real listings.

Google aggressively sells space on its search results pages. But several aspects of Google's ad business distinguish it and make it amazingly popular:

✔ The ads are clearly separated from search results, keeping Google's integrity untarnished.

✔ Google enforces language and style guides that create accurate promotions in the true spirit and tone of the search results page.

✔ Anybody can get in on the game, at a price of their own choosing.

✔ The ads are distributed across all Google search areas and a wide network beyond, enhancing their impact and effectiveness.

✔ The ads running on Google's pages are text-only presentations, which don't slow the display of search results. Ads running on the wide network beyond Google's pages may be either text or nonflashing banners.

✔ Most ads are not charged upon display. Advertisers pay only when an ad works — that is, upon clickthrough. This policy differs from traditional online advertising, which is billed by *impressions* — in other words, whenever an ad is displayed. (At the time of this writing, Google had just inaugurated a pay-per-impression program designed for large companies. Smaller companies and individuals are expected to continue using the pay-per-click system.)

✔ The process of purchasing an ad is almost totally automated and interactive, putting all control of price and display frequency in the hands of the advertiser.

This chapter concentrates on traditional AdWords — the pay-per-click system using text ads. This book has space for only a basic outline of features. Readers who are intrigued by the possibilities might want to look at my *Building Your Business with Google For Dummies* (published by Wiley), which devotes five chapters to Google AdWords.

Understanding the AdWords Concept

A business of any size, even an individual just starting out, may purchase AdWords. There is no exclusivity based on type of business, amount of revenue, promotional budget, or any other criterion. You do need a Web page. You do not need to be selling something, though there is probably a low limit on the amount of money anybody would spend on advertising a hobby site. Still, many Webmasters use AdWords to promote sites which make their money by running advertising.

Beginning an AdWords campaign consists of four main steps:

1. Sign up for an AdWords account.
2. Write an ad.
3. Choose keywords with which your ad will be associated.
4. Price your ad and decide on an overall payment budget.

You may create the account and your ads before committing to the program.

Step 3 — choosing keywords — is crucial. AdWords operates by displaying ads on search results pages generated by users querying with keywords that match the advertisers' keywords. To put it another way, your ads are triggered when somebody searches on the ad's keywords. Choosing keywords relevant to your ad and to your *landing page* (the page viewed by anybody who clicks your ad) is of supreme importance. If your keywords are off the mark, you probably won't get many clickthroughs, and the visitors you *do* get from your ad will probably be mismatched to your content.

AdWords text ads are nothing more than blurbs. With no graphics and minimal text, they fit concisely along the right side of search results pages. Figure 17-1 shows a results page with several AdWords placements.

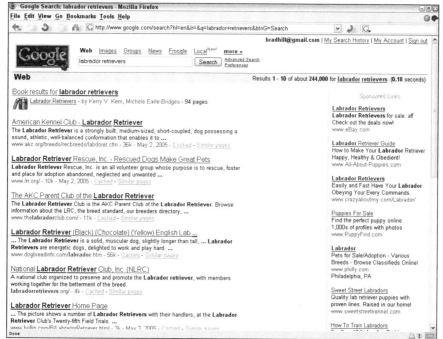

Figure 17-1:
AdWords ads appear in a column on the right side of a search results page.

The essential item that you create in an AdWords campaign is the ad group. An *ad group* contains one ad, its keywords, and its underlying cost structure. (In truth, an ad group may contain more than one ad, but just one set of keywords targeted by the ads. In the interest of keeping things simple, this section considers an ad group as containing a single ad.)

Following is a breakdown of every element in an ad group:

- **Headline:** Each ad starts with a headline that links to the target page.

- **Description lines:** Two very short lines. That's all you get in the way of descriptive content. Concise writing is crucial.

- **Destination URL:** Each ad spells out the target page address, which is the same as the Headline link address.

- **Keywords:** Every ad is associated with search keywords that cause its appearance on a results page. Keyword phrases may be used. You can change the keywords at any time.

- **Cost-per-click (CPC):** You decide how much the ad is worth by deciding the price you'll pay whenever somebody clicks it. Google enforces minimums for some keywords. (The total CPC price range for all ads is $.05 to $50.00.) Your ad competes with other ads associated with the same keyword(s), and advertisers willing to pay more get better (higher) positioning on the page.

Google's international sensibility is reflected in AdWords; you may specify a language and a country for your ads. (More specifically, you may also determine a metropolitan region of the United States.) Google determines, more or less successfully, the country (or region) from which each user's computer is logged in. The language requirement is more certain: Google shows your ad to users whose Preferences language setting (see Chapter 2) matches your chosen language.

You control the cost of your advertising in two ways: by establishing a CPC (cost-per-click) price for each ad you create and by creating a daily expenditure budget. If you get many clickthroughs on a certain day and hit the top of your budget, Google pulls your ad for the rest of the day.

Here's how it all works. You create an ad (or ads). You choose one or more keywords (or phrases) to associate with each ad. You decide how much to pay for visitors clicking through each ad. You establish a limit on your daily expenditure on Google advertising. Then, if and when you *activate* your ad, Google places it on search results pages when people search for keywords associated with your ad. Your ad's visibility (placement on the results page) depends on your CPC price compared to that of other advertisers sharing your keyword(s). Higher bids generally get higher placement on the page, though the ad's success also influences placement. (See the sidebar titled "Google's placement formula.") In many cases, the placement of an ad varies over time as advertisers come and go, or as they adjust their CPC prices.

The CPC price you set is a *maximum* price. Google charges less if it can. Over time, in most cases, your average CPC price is less than the price you set. In this regard, AdWords is like an eBay auction, in which you're bidding for high placement on a Google search results page. By setting a maximum CPC price, you authorize Google to go up to that price for the top spot. But in reality,

---

Google's placement formula

Nothing succeeds like success, the old saying goes — and it holds true for ad placement on Google's search results page. The cost you assign per clickthrough is a big part of the story, but it's not the only part. Google rewards successful ads by placing them higher on the page and reducing their clickthrough costs. Success is measured by clickthrough rate — that is, the number of clickthroughs an ad attracts compared to its display rate.

Google rewards high clickthrough rates by lowering the *effective* CPC price assigned to that ad. This means the more popular ad might get top placement even when competing with an advertiser who bid a higher CPC price. Google does not divulge the exact formula that determines ad placement. Generally, though, ad placement depends on a combination of CPC price (your bid) and clickthrough rate (your ad's success).

This formula has a flip side. Just as Google rewards success with higher placement, it punishes failure with reduced distribution. That means if an ad doesn't generate a certain clickthrough level (usually one percent for new advertisers, but lower in some circumstances),

Google reduces the rate at which it's displayed. This measure might seem harsh, but Google is primarily concerned with the experience on people using the search engine, so it wants useful, magnetic ads appearing in the right column of its results pages. If the clickthrough rate gets too low, Google assumes that the ad isn't relevant to its keywords and doesn't want the ad on its pages.

Google sends a notice to the control center of any advertiser whose ad has been knocked into reduced circulation. You can restore full delivery with a button click, and Google provides tools and tips for improving the clickthrough rate. If Google again pushes aside your ad, and you restore full delivery a third time, Google charges a $5 reactivation fee. More drastically, Google doesn't hesitate to knock your ad off the pages of certain keyword results entirely if, after one thousand impressions, the clickthrough rate isn't up to par. After a keyword in an advertiser's campaign has been disabled in this fashion (meaning that the advertiser's ads no longer appear on that keyword's results page), it's very hard to reactivate that keyword. Google plays tough.

you pay only one penny more than required to get that top spot (in other words, one penny more than the top CPC rate set by competing advertisers). If your top bid is less than the top CPC price of two other advertisers, for example, you earn third place in the placement sweepstakes.

You control your Google advertising activity through a personal set of reporting and management tools attached to your account. There, you activate and deactivate individual ads, change keywords, adjust cost settings, pause and restart portions of your overall campaign, and develop new strategies.

Creating an Account and Your First Ad

Feel free to check out the AdWords tools before deciding whether you want to advertise. You can open an account and create ads without making a commitment. Your ads don't go into play until you *activate* the account.

Get started by beginning an AdWords account:

1. **Go to the following Welcome to AdWords page:**

   ```
   adwords.google.com
   ```

   After you create your account, you can continue to use this page for logging in.

2. **Click the Click to begin button.**

   Google gets you started by creating an ad group. Nothing about this process requires money or payment information.

3. **Under the Step 1 of 4 banner (see Figure 17-2), select your language and type of geographic targeting.**

   These options determine who will see your ads. Users whose Preferences settings match your language selections see your ads. Google uses the computer's IP (Internet Protocol) address, which is roughly accurate, to determine a person's location by country. You may select more than one language by pressing the Ctrl key while making selections. If you select the Regions and cities regional targeting class or the Customized targeting class, Google displays two extra pages on which you choose specific countries and metropolitan regions. In this example, we're choosing the Global or nationwide option.

4. **Click the Save & Continue button.**

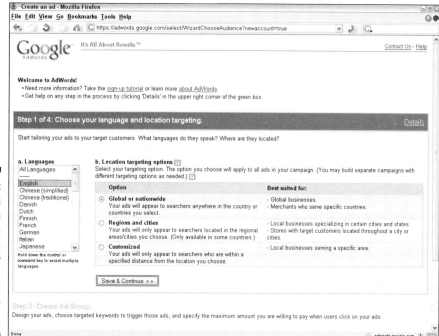

Figure 17-2:
Use this
page to
select the
language
and country
of people
who will
view your
ads.

5. **Under Step 1b, select one or more countries with the Add button, or select All Countries, and then click the Save & Continue button.**

6. **Under the Step 2 of 4 banner (see Figure 17-3), choose a name for your ad group and create an ad.**

   This is where you write a headline, description, and target page URL. The display URL may be different from your target URL. Google offers this flexibility so the ad isn't cluttered with a long, complicated URL. Display URLs are usually short, containing the domain only, eliminating whatever long address might actually take the visitor to the destination page. Take some time here. Google has strict editorial guidelines that must be followed; click the Editorial Guidelines link to understand them. The limited description space requires you to be extremely concise, and I can tell you from personal experience that pithiness is a lot harder than wordiness. Take the time to make every word count.

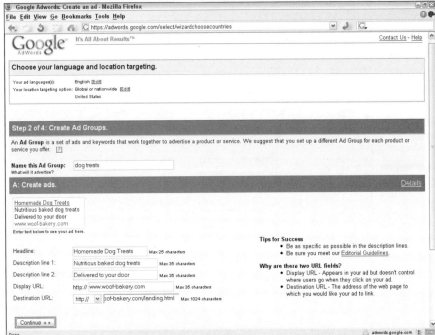

Figure 17-3:
Write your
heading,
description,
and URL in
these fields.
The display
URL may be
different
than your
target URL.

7. **Click the Continue button.**

8. **On the next page, choose your keywords.**

   People searching on the keywords you place here will see your ad. Type one keyword or phrase per line; press the Enter key to add each subsequent keyword. Later, you'll be able to adjust your keyword selections based on Google's estimate of how much your choices will cost. Assigning keywords is a crucial part of the success and budgeting of an AdWords campaign, but the words you type on this page are not etched in stone; you can change them later.

9. **Click the Save Keywords button.**

10. **On the next page, choose the monetary currency to use to pay for AdWords and choose the maximum CPC for your keywords.**

    You are not committing any money at this point, nor are you activating your ad. Google opens this page with a suggested CPC price; that number is a competitive price based on other advertisers who are using your keywords. Feel free to override the suggested price (which is usually arbitrary and insanely high) and lower it.

11. **Click the Calculate Estimates button.**

    Google reloads the page with the CPC chart filled in with estimated costs of your ad campaign, broken down by keyword. Google estimates the number of clickthroughs based on current data from advertisers using the same keywords. In the Average Cost-Per-Click column in Figure 17-4, note that the estimates are lower than the assigned maximum cost that you set above the table — quite a bit lower. These numbers are based on competitive prices from other advertisers and give you an opportunity to adjust your maximum accordingly. (Remember, Google will always charge you the least amount below your maximum to deliver the top spot on the page.) The cost estimates are your first indication of how you should budget your campaign.

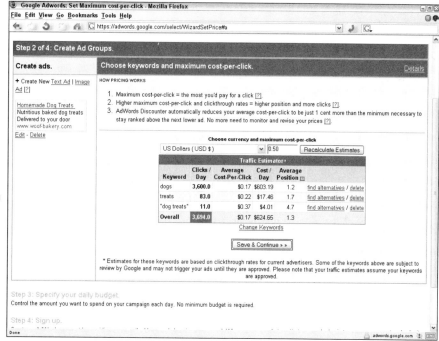

Figure 17-4: Google estimates the click-through rate and cost of your campaign.

12. **Click the Save & Continue button.**

    Before continuing, Google gives you a chance to create another ad, starting this process over. Feel free to do so. I'm moving on to the daily budget section.

13. **Click the Continue to Step 3 button.**

14. **Under the Step 3 of 4 banner, enter a daily maximum you want to spend.**

    Creating a daily budget instead of using a longer time frame keeps your ad's exposure fairly even throughout the month (Google's billing period) even if you don't want to spend much. Notice that Google displays this page with a figure already loaded, and that it's higher than your estimated daily expense shown in Step 10 of this list. The higher amount is meant to give you some breathing room and ensure that your ads appear maximally. Feel free to lower the number.

15. **Click the Save & Continue button.**

16. **On the next page, scroll down to the Step 4 of 4 banner and fill in the fields below it.**

    Nothing on this page, including clicking the button in the following step, commits you to running your ads. This page creates the account that holds the ads you just created, which may remain inactive for as long as you want.

17. **Click the Create my AdWords account button.**

    Google send a verification letter to your e-mail address. It should arrive within seconds.

18. **In the e-mail you receive from Google, click the provided link.**

    Clicking the link displays an AdWords welcome page in the browser window you were using or a new one, depending on your browser and e-mail settings.

You're set. From this point on, log in to your control center by going to the AdWords login page:

```
adwords.google.com
```

There, type your e-mail address and password to enter your account.

Activating Your Account

The AdWords account is activated by providing credit card information for payment. When your credit card is verified (which takes mere seconds), your ads immediately begin running.

 Given Google's continual tidal wave of search traffic, chances are good that your ads and their potential clickthroughs will start appearing before you make any adjustments to your campaign. Therefore, you should make those adjustments before giving Google your billing information. If you're confident of your campaign expenses, go ahead and activate the account. But if you created an ad as an experiment and are unsure whether to proceed, *do not* fill in your billing information.

Activate your account with these steps:

1. **Go to your control center at `adwords.google.com`, type your e-mail address and password, and then click the Login button.**

2. **Click the <u>Edit Billing Information</u> link.**

3. **On the Edit Billing Information page, fill in your credit card and address information.**

4. **Using the drop-down menus, choose a primary business type.**

5. **Click the Record my new billing information button.**

Google charges $5 to activate your AdWords account.

Managing Your Campaigns

The AdWords control center lets you control five main areas of the AdWords experience:

✔ View the details of your ads and campaigns

✔ Display activity reports showing your ad impressions and clickthroughs

✔ Change keywords and prices

✔ Create ads and campaigns

✔ Track expenses and manage your billing arrangements

This section gives you a brief tour of the control center; the main page of the control center is shown in Figure 17-5.

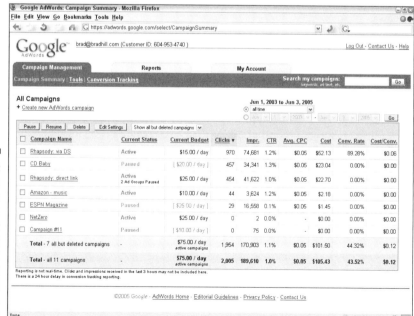

Figure 17-5: The AdWords control center displays and edits all aspects of your ad campaign.

Viewing your campaign reports

Google provides a summary of all your campaigns on one page. This summary view appears whenever you first enter the control center (see Figure 17-5). The following elements go into the summary report:

- ✔ **Campaign selector:** Use the top drop-down menu (it displays the default selection "Show all but deleted campaigns") to select which campaign you'd like summarized. The default selection shows summaries of all current campaigns. Clicking a single campaign automatically reloads the page with a full report of the selected campaign.

- ✔ **Date range:** Use these drop-down menus to select a date range for which Google will summarize your report. Click the lower radio button to choose your own date range.

- ✔ **Campaign Summary table:** In this green-highlighted table are vital statistics of your campaign's performance, detailed in the following items.

- ✔ **Clicks:** The numbers in this column represent clickthroughs on your ad. See the full report for a breakdown of clickthroughs per keyword.

- ✔ **Impr.:** This abbreviation stands for impressions and is a measure of the number of times your ad has been displayed on search results pages.

- ✔ **CTR:** This all-important figure represents your clickthrough rate. The CTR is expressed as a percentage; if one out of a hundred people who are shown your ad click it, your clickthrough rate is 1 percent. If that rate falls too low, Google restricts the distribution of your ad.

- ✔ **Avg. CPC:** This dollar (or other currency) figure tells you the average cost-per-click accounted to your ad.

- ✔ **Cost:** This column displays the total cost of your clickthroughs to date.

- ✔ **Conv. Rate:** Google helps you track not only clickthroughs but also your site's success at convincing visitors to take a planned action. You decide what that action is — perhaps signing up for a newsletter or buying a product. Google provides HTML code for Webmasters to place on the result page of that action; such a page might be a thank-you for newsletter sign-up or an order-confirmation page after a purchase. That HTML code then reports back to your AdWords account and translates your accumulated conversions over time to a cost-per-conversion figure. If all this seems too complex for a simple marketing campaign, feel free to ignore it. You do not need to use the feature or pay attention to the Conv. Rate column.

- ✔ **Cost/Conv.:** Google computes how much you spent per conversion in that campaign, helping you manage your AdWords expenses and profit margin.

Google's reporting is reasonably quick but hardly instantaneous. Take into account a time lag that could be as long as three hours.

Editing your campaign

Click any campaign title to see a full report for that campaign. The full report contains all the information in the summaries, but itemized by ad group, as shown in Figure 17-6. Further, from the report page you can make changes to the campaign's ad text, keywords, costs, and timing.

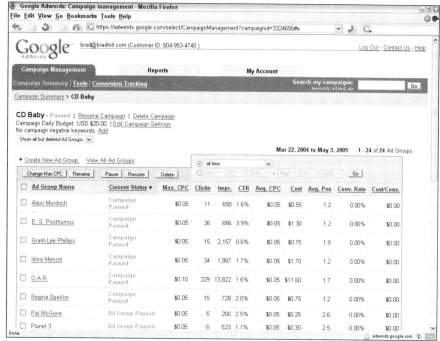

Figure 17-6:
A full report of a single AdWords campaign. Click any ad group title to see a keyword-based report.

Following is a rundown of editing features you can launch from the report page:

- ✔ **Edit Campaign Settings:** Click this link to alter crucial basic information about the campaign, including its name, daily budget, start and end dates, language and country settings, and network distribution settings. These are the settings you established before activating the account; you always have the opportunity to adjust them. Figure 17-7 shows the options on the Edit Campaign Settings page.

- ✔ **Delete Campaign:** This self-explanatory link not only halts the campaign from running (see the Delete item in this list) but erases your ad and all campaign settings. Although Google allows you to view deleted content in AdWords, it doesn't allow you to restore deletions. So be careful. If you want to stop advertising but preserve the campaign for later reactivation, use the Pause Ad Group option.

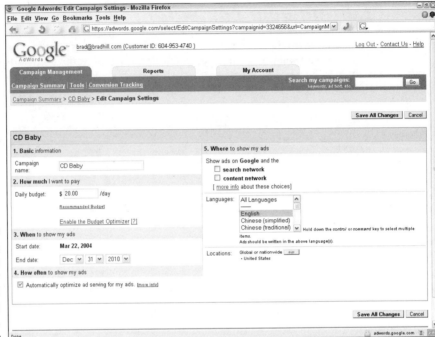

Figure 17-7:
Use this
page to alter
your general
campaign
settings.

✔ **Pause:** Clicking this button instantly removes the ads associated with the currently displayed keywords from distribution. Big brown letters indicate that the ad group is paused, wherever the ad group is listed or referred to in the control center. Click the Resume Campaign link to get it going again.

✔ **Delete:** A dangerous button, this one eradicates any checked ad group in the currently displayed campaign.

✔ **Create New Ad Group:** This link takes you to the same ad-creation page you went through before setting up the account. There, you can write a new ad (headline, description, and URLs) to associate with a new set of keywords.

Keywords and cost-per-click remain constant across an ad group, regardless of how many ads are in the group. You may use the same ads in different groups, associated with different keywords and costs. In fact, doing so is a good way to test the performance of certain ads when displayed against different keyword sets.

Starting a new campaign

In the control center (refer to Figure 17-5), click the <u>Create new AdWords Campaign</u> link to start a new set of ad groups. Remember the hierarchy in AdWords: one or more ads in an ad group (all associated with the same keywords and cost-per-click), and one or more ad groups in a campaign.

Creating a new campaign takes you through the same process (assigning languages and countries, writing the ad, and establishing costs) described previously in this chapter.

More About Keywords

AdWords places a huge emphasis on choosing effective keywords. Getting your ad on the right results pages, where it can be noticed by the right people, is the free method of increasing your clickthrough rate. (The only other method is to raise your placement level, which usually costs more money.)

When choosing keywords, an inherent tradeoff is at work between traffic and placement. Here's how it works. If you choose popular keywords, you have more competition from other advertisers. That means you must bid with a higher cost-per-click price to get good placement. If you choose more obscure keywords with less competition, you can get higher placement more cheaply, but you sacrifice the raging river of traffic searching for high-profile keywords. Of course, with Google's overwhelming level of traffic, even a relative trickle might be sufficient.

The answer to this tradeoff is to think in terms of precision, not popularity. Spend time finding the exact match between keywords and what you're offering.

Just as Google understands certain search operators when trolling the Web, Google AdWords understands certain keyword modifiers when applied to your ad groups. Of course, you may list single keywords and multiple-word strings. In addition, remember these conventions:

✔ **Quotes:** Exact phrase quotes work in AdWords as they do in the search area. Put quotation marks around any set of two or more keywords to denote an exact phrase. Google places your ad on results pages that searched for that exact phrase *plus* any other words the user might have included in his or her search string. For example, *"leather belts"* would force the ad to display on results pages for *leather belts* and also *leather belts handbags*.

- ✔ **Brackets:** Use square brackets around any phrase to keep it exact *and* to exclude any other words in a search string. This tactic limits the appearance of your ad to results pages for your phrase standing alone as the entire search string. For example, *[leather belts]* forces the ad to appear only on results pages for *leather belts*.

- ✔ **Negative keywords:** Exclude keywords by placing a minus sign directly before them. This modifier is identical to the *NOT* search operator (see Chapter 2). When the excluded keyword is used by someone searching Google, your ad does not appear on the results page. For example, *"leather belts" -handbags* means the ad won't appear on results pages for *leather belts handbags*.

Chapter 18

Rescuing Your Revenue with Google AdSense

. . . .

. . . .

*I*n Chapter 17 I observe that Google is like two companies: a search engine and an advertising company. As you might guess from the name, AdSense is part of the advertising side. AdSense is related to AdWords; it is a program in which a far-flung network of Web sites displays AdWords ads.

When an advertiser signs up for AdWords, that advertiser has two broad choices: to limit the placement of ads to Google search results pages, as discussed in Chapter 17, or to broaden the placement of ads beyond Google to thousands of other sites. Most of those other sites belong to what Google calls the *content network*. It is so called because Google determines the content of those sites before placing relevant ads on them. Ads that appear on Google search results pages are determined by the keywords searchers use to bring up results pages. Ads that appear on the content network pages are determined by Google's interpretation of those pages' subject matter.

There is no shortage of advertisers choosing to broaden their reach by having Google place ads on the content network. And, as you know if you've searched around the Web much, there is no shortage of sites eager to run those ads. Figure 18-1 and 18-2 show two pages — one a large news site and the other a personal Web journal — that participate in AdSense. The now-famous "Ads by Goooooogle" (don't ask me about all the o's) is a sign of an AdSense content site.

Figure 18-1:
A major
news site
runs a
vertical
column of
AdSense
ads.

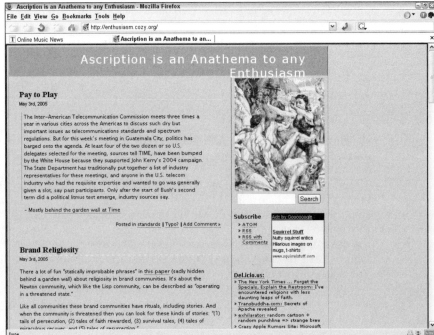

Figure 18-2:
This blog
page carries
a single
AdSense
ad.
AdSense
publishers
choose from
several ad
layouts.

This chapter covers the essentials of AdSense in theory and practice, while regretfully omitting some of the deeper complexities to save space. Any readers interested in a full treatment might want to look at my *Building Your Business with Google For Dummies* (by Wiley).

The AdSense Overview

Google AdSense is an extension of AdWords that allows Web sites to earn advertising revenue. At best, AdSense is a nearly effortless way to make good money. At worst, AdSense requires a little time to figure out, takes some space on your pages, and ends up paying almost nothing. Your fortunes with AdSense depend on three factors:

- ✔ How well optimized your site is (see Chapter 16)
- ✔ How much traffic your site has
- ✔ What subjects your site is focused on

That second one — your traffic volume — is usually the most important. AdSense *publishers* (the Webmasters who participate in the AdSense program) are credited every time a visitor clicks a Google ad displayed on their sites. The advertiser pays Google for every clickthrough (see Chapter 17 for an explanation of AdWords), and Google shares that money with the Webmaster. It might seem incredible that Google can keep track of all this on thousands of sites, but it's not a problem. That kind of tracking technology has been in place for years.

The big question is this: How much of the clickthrough payment does Google give to the Webmaster — what's the split? Nobody knows. Oh, I suppose somebody knows, perhaps Alan Greenspan or the Dalai Lama. But nobody else outside Google knows, and this secrecy has been a point of contention since the start of AdSense. However, Google does not appear to be stingy. AdSense publishers are forbidden (by the Terms of Service agreement) to divulge their clickthrough volume or clickthrough payments, but they are allowed to reveal overall revenue earned through AdSense. Some publishers are doing very well, to the tune of thousands of dollars a month. You need to be processing a great deal of Web traffic to accumulate that kind of payout — along the lines of hundreds of thousands of visitors per month or more. But the point is that Google has built AdSense into a successful program by sharing generously with its publishers.

The subject of your site has some bearing on the AdSense payout. Google places relevant ads on your pages, and some subjects are in great demand among advertisers who are willing to pay high clickthrough rates. For example, at this writing, the mortgage industry was paying high premiums for clickthrough advertising, so a mortgage site running AdSense might enjoy high payouts per clickthrough. At the same time, competition is high in that field, so building traffic is more of a challenge. (Please see Chapter 17 for a fuller discussion of how advertisers bid for ad rates in AdWords.)

Site optimization is important to AdSense success. (Please attempt to say "AdSense success" quickly, several times. Thank you.) If you follow the principles laid out in Chapter 16, your site will draw ads from Google that relate closely to your page content. Your visitors will find them relevant and interesting; some visitors will click through. Irrelevant ads are your biggest enemy, so make sure every page upon which you place AdSense ads is fine-tuned and focused. Check the ads (don't click them; just look at them) to see if they are relevant. If not, the problem might be that the Google AdSense crawler doesn't understand the page, and that's probably an optimization issue.

What You Need to Know to Run AdSense

Once put in place, AdSense runs itself for the most part. The money you make with AdSense is called *passive income* for a good reason: You remain passive (perhaps reclining with a glass of wine) while the money rolls (or trickles) in. I don't want to mislead anybody. AdSense is not a get-rich-quick scheme. The Webmasters making the most money have paid their dues in numerous ways. For most publishers, AdSense revenue is like found money: not very much but gladly received. Serious publishers with modest but substantive sites can reasonably hope to pay for their domain and Web-hosting expenses through AdSense.

In exchange for this easy money, you must know enough HTML (the basic underlying language of Web sites) to insert the AdSense code into your pages. If you build your pages using a graphical program such as Macromedia Dreamweaver or Microsoft FrontPage, the HTML can remain hidden. Most programs allow you to see and directly manipulate the HTML code, but if you don't know what you're doing, your AdSense ads might appear on the wrong part of the page until you get it right. You do *not* need to know how to write HTML. The process involves copying and pasting about a dozen short lines of code from your AdSense account to your Web page(s).

Determining Your Site's Eligibility

Before you get stars in your eyes, dreaming about earning money for posting pictures of your cat, you should know that Google reserves AdSense participation for serious content sites. That doesn't mean you must be a professional Webmaster. Google is pretty accommodating, but there is an acceptance process, and some sites get rejected. After all, Google is trying to provide value to its advertisers, so the publishers in the content network must provide the type of page likely to deliver viable clickthrough business to the advertisers.

AdSense for feeds: Money for Weblogs

Just before this manuscript was completed, Google launched an AdSense experiment called AdSense for feeds. AdSense for feeds is designed for bloggers — the millions of individuals who write online journals called Weblogs, or blogs. There are two ways to read a blog: Visit the blog site and read the entries, or use a program called a newsreader to display the blog's feed. A *feed* is a type of syndication; in short, it brings Web sites to you so you don't have to click your lazy way to them. Just kidding about the laziness; feeds are extremely convenient, and if you're not using them now, I can promise that eventually you will be using them. Feeds are now used by nearly all major news outlets in addition to personal bloggers. For many people, the feed-displaying newsreader has become the new home page.

Because feeds are a new type of online publication, and some forty million people author blogs as of this writing, it makes sense for

Google to provide an opportunity to make a little money from the feed, just as Google does for Webmasters running traditional sites. That goal is the point of AdSense for feeds, which simply places AdWords into the feeds displayed in newsreaders. The figure in this sidebar, showing the feed of my Google blog, illustrates what those ads look like.

Participating in AdSense for feeds requires a separate application process from AdSense (for Web sites). Of course, a blog is also required, and Google is currently requiring a certain level of feed distribution to qualify (as of this writing; it could change). In other words, if you can't demonstrate that more people beyond your mother and best friend read your blog, you might not be accepted. Eventually, though, I expect AdSense for feeds to be as open as AdSense. To apply, go here:

```
services.google.com/ads_inquiry
/aff
```

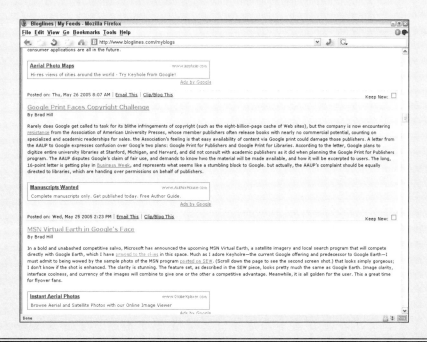

Here are the important points to remember:

- ✔ **Vanity sites are not allowed.** Generally speaking this is true, but with important exceptions. Confused yet? Well, AdSense eligibility is not an exact science. The site should convey information beyond the strictly personal. Pages devoted to photos of your college buddies will probably not make the cut. But a hobby page about Civil War reenactments certainly would be admitted. AdSense sites don't have to be commercial, but they must contain content of some substance. Weblogs have added an interesting twist, because any blog is likely to vary greatly in quality from page to page, and entry to entry. Many blogs run AdSense. I haven't heard any complaints of rejection from bloggers. However, you need to control the code of your blog pages, so hosted solutions that prevent direct access to the page's HTML code do not provide an AdSense opportunity.

- ✔ **Keep it appropriate.** The usual rules apply to your content, the same as you're likely to see on any hosting service. Google's guidelines prohibit running AdSense on sites that promote illegal behavior, pornography, or gambling. Excessive profanity can be a problem. Espousing hate and violence can get the site in trouble. Avoid copyright infringement.

- ✔ **Keep the site functioning.** All links must work. The site itself must be available to visitors without undue delay. If Google can't crawl the site after you apply to AdSense, the site will be rejected.

- ✔ **Don't mention the ads.** This is important: Do not reference the AdSense ads in your page content. Do not plead with your visitors to click them. Do not click the ads yourself. (More on this last point later.) Do not offer incentives to click ads. Simply do not talk about the ads at all. You probably get what Google is driving at here. Google's advertisers need to know that clickthroughs derive from genuine interest in the ad, not from coercion. The advertiser is paying for each clickthrough, so each one must be legitimate. If you dilute the quality of your clickthroughs and Google detects it (yes, it has ways), Google will cut you off like a stern bartender at closing time.

The quickest way to get kicked out of AdSense is to click your own ads. You might be tempted. Each click earns you money, and who's to know? Google knows. *Click fraud* is a serious topic in search advertising, and Google takes serious measures to detect it and remedy it. Don't click any ads that appear on your pages. Don't tell your friends to click them. Don't tell your site visitors to click them. Generating fraudulent clicks is considered a heinous abuse of the AdSense system, unworthy of lenience or second chances. Out you would go.

Getting Started: Opening an AdSense Account

The first step in becoming an AdSense publisher (besides owning a Web site) is applying for and starting an AdSense account. Opening the account doesn't obligate you in any way and doesn't cost a dime. In fact, nothing about AdSense ever costs anything.

You don't need to provide credit card information to join the AdSense network, but you must supply tax information so Google can pay you. That information consists of your EIN (Employer Identification Number) or Social Security number. Most people don't have an EIN, so they provide the SS number.

If Google doesn't know you through AdWords (if you are not a Google advertiser in that program), you must apply for an AdSense account. The application process is brief, but the acceptance process can sometimes stretch out for a few days. (Getting in is sometimes much quicker. It's unpredictable.) If you're an AdWords advertiser, your AdSense account becomes verified immediately.

To get going, follow these steps:

1. **Go to the AdSense page here:**

   www.google.com/adsense

2. **Click the Click Here to Apply button.**

3. **Fill in the Email address and Password boxes, and then click the Continue button.**

   If you have an AdWords account, you can use that information here. If not, create a password; it may be the same password you've used for other Google accounts, such as Gmail or Google Groups. For this series of steps, I assume you do not have an AdWords account.

4. **Use the radio buttons to choose whether you are the sole proprietor of your business or will be entering an EIN. Then click the Continue button.**

5. **Fill in all the contact information on the displayed page, and then click the Submit button.**

   Google sends a verification e-mail to the address you supply.

6. **Open the verification e-mail from Google and click the supplied link.**

   This step is a standard verification process and lets Google determine that you are real. If you are not real, it's probably time you came to grips with that.

7. **Wait for Google's acceptance e-mail.**

   When you receive the acceptance, you can log in to AdSense with the password you chose in Step 3.

You may publish AdSense ads on more than one site. I don't mean multiple pages within a site; I mean multiple domain names. If that is your intent, you must still open just one AdSense account. If you start a new account for each site and Google connects the dots between them, Google might close all your accounts. Use reporting channels (covered later in this chapter) to keep track of AdSense results across different pages and sites.

Useful AdSense Terms to Know

After your AdSense account is active, your AdSense experience will be clearer, and this chapter will make more sense if you're familiar with several important terms. Either read through this section or refer to it as needed.

Ad layout: An ad configuration for AdSense publishers. Google offers ten ad layouts; you can choose horizontal or vertical layouts containing one, two, four, or five ads. AdSense publishers can't alter the configuration of ads within the bars and banners that constitute ad layouts, but they may change the colors in which text and borders are displayed.

Ad unit: One set of AdSense ads displayed in an ad layout.

AdSense code: The snippet of HTML and JavaScript that Webmasters paste into their pages to begin serving AdWords ads.

AdSense channel: A tracking division that allows AdSense publishers to separate their revenue statistics according to page, site, ad style, or other distinguishing factors.

Alternate ads: AdSense publishers may specify non-Google ad sources for the space occupied by an ad unit, in preparation for those occasional times when Google can't deliver ads. Once specified, the alternate ad source is bundled into the AdSense code, and the replacement of Google ads by alternate ads occurs automatically if Google has no relevant ads to serve. (See Chapter 13.)

Banner: One type of ad layout. Three banners are available, one vertical and the other two horizontal. Each banner contains multiple ads.

Button: A type of ad layout that holds a single ad.

Clickthrough rate (CTR): Calculated by dividing the number of clicks by the number of displays (impressions). AdWords advertisers are charged for clicks through their ads. AdSense publishers are paid for clicks through the ads they host, sharing the revenue with Google.

Color palette: Individually adjusted colors for each of five elements in AdWords ads: headline text, ad text, URL text, border, and background. Google supplies several preset color palettes.

Content-targeted advertising: The generic name for Google's distribution of AdWords ads to AdSense sites. The AdSense network is also known as the *content network*. The word *content* is important in this context because Google uses its analysis of an AdSense page's content to determine which ads should be served on it.

Cost-per-click (CPC): A monetary amount charged by Google, and paid by the advertiser, when a user clicks through an ad. Advertisers bid for placement by offering a maximum CPC per keyword; Google charges the minimum amount beneath that amount (called the *actual CPC*) required to hold the best possible page position for the advertiser. (See Chapter 17 for more on this fine point.) AdSense publishers are paid an undisclosed percentage of the actual CPC.

Cybersquatting: The practice of unfairly capitalizing on ownership of a domain name that infringes a trademark or copyright. Google doesn't allow AdSense publication on a cybersquatting Web page.

Destination URL: An underlying URL in an AdWords ad that specifies the destination of clickthroughs. The destination URL is not necessarily the same as the URL displayed on the ad (called the *display URL*). When you set up a URL filter, the destination URL is blocked (see Chapter 13).

Distribution preference: Set by AdWords advertisers to include, or exclude, the content network of AdSense sites. AdSense publishers run AdWords ads only when those advertisers opt to have their ads appear on those publishers' pages.

Double serving: The practice of placing AdSense code in more than one location on a single page. Doing so violates Google's terms of service and is grounds for a warning and possibly expulsion from AdSense.

Image ads: Optional replacements of text ads, image ads are banner advertisements created by some AdWords advertisers and allowed by some AdSense publishers.

Impressions: Ad displays. AdSense measures and reports the impressions of all your ad units.

Inline rectangle: A type of ad layout meant to be placed within bodies of text, not in sidebars. Google offers four configurations of inline rectangles.

Leaderboard: A type of ad layout featuring four AdWords ads arranged horizontally. Leaderboards are designed to be placed at the top of Web pages but can be placed anywhere on the page.

Public service ad (PSA): Used to fill an AdWords ad before an AdSense site is crawled for the first time or if topical relevancy can't be established for some reason.

Publisher: An AdSense account holder and operator of a content site.

Skyscraper: A vertical arrangement of ads. Two skyscrapers are available; one holds four ads and one holds five.

Towers: All the vertical ad layouts: two skyscrapers and one vertical banner. Towers are usually placed on AdSense pages in the sidebars.

Typosquatting: The practice of purchasing and capitalizing on a misspelling of a prominent domain name, such as googal.com.

URL filter: A means of blocking specific AdWords ads from displaying on an AdSense site. This feature is normally used to prevent competitors from advertising on your site and taking away your visitors. Webmasters need to know the destination URL of any ad to block it. (See Chapter 13.)

Creating Your AdSense Ads

Strictly speaking, you don't create the ads that appear on your AdSense pages. The AdWords advertisers create the ads, Google determines which ones are appropriate for your site, and Google serves the ads to your pages. Your part in this is to decide what style of ads will appear and make some color choices. (You also must determine where on your pages the ads will be placed, but you do that part in your page-designing software, not on the Google site. This section is about using the AdSense account to create the code that you insert in your pages.)

AdSense is a simple, automated program. You need only place a snippet of code into your page's HTML, and then let the ads appear. When your page is visited and loads into a visitor's browser, the code reaches into Google and pulls the appropriate ads onto your page. As with other ad servers, your page content comes from two locations. The editorial content originates from your server, and the ads come from Google's server. This mechanism is invisible to the visitor, and Google ads load extremely fast, thanks to the absence of graphics (if you choose to run text ads).

As I walk you through the creation of AdSense code and describe how to paste that code into your page, you might get the impression that you may use only one code sample. Far from it! You may use variously altered versions of the basic code throughout your site — a different layout and different colors on each page, if you like.

Choosing an ad type and ad layout

When you first visit your AdSense account pages, the Reports section is displayed. At the beginning there is nothing to report, so your Reports section is empty. Start building your AdSense participation by clicking the Ad Settings tab. Figure 18-3 shows the Ad layout code page of the Ad Settings tab, where you create the code that will eventually get inserted into your page(s). Many AdSense publishers return to this page again and again to create different code snippets for different pages, or to create code that will alter the appearance of ads already running. This page is your workshop for choosing a layout style (horizontal, vertical, or single-ad), the ad type (text, images, or links only), and a color combination.

You have two basic choices of ad type:

- Ad unit
- Link unit

Ad units are horizontal, vertical, or single-unit blocks that contain between one and five text ads. Some (but not all) ad unit designs may also contain image ads. Look back at Figures 18-1 and 18-2 to see examples of ad units.

Link units contain no text except that contained in the links; they are extremely compact advertising designs. Link units are less attention-grabbing than ad units, but they also look less like ads, which might increase their clickthrough attractiveness on some pages. Figure 18-4 illustrates the several styles of link unit available.

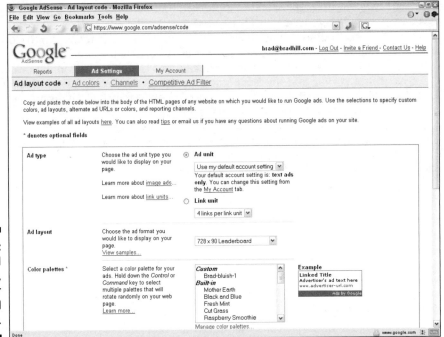

Figure 18-3:
In the Ad Settings tab, choose your ad type and layout style.

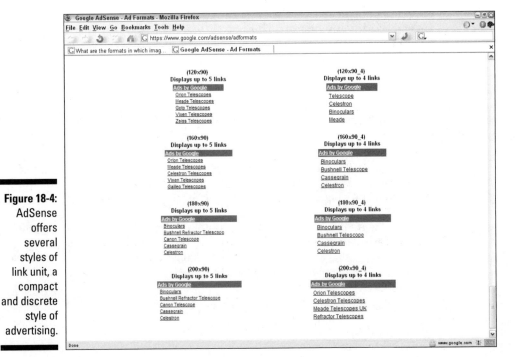

Figure 18-4:
AdSense offers several styles of link unit, a compact and discrete style of advertising.

All ad design possibilities are illustrated at the following page:

```
www.google.com/adsense/adformats
```

Choose an ad layout style that fits your page, but remember that no decision is ever carved in stone. You may change ad styles anytime. Experimentation is often necessary to find the right style. Furthermore, "the right style" is partly determined by observing which styles generate more clickthroughs. Finally, some Webmasters change styles periodically simply to freshen up their pages and to combat "ad blindness" — the tendency of frequent site visitors to block out ads if they know where they are and what they look like. When you do change an ad style, remember that making the settings on this page is not, by itself, going to do it. You must clip the resulting code and insert it in your Web page. (The code resulting from your selections on this page is presented at the bottom of the page. You can't see it in Figure 18-3; scroll down to find it.)

Overall, you want to strike a balance between attracting attention to your ads and irritating your visitors. If you overwhelm the page with large ad units or banners, you might achieve nothing more than driving away your visitors. In that case, you might retain your traffic *and* get better clickthrough rates with link units, inconspicuous as they are.

If you choose ad units, not link units, you face another choice. Do you want to run text ads, image ads, or both? If you choose both, Google will unpredictably send both; you'll never know which type of ad will appear on any given page view. Image ads fit into only certain ad unit designs: leaderboard, banner, skyscraper, medium rectangle, and wide skyscraper.

After choosing an ad type, select your layout. The choices available to you in this second portion of the Ad layout code page are determined by what you selected for an ad type. Use the pull-down menu to see the available selections. Click the <u>View samples</u> link to see illustrations of all selections.

Choosing colors

If you chose Image ads only as your ad type, you don't get to choose colors. Sorry. Spend this free time overcoming your bitterness; nobody likes a sourpuss. The rest of you: pay attention.

AdSense color palettes determine the hues of the ad unit's border, the background color, and the colors of the text, title, and URL. Click any preset combination in the scrollable color palette list to see the resulting combination next to the list. Each time you select a preset combination, the HTML code at the bottom of the page changes to reflect that change. When you make a final (for now) selection, you need do nothing to lock it in; the HTML code has incorporated your choice.

Click the <u>Manage color palettes</u> link to have more control of the color of each element. Figure 18-5 shows how this works; you pinpoint a hue for the border, background, text, title, and URL.

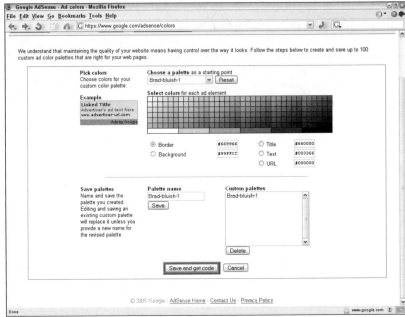

Figure 18-5:
Use this
page to
control the
coloring of
each of the
five ad
elements.

At this point, having selected an ad type, an ad layout, and a color combination, you've done everything you need to do before clipping the code, placing it in your page's HTML, and sitting back and waiting for the big bucks to roll in — that is to say, watching ads appear on your pages and hoping that over time you'll earn a bit of extra cash. So . . . clip the code! Do this:

1. **Scroll down to the bottom of the Ad layout code page.**

2. **Click anywhere in the Your AdSense code box.**

3. **Press Ctrl+A.**

   Doing so selects and highlights all the text in the box. Using the keyboard combination is safer than dragging the mouse, which risks missing a bit of highlighting.

4. **Press Ctrl+C.**

   Doing this copies the code to the Windows clipboard.

5. Press Ctrl+V to paste the code into your Web page's HTML source code.

Before pasting, position the mouse cursor at the position in your page's source document that will properly place the ad on the finished page.

AdSense Channels and AdSense Reports

AdSense gives you one hundred channels for tracking the effectiveness of your AdSense publishing. A *channel* allows you to gather ad units into distinct reporting groups. Say you have two sites residing at two different domains. Each site can be assigned a channel, enabling you to track earnings of the two properties separately. Now imagine that you have one site containing fifty pages; you may use channels to individually track the effectiveness of ads on each of those fifty pages. One more mental exercise: Imagine you have five hundred pages in your site, and you plan to run an AdSense ad unit at the top and bottom of each page. You may assign all the top-of-page ad units to one channel, and assign the bottom units to a second channel, letting you track the effectiveness of top and bottom placement across the entire site.

Each AdSense channel is defined by shared code. That's the HTML code you snip and clip into your page. If you select a channel on the Ad layout code page while selecting your ad layout and color scheme, that channel selection gets embedded in the code. That single line of code enables Google to track the performance of those ad units separately from differently coded ad units.

Creating a new channel is as easy as naming it, which you do on the Channels page under the Ad Settings tab in your AdSense account. Google suggests that you name your channels with URLs, but doing so is not necessary and doesn't make sense if one page contains ad units belonging to two different channels.

After you have created (named) one or more channels, those channels appear in the drop-down menu next to Channel on the Ad layout code page. When creating your code (ad type, ad layout, and colors), also select a channel. That channel selection gets embedded in the code, and any ad unit resulting from that pasted code, anywhere on your site, is reported in that channel.

AdSense reports break down the number of impressions (displays), the number of clicks, the clickthrough rate, earnings, and other information. The presentation is fairly flexible. You can sort the information by day, time period, and channel. AdSense rules prevent me from showing a report with actual numbers in it, but Figure 18-6 shows the Ad Performance page in the Reports tab with no performance data displayed.

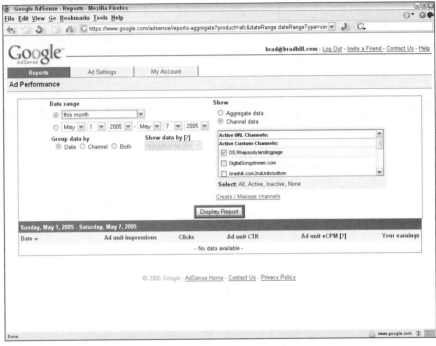

Figure 18-6:
AdSense
reporting
tools
provide
earnings
information
by date,
channel,
or both.

Removing Ads and Exiting the Program

Just as adding new pages and sites is hassle-free, Google puts up no barriers to exiting the AdSense program or reducing your involvement with it. AdSense is entirely configurable on this point; you may publish ads on one page of a large site, on all pages, on some pages, or across as many domains as you deem productive.

Simply remove the AdSense code from any page that you want to be ad-free. Removing a page from the program doesn't penalize other pages or change the quality of ads delivered to your pages. To stop your involvement with AdSense altogether, dump all the code. There's no way to close your AdSense account, nor is there any need to. It remains there, in case you decide to publish ads again in the future.

When you remove AdSense code, remember to adjust your page code to fill the hole you've just ripped in it. If you created a table cell to hold your ad unit, for example, eliminate the cell or put something else in it.

Part VI
The Part of Tens

The 5th Wave   By Rich Tennant

"Guess who found a Kiss merchandise site on the Web while you were *gone*?"

In this part . . .

The book draws to a reluctant close here. Unless you've come to this part first, in which case . . . well, hi! Do you walk backwards, too? Actually, I often start reading a *For Dummies* book with The Part of Tens.

This part contains two chapters that will open your eyes to new ways of Googling. Google freely gives away its most valuable asset: access to its index. The result is a host of alternate Google sites that deliver the same search results as Google.com but through a variety of different interfaces. The TouchGraph browser described in Chapters 19 and 20 will twist your mind into a new perspective on the living network surrounding every Web site. Chapter 21 lightens the intensely determined mood in which most of us search by presenting online games based on poking the Google index in new ways. You would never think the Googlebeast was so playful. Chapter 22 is devoted to sites *about* Google: Weblogs and resource sites that are both praiseful and critical.

If you read this book from start to finish, these pages will top off the renovation of your Googling mindset. If you're reading this book out of order, perhaps the items in these chapters will motivate you to explore other chapters. Either way, drink plenty of coffee and remember: Don't let an entire day happen without Google. [Editors' note: Brad has slipped into a fitful slumber, tormented by caffeine-generated dreams of battling the ferocious thrashing tentacles of the Google index. We pity him and hope for regained coherence before he writes his next book.]

Chapter 19

Ten Alternative Googles

*M*ost of this chapter, and the next, strays outside Google, yet remains within. Googles have sprouted up all over the place, delivering authentic Google results from search pages that don't look much like Google. These alternative Google interfaces are not endorsed by Google, for the most part, and don't enjoy any official relationship with Google, the company. But every search engine described in this chapter enjoys a close relationship with the Google index, which disgorges its treasures to any developer with the know-how to program into it.

Think of this chapter as a big, unofficial Google Labs, whose experiments are transpiring on the desktops of individuals and small companies. We, the lucky users, get to try them out. And let me tell you something startling: A few of these things are better than the original in certain ways. Google's innovative power resides in the index and the intelligence algorithms that power it. But as an interface design company, Google is more efficient than elegant, more brusque than thorough. If these characteristics can be called weak spots, they represent an opening for resourceful programmers.

For this chapter and the next I selected sites that are free to use, mostly easy, and worth whatever small efforts are required to use them. Some of these alternative Googles concentrate on delivering a single Google service better (or differently) than Google does. A few rope together many of Google's engines into a single glorious interface.

Onward, then, into realms of Googleness that you never dreamed of!

Bare-Bones Results

www.google.com/ie

You wouldn't think Google could be simplified. The home page is spare to the point of being stark, with no ads or miscellaneous graphics whatsoever. But there is room to make it simpler still, by removing the Images, Groups, Directory, and News tabs. Then strip away the links to Advanced Search, Preferences, and Language Tools. And get rid of the miscellaneous corporate links. Finally, clear out everything on the search results page except the target site links — no descriptions, ads, summaries, or anything else.

This first destination in a mostly non-Google chapter is an official Google page. But it's one that Google doesn't promote, and in that sense it's an alternative search experience.

Figure 19-1 shows what a search looks like through this interface. You don't get much information, but you also don't get a heavy page load. This point is important if you have your Preferences set to deliver one hundred hits per results page (see Chapter 2).

This simplified search format supports the search operators described in Chapter 2 and the specialized operators explained in other chapters. Basically, you can conduct any search on this page that you can on the regular Google home page. The phone book and dictionary described in Chapter 3 work here, too.

Run your mouse cursor over the compact results to see a snippet from each target page in a small pop-up blurb. This tip works in compact search results in other sites, too.

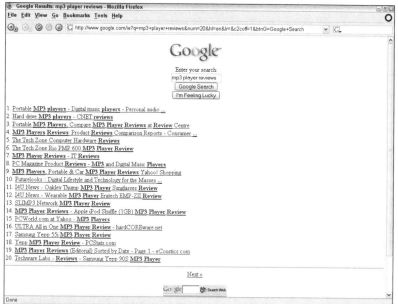

Figure 19-1:
A bare-
bones
search
result.

Finding the Freshest Google

www.researchbuzz.com/goofresh.shtml

Google is not particularly strong at letting you determine the freshness of search results. The vagueness surrounding page freshness is due to several reasons:

✔ Google uses more than spiders to crawl the Web, and more than one *type* of spider. (See Chapter 16 for more about spiders and Web crawling.) These crawlers operate at different speeds and different depths. It's possible for a newly created Web page to go undetected by one crawl and then turn up in the index two weeks later after a deeper crawl.

✔ Google uses more than one server (Internet computer) to deliver search results. The servers are not perfectly synchronized. At any moment, one server might give slightly different search results from another server.

✔ The freshness of a page is determined by the time it was created, or the time it was added to Google's index, or both.

Google does enable a certain degree of freshness filtering on the Advanced Search page in a Web search. (An advanced search in Google Groups lets you specify dates because newsgroup posts are dated more precisely than Web pages. See Chapter 6.) On the Advanced Search page, you can ask for Web pages updated within the past three months, six months, or year. These large time frames are safe for Google because the three variables just listed cause confusion only within time periods shorter than three months.

An alternate Google engine called GooFresh invites you to fine-tune the freshness setting by drastically narrowing the time frame. GooFresh accomplishes the time-narrowing trick by using the *daterange* operator. I don't discuss this operator much in this book because *daterange* doesn't understand dates formatted in a typical fashion — month, day, and year. Google understands only the Julian date system, which involves long and cryptic strings of numbers.

Assuming that your freshness needs aren't too precise or imperative, GooFresh is a fine alternative. Figure 19-2 shows the GooFresh page ready to launch a search. The search results look completely normal and are drastically narrowed compared to an undated search. A recent search for the keyword *internet,* which normally returns hundreds of thousands of results, yielded only three when GooFresh looked for pages added on the current day.

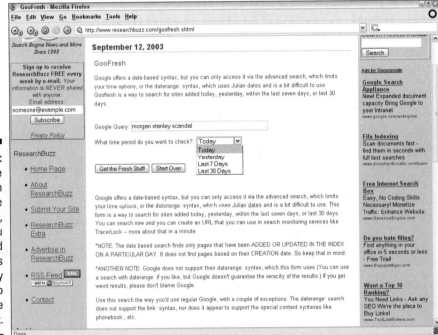

Figure 19-2: The GooFresh interface to Google, where you can find Web sites freshly added to the Google index.

Widen your search results by enlarging the time frame. Selecting Today from the drop-down menu (see Figure 19-2) delivers the fewest results. Also, because of the restricted time frame, you get better (or, at least, more) results by using fewer keywords. At the same time, limit your use of operators, especially when choosing Today or Yesterday. In other words, give Google some breathing space: Be less demanding in your keywords when you're more demanding about the time frame.

GooFresh provides results based on when pages were added to the Google index, not when the pages were created.

The Amazing TouchGraph

For a truly unusual and stunning graphical representation of Google search results, dig into this section and get familiar with TouchGraph GoogleBrowser. TouchGraph uses the Java programming language to create alternative displays for databases. When you type a URL in TouchGraph, it displays sites related to the URL — just as if you had clicked the Similar pages link of a Google search result.

In this section, you first explore TouchGraph GoogleBrowser, which displays Google's Related Sites feature (see Chapter 2) in an entirely new way. After exploring the TouchGraph Google Browser, I discuss a similar site, Google-set-vista, created by different individuals but using the TouchGraph browser technology.

Visualizing related sites

    www.touchgraph.com/TGGoogleBrowser.html

You should understand one thing from the start: TouchGraph GoogleBrowser does not perform keyword searching. You do not get a visual representation of a standard Google search here. The TouchGraph system is all about displaying related items (Web pages, in this case). In a keyword search, all the hits relate in the same way: They match the keywords. TouchGraph reveals constellations of sites surrounding the related sites, and you can extend the model outward again and again. This type of multiple-universe display doesn't lend itself to straight keyword matching, but I hope to be proven wrong very soon.

For now, though, go to TouchGraph to see URL relationships that aren't easily apparent in a long list of text links — and for the sheer delight of playing with one of the coolest Java interfaces around.

When typing the TouchGraph GoogleBrowser URL in your browser, note the uppercase letters in TGGoogleBrowser. Because they are part of a filename (not part of a domain name), they must be typed exactly as they appear here. Otherwise, the page will not load. And your computer will explode. (Sorry, my inner demons made me say that.)

TouchGraph requires a certain Java component called a plug-in (specifically, Java plug-in 1.3). Fortunately, you don't need to know whether you have that component; if you don't, the site tells you and helps you get it. So, in blessed ignorance, hop over to the TouchGraph GoogleBrowser site, type a URL in the search box, and click the Graph it! button.

A URL consists of three parts separated by periods: the *www* part, the *domain* part (often the name of the site or a company), and the *domain extension* part (such as *.com* or *.org*). An example, pulled randomly from the millions of Web URLs, would be:

```
www.bradhill.com
```

TouchGraph GoogleBrowser allows elimination of the *www* part, just like most Web browsers do. But don't leave off the extension.

If you don't have the Java plug-in 1.3 component, a Security Warning window pops open, asking whether you want to install and run Java plug-in 1.3. The required Java plug-in is free of charge and third-party hassles. It's a safe download and installs easily with the assistance of a few mouse clicks on your part. TouchGraph GoogleBrowser is one good reason to get the 1.3 plug-in, but not the only reason: If you surf a reasonable amount, you're bound to find other sites that use it.

On some computers, the download proceeds without the Security Warning pop-up, but that is rare. Assuming you do get the Security Warning window, proceed as follows:

1. **In the Security Warning box, click the Yes button.**

   The plug-in is more than 5 megabytes in size, so if you're using a dial-up telephone modem, now is a good time to brew a double mochaccino. After the download, an autoinstallation program runs.

2. **In the Select Java Plugin Installation window, choose a locale and region, and then select Install.**

3. **In the License Agreement page, click the Yes button.**

   It's always a good idea to read the terms before agreeing. In this case, I doubt you'll find anything objectionable.

4. **In the Choose Destination Location window, click the Next button.**

   Use the Browse button if you want to change the default location of the Java plug-in. I don't see much point to changing it — this isn't a stand-alone application that you access outside the browser.

5. **In the Select Browsers window, check one or more boxes and click the Next button.**

   There's no harm in selecting all listed browsers, but at least select the browser you're currently using.

At this point the Java plug-in installs. After a few seconds, the installation program disappears, and you're returned to the TouchGraph browser window. This window is a new one, leaving your original window anchored at the TouchGraph Web site.

This rigmarole might seem like a lot of work to experience an alternate Google, but it's worth it. And I should emphasize that many browsers have the necessary Java plug-in. If the site doesn't tell you that anything is missing, you're good to go; ignore the preceding instruction list.

Figure 19-3 shows TouchGraph in action, displaying search results for the `www.nytimes.com` URL.

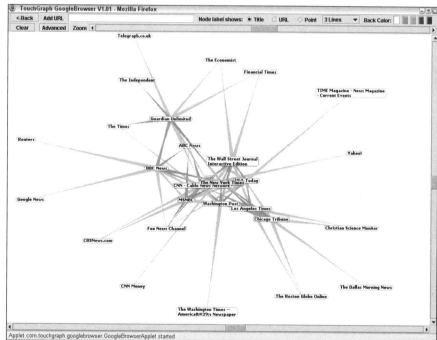

Figure 19-3: TouchGraph GoogleBrowser displays clusters of related sites. Drag any site to shift the cluster's shape.

The TouchGraph display is interactive. As you run the mouse over its screen, two things happen to indicate relationships between sites (called *nodes* in the TouchGraph system):

- ✔ The strands connecting nodes light up when a strand or a node is touched by the mouse cursor.

- ✔ When you touch a node, the node label expands to show the full site title (as long as the node label is in URL or Point mode, as I describe a bit later), and the strands between the touched node and its related nodes light up. Pink strands indicate outgoing links. Blue strands indicate incoming links. A small green info button also appears above any mouse-touched node label. Click that button to see more information about the site.

You may click and drag any node. You must try this, in fact, — it's fun to see the entire web of related sites shift, like a living being, to accommodate the dragged node's movement.

Figure 19-4 shows lighted strands of relatedness and the information window that opens when you click the info button of the expanded label. The information window contains some of what you'd get in a regular Google search result, without the capability to display a cached page. Because the TouchGraph display is all about showing similar pages, there's no link to display similar pages.

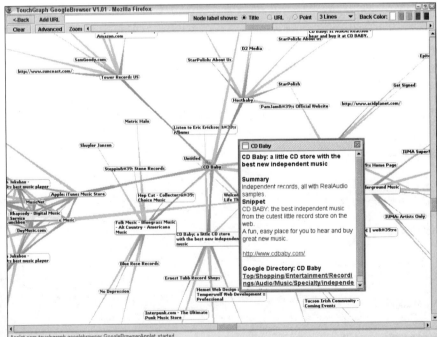

Figure 19-4:
Clicking the info button opens a window with search result information.

You can order up a new constellation of related sites around any node on the graph by simply double-clicking the node. When you do, a small red tab pops up from the node, titled 0-10. TouchGraph receives the first ten results from Google and displays them. If you double-click that node again, the red pop-up reads 11-20, and so on for every double-click. Keep doing this, or move from node to node opening new clusters of relatedness, and you can end up with a seething mass of nodes and connecting strands (see Figure 19-5).

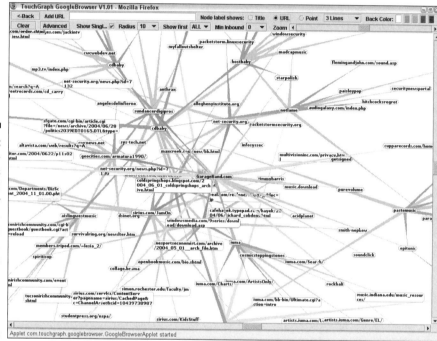

Figure 19-5:
Add con-
stellations
of related
sites by
double-
clicking
nodes.
In this
screen, the
Advanced
controls are
toggled on.

The display of node clusters might extend beyond the window, especially on small monitors or screens running low resolutions, such as 800 x 600. The illustrations in this section were taken on an 800 x 600 screen and, as you can see, the TouchGraph strands reach out beyond the window's boundaries. My larger screens aren't big enough either, after I start double-clicking nodes. Notice the scroll bars at the bottom and right edges of the TouchGraph browser. Use them to scroll from side to side, and up and down.

Use the Zoom bar in the TouchGraph toolbar to pull back, getting all your node clusters into view. Figure 19-6 shows a zoomed-out screen with all nodes labeled as points instead of titles or URLs. Note the radio buttons in the TouchGraph toolbar with those choices. The point labels display the first two letters of the site's title. Run your mouse cursor over any abbreviated node to see its title.

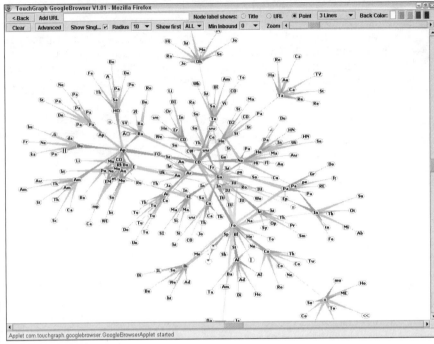

Figure 19-6:
Use the
Zoom
function and
relabel
nodes as
points to
present a
coherent
overview.

Other control features of the toolbar follow:

- ✔ **Back:** The Back button highlights the previously highlighted node.

- ✔ **Add URL:** Use this search box to launch a new search. If you don't click the Clear button first, TouchGraph puts the new search results right on top of the old graph. There might be no relatedness whatsoever between the two sets of results, in which case the graph holds them both with no connecting strands between the two sets of constellations.

- ✔ **Node label shows:** Use the options here to determine how the node labels appear. The Title setting creates the most cluttered display. The URL setting shortens most node labels a bit. The Point setting displays only the first two letters of the site title and is great when the screen gets packed with nodes. Run your mouse cursor over the nodes in URL or Point mode to see their titles.

- ✔ **Number of lines:** Note the drop-down menu whose default selection reads 3 Lines. Use it to select 1 Line, 2 Lines, 3 Lines, or All Lines; these choices determine the number of text lines appearing in TouchGraph node labels; some titles and URLs are quite lengthy, and you might not want to see the node labels stretched to accommodate them.

- ✔ **Back Color:** Click one colored box to change the graph's background color. If you stare at this thing for as long as I do, the change of hue relieves the eyes.

- ✔ **Clear:** Beware of this button. It clears the entire screen, potentially wiping out a long session of playing around . . . I mean, of productive searching.

- ✔ **Advanced:** This button toggles the advanced controls on and off.

- ✔ **Show Singles:** When checked, this feature expands the node clusters by displaying those nodes with only a single link to the central URL in addition to the nodes with multiple links to the central URL. Uncheck this box to reduce screen clutter.

- ✔ **Radius:** This setting determines the number of edges surrounding the URL you've searched. Reducing the number lowers the number of related constellations around your main cluster.

- ✔ **Show first:** This option determines how many search results are displayed. I usually keep this set to All, greedy searcher that I am.

- ✔ **Min Inbound:** The lower this number, the more numerous your results. The default setting is 0. The setting determines the minimum number of incoming links a site must offer to register on the graph. When no incoming links exist from one site to another, Google sometimes assigns relatedness based on other factors in the index.

In addition to being insanely fun, TouchGraph GoogleBrowser provides a good way to find new Web destinations of interest. When you click an info tab, the pop-up box always displays a link to that Web site, and clicking that link opens a new browser window for that site.

The next section discusses the same TouchGraph technology as applied to Google Sets.

Visual keyword sets

```
www.langreiter.com/space/google-set-vista
```

Keyword sets are discussed in Chapter 11. One of Google's technology experiments open to the public, Google Sets are collections of related keywords. Type one or more words (presumably related in some way), and Google finds many other words related in the same way. (Reminiscent of the standardized tests you took in high school, isn't it? Don't panic. You're not being graded.)

Google Sets provides a perfect application for TouchGraph viewing, which specializes in showing relatedness. Launching the TouchGraph viewer and installing the Java plug-in are identical here as with TouchGraph GoogleBrowser, described in the preceding section. If you installed the Java plug-in 1.3 component for GoogleBrowser, you don't need to install it again here (or ever again at any site).

This Google Sets tool, created by Christian Langreiter, is called google-set-vista. Easy as it is to use, it differs in important ways from TouchGraph GoogleBrowser and from the Google Sets home page at Google. Follow these steps to get started:

1. **On the google-set-vista home page, type a word in the box marked Term.**

   Type not a search keyword but a word or phrase that will generate related words. The results are not Web pages; they're groups of words or names. It is important that you start with either just one word or a phrase — not unrelated words. Google lets you enter several related words, but google-set-vista doesn't understand multiple words and thinks they're one big hybrid word.

2. **Click the Set me some! button.**

   The site activates the Java applet (which takes a few seconds) and displays results (see Figure 19-7). Notice that google-set-vista displays the TouchGraph viewer within the browser rather than opening a special window.

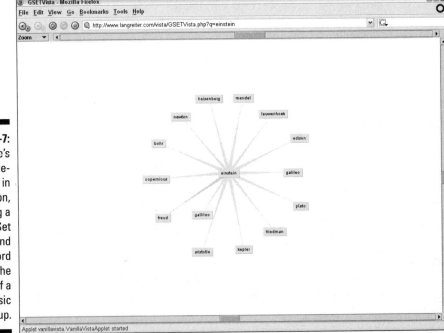

Figure 19-7: Here's google-set-vista in action, displaying a Google Set around the word *Einstein,* the name of a music group.

The google-set-vista tool makes substantial changes to the TouchGraph viewer as deployed in GoogleBrowser. The basic display is the same, in that you can grab a node (a word in this case, not a Web site) and drag it around, pulling the whole set with it. The strands connecting words do not behave with the same color-coded responsiveness as in GoogleBrowser, naturally, because a Google Set has no incoming and outgoing links. The same scroll bars are found along the bottom and right edges, for viewing portions of a large array of sets.

There's no Clear button in google-set-vista, as there is in GoogleBrowser. Nor is there an entry box. So, you can neither clear the screen of its current search nor launch a new search within the TouchGraph window. To start a new search, click your browser's Back button, returning to the google-set-vista home page. Unfortunately, this process requires a reload of the Java applet with each new search. (That's not the same as downloading Java plug-in 1.3, which you do only once. Loading the applet takes just a few seconds.)

As in GoogleBrowser, google-set-vista nodes can be expanded. Simply double-click any node to create a set around that word. It's interesting to see how two sets are connected — in other words, which words belong to both sets. Continue expanding nodes repeatedly to get a complex web of Google Set connections (see Figure 19-8).

Figure 19-8:
Overlapping and contiguous Google Sets, TouchGraph style.

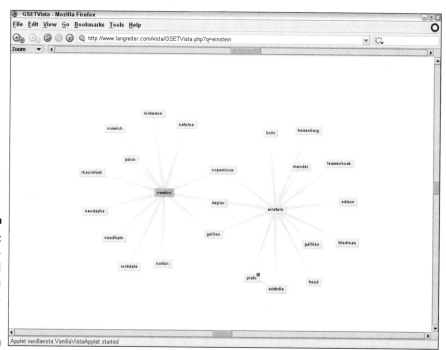

The Zoom bar atop the google-set-vista viewer has three functions, only one of which is displayed and functional at any time. Set the function of the Zoom bar with the drop-down menu to its left. Its three functions are

- ✔ **Zoom:** Set the slider here to zoom in and out of your field of nodes.
- ✔ **Rotate:** Handily, you can use the slider to rotate the entire network of nodes. Doing so can bring a partially hidden field into view without zooming.
- ✔ **Locality:** This is where I normally keep the scroll bar set. Moving the Locality slider to the left folds the node groups into themselves, one by one, simplifying the screen. Moving it to the right expands the node clusters again, revealing all connections.

When I first encountered google-set-vista, I thought it was a poor second cousin to TouchGraph GoogleBrowser. My prejudice was due partly to my disaffection for Google Sets, which seemed like one of the more boring Google Labs experiments, and partly because google-sets-vista didn't have all the toolbar bells and whistles of GoogleBrowser. I quickly changed my mind, though, and now I turn to the two TouchGraph sites equally. The google-set-vista tool refreshed my attitude about Google Sets, which I now use often as a way of discovering new bands, books, movies, and ideas. But I never use the official Google interface — only google-set-vista. I only wish the right-click menu included a Search option for launching a Google keyword search.

Google by E-mail

`www.google.com/alerts`

If you repeatedly search Google with the same keyword strings, you might wish for a way of receiving search results without having to visit Google every day, or week, or however frequently you remember to repeat the search. Google recently launched a service that provides updates to previously seen search results for your keyword or keyword string. The updates are delivered as e-mails. Furthermore, because repeated search queries are often news-oriented, Google offers the choice of repeatedly search Google News, or Google Web, or both.

Figure 19-9 shows the Google Alerts page. You do not need a Google account to sign up for a Google Alert, but having an account, and signing in to it, enables better management of your alerts. You can set up multiple alerts, each with its own frequency (from a list of three choices), source (Web, News, or both), and — naturally — its own keyword or string.

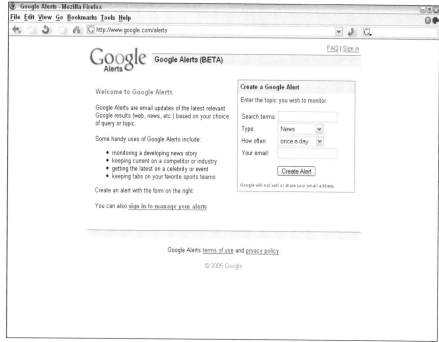

Figure 19-9:
The Google
Alerts home
page. You
don't need a
Google
account to
receive
e-mail
alerts.

If you don't have a Google account, simply fill in the fields shown in Figure 19-9, and click the Create Alert button. Google sends you a verification e-mail. When you click the verification link in that e-mail, Google accepts your alert and starts sending them to that e-mail address at your specified frequency.

If you do have a Google account, click the Sign in to manage your alerts link near the bottom of the Google Alerts home page (shown in Figure 19-9). After signing in on the next page, you see a page resembling Figure 19-10. There, you can define new alerts, change the features of existing alerts, and delete existing alerts. Use the pull-down menus to set the alert source (Type) and frequency (How often).

Google Ultimate Interface

Google offers advanced search pages in most of its engines. But the Web-search advanced page lacks power, as anyone would agree after seeing Google Ultimate Interface and Soople (see Chapter 20). In a reasonably concise format, the Google Ultimate Interface reaches into the Google index with exceptional flexibility. If this page were represented on the Google Toolbar, you'd probably use it routinely as your primary Google interface. In fact, you might use this page every day even though it's absent from the Toolbar. For a quick, darting search, it doesn't make sense. But when you want nearly all of Google gathered onto a single page, the Google Ultimate Interface site lives up to its name.

Figure 19-10:
Use this page to create, edit, and delete alerts.

Google Ultimate Interface is located here:

```
www.faganfinder.com/google.html
```

The preceding address is for the Internet Explorer browser. If you're using Firefox or Netscape, go here:

```
www.faganfinder.com/google2.html
```

Figure 19-11 shows Google Ultimate Interface in its default state. This view is just one of the available forms. You're two clicks away from equally impressive forms for launching searches into Google Groups, Images, Directory, Answers, Glossary, Froogle — nearly every Google engine documented in this book.

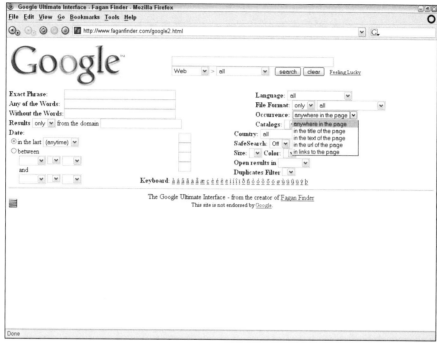

The following points discuss the important features of the Web search form shown in Figure 19-11. Advanced features that duplicate Google's Advanced Search page in a Web search are described in Chapter 2:

- **Scope:** Use the upper-right drop-down menu (shown in Figure 19-11 with *all* as a default setting) to select compact results, one of the specialty searches introduced in Chapter 9, or even a specific Google server.

- **File Format:** Use these menus to include or exclude certain file formats.

- **Window:** Use the Open Results In menu to choose whether to open a new window for search results or use the original window. I strongly recommend using a new window, especially because using the Back button to retrace your steps from the search results page is sluggish. (The complex and form-intensive search page takes time to reload.)

- **Date:** This feature seals the deal. The Google Ultimate Interface is where you come for easy, intuitive date-range Web searching. The top menu (labeled *in the last*) duplicates the broad ranges Google provides on its Advanced Search page. For more precision, click the *between* option and use the drop-down menus to determine a date range within which your search results must fall.

✔ **Country and Language:** Google's Advanced Search page provides a language setting but not a country setting. (Both settings are included in Google Ultimate Interface.)

✔ **Duplicates Filter:** Use this menu to toggle Google's filter for removing duplicate and near-duplicate search results.

✔ **Keyboard:** In a fantastic, even show-offy stunt, Google Ultimate Interface provides special characters to include in your search string. Click any one of them, and it appears in the keyword box. This feature is great when searching for pages in some non-English languages.

This interface reaches into the Google engine, of course, so search results are identical to those in a standard Google search.

When searching within a date range, Google can determine only when a Web page was added to its index, not when the page was created. There can be a lag of weeks between the two dates.

Now look at that Web menu below the search box. Pull it down to choose one of Google's other search engines. Click a selection, and Google Ultimate Interface changes its configuration, becoming an advanced search page for that search engine.

For basic, thorough searching, Google Ultimate Interface is the site in this chapter that should be taken most seriously. I find it indispensable.

GAPS, GARBO, and GAWSH

That section title should get your attention. The GAPS, GARBO, and GAWSH search engines are presented by the same site and provide three distinct search experiences, each valuable in its own fashion.

If you have a Google license key (see the "Getting the Google license key" sidebar), have it handy as you cruise among the sites in this <u>section</u>. Very few alternate Googles insist on a bring-your-own-license policy, but some request that you "pay" your own way, and others surreptitiously position an entry box for the key number with the hope that you'll use it. Be polite to other users and put your searches on your own key's quota, thereby saving the site from burning quickly through its own quota and shutting down until the next day.

Unlike too many alternative Google sites, this one provides detailed explanations of its features. Click the <u>Read Me</u> link on the GAPS, GARBO or GAWSH pages to get some help with the particular engine. The following sections convey the basics, certainly enough to get you started.

Getting the Google license key

Google offers a free license to software developers to access the Google Web index. This license enables alternate Google sites to deliver Google search results through new interfaces. Developers download a software kit that includes the Google Web API (Application Programming Interface). An API is necessary whenever one program or Web site hooks into a necessary underlying system, such as Google or the Windows operating system. If your computer runs Windows, every application program you have uses the Windows API. Similarly, every alternate Google interface uses the Google API.

Developers using the Google API also must obtain a Google license key, which is used every time somebody conducts a search through the alternate site. If Google doesn't "see" the license key (which is just a string of letters and numbers), it will not perform the search.

All this might seem irrelevant if you're not planning to develop a new Google search site. But anybody can get a license key, even people with no intent to program. The license key is separate from the developer's kit. And it's a good idea — even good manners — to own a free license key. The reason is that each license key allows the owner a certain number of searches per day. That number is currently set at 1000, which might seem like a lot. But in a public site, a daily quota of 1000 searches can be used up quickly, disabling the site for other users until the next day. So many sites in this chapter provide a space for entering your license key. By doing so, you "pay" for your own searches out of your quota. (All this is completely free of charge, of course.)

You don't need to download a developer's kit to get the license key; you merely need to create a Google account in the Web APIs section. Follow these steps:

1. **Go to the Google Web APIs page here:**

   `www.google.com/apis`

2. **Scroll down to Step 2, Create a Google Account, and click the create a Google Account link.**

3. **Enter an e-mail address and password, and then type the word *verification*.**

   If you've already created a Google account for Google Answers (see Chapter 10) or Google Groups (see Chapter 6), click the Sign in here link at the bottom of the page and use the username and password you established then. You must sign in (or create a new account) from the Google Web APIs page before Google sends you a license key.

4. **Click the "I have read and agree to the Terms of Use. Create my account." button.**

If you create a new account this way, or if you sign in to an existing Google account through the Web APIs page, Google sends your license key to your e-mail address. The e-mail includes the Terms of Service for the Web API program, which are distinct from the Terms of Service you (presumably) read and agreed to when creating a Google account.

The license key contains more than thirty characters, so obviously you shouldn't try to memorize it. Keep it in a safe place in your computer, ready to copy and paste into alternate Google sites that request it.

Proximity searching with GAPS

`www.staggernation.com/cgi-bin/gaps.cgi`

Google API Proximity Search (GAPS) invites you to search for two keywords that occur within a certain proximity. This tool strikes a useful middle ground between two extremes: keywords that might be located anywhere on the page, and keywords located directly next to each other, as in the case of an exact phrase. Putting the keywords close to each other but not necessarily next to each other encourages relevance without the restriction of an exact phrase. Figure 19-12 shows the GAPS form.

Figure 19-12: Locate Web pages with two keywords in close proximity.

Follow these steps to design and launch a GAPS search:

1. **In the Find search boxes, type a single keyword in each box.**

2. **Use the drop-down menu between the keyword boxes to select a proximity range.**

   The GAPS engine is currently limited to finding keyword pairs separated by no more than three intervening words. Google doesn't insist on this limitation, but GAPS enforces it to contain search results.

3. **In the first drop-down menu, choose In either order.**

   The alternate choice, In that order, reduces results by forcing Google to match your first and second keywords in that order.

4. **In the next drop-down menu, choose Sort by ranking.**

   Ranking is Google's assessment of relevance. You may also sort by URL, page title, and keyword proximity. It's easy to reset the search parameters after you see the results.

5. **In the Additional terms box, type any other keyword that you want as part of the search string.**

   Here you may use operators, exact phrases, and multiple keywords.

6. **In the Show menu, select how many results you would like overall.**

   I leave this setting in its default All state.

7. **In the next drop-down menu, choose how many results should be listed for each query.**

   This might seem confusing. With a proximity search using these features, you're forcing Google to perform multiple searches, one for each combination of keyword order and proximity. The two keywords can be three words apart, two words apart, one word apart, or next to each other — and furthermore, they could match any of those conditions with their order reversed. This setting determines how many search results you see for each of those distinct searches.

8. **Click the Filter each query option.**

   This setting refers to Google's duplicate filter, which eliminates multiple hits from the same site.

9. **Click the Search button.**

   GAPS displays results in normal fashion, with no separation of individual searches. Your sorting option determines how the results are ordered. Conveniently, GAPS reproduces the entire search form atop the search results page, so you can modify your parameters or launch a new search without backtracking.

You may use the exact phrase (quotes) operator in either of the two proximity keyword boxes. Google treats the phrase as a single keyword that must exist within a certain proximity to the other keyword. The two keywords can both be phrases, for that matter. I like doing that to search for articles about two closely paired public figures. Try searching this way for "Carrie Underwood" and "Bo Bice," the two most recent (as of this writing) *American Idol* winners.

Relation browsing with GARBO

www.staggernation.com/garbo/

The GARBO engine performs the same sort of search as TouchGraph GoogleBrowser, described previously in this chapter — namely, searching for sites related to a certain Web domain. Google API Relation Browsing Outliner (GARBO) adds a twist by also enabling you to search for sites that link to a certain page (using Google's *link* operator). Instead of displaying results in an interactive graphical spread, GARBO delivers text results that are unusually customizable. In fact, the intelligence of the results display makes GARBO particularly useful.

As with TouchGraph GoogleBrowser, you type a URL, not keywords, into GARBO.

The search form, shown in Figure 19-13, contains three main elements:

- ✔ **Search box:** Type a URL here.

- ✔ **Related pages or linking pages:** You can select related pages (Google's Similar pages feature) or linking pages (which delivers sites containing links to your search URL). Google allows one of these searches at a time; you can't do both.

- ✔ **Snippets and URLs:** I prefer to keep the search results clean in GARBO, so I leave both these options unchecked. (Snippets and URLs both appear in search results derived from Google.com. Snippets are bits of content containing your keywords from the result site, and the URL is the result site address.) GARBO then displays a concise and useful folder-like results page.

The beauty of eliminating snippets and URLs is revealed on the search results page, which comes up with economical élan. The results look and behave like a list of folders. Click a triangle next to any item to open it, revealing more detailed results within.

Engagingly, GARBO encourages secondary searching on the search results with the <u>View in Google</u> link next to each opened folder when you search without snippets and URLs. Doing so conducts a relation search (or a link search, if that's how you started) on the result URL. *That* is cool.

Search by host with GAWSH

`www.staggernation.com/gawsh/`

Rounding out this invaluable trio of alternate Googles is Google API Web
Search by Host (GAWSH). This engine takes the folder approach to results
available in GARBO and makes it the default, irrevocable result format. Here,
you search by keyword (with operators) and get results organized by Web
domain. Each domain in the search results list can be opened, like a folder,
revealing matching pages that come from that site. These revealed inner
results are displayed in traditional Google format, within the opened GAWSH
folder.

GAWSH is not as trivial as its description might sound — or as it might look
when you first visit the search page. The search form consists of nothing
more than a keyword box and a Search button. The action is in the results
page, shown in Figure 19-14. In this screen shot, I expanded one of the folders
to illustrate the mixture of GAWSH formatting and Google formatting.

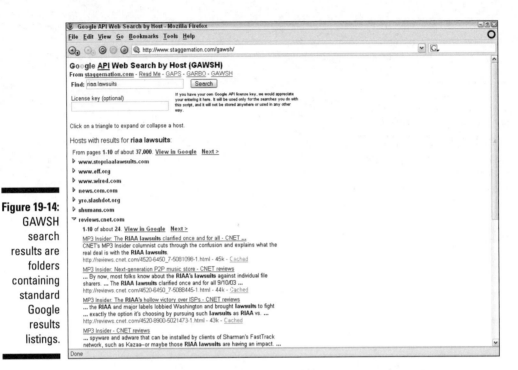

Figure 19-14:
GAWSH
search
results are
folders
containing
standard
Google
results
listings.

GAWSH is fantastic for bundling essential search result information into a small space for quick scanning. Most of us prefer getting information from favorite sites but don't want to specify those sites every time we search. GAWSH reveals at a glance which sites have pages matching your keywords, enabling you to zoom into favored domains for exact matches. Every time you click an expanding folder triangle, GAWSH launches the search again, limiting it to the selected domain.

GAWSH provides the perfect environment in which to use the negative *site* operator (see Chapter 2). Eliminating obvious host matches makes the resulting host list even more valuable. Try this search:

```
boycott RIAA -site:www.boycott-riaa.com
```

Chatting with Google

Is no medium safe from Googling? Well, instant messaging isn't, that's for sure. Instant messaging is a popular online discussion medium through which people chat in pop-up windows that appear on the screen. As with e-mail, most instant messaging users keep a list of contacts, to whom they can shoot a "Hello!" or "How are ya?" at any time. The transmission of these lines is, well, instant.

At least three developers have contrived to let you conduct a basic Web search in Google, through one of the three major IM programs:

- AOL Instant Messenger (AIM)
- MSN Messenger
- Yahoo! Messenger

Each one works the same way. You use your IM program's features to see whether the Google search service is online, and then simply send your keyword string as an instant message. The problem is, these services are very often *not* online. Remember, this isn't Google itself, which is always available. These instant-messaging searches are third-party services, alternate Googles, and the developers are regular folks who go online and offline just like you and I do. (Actually, I never go offline. Nor do I venture outside. I am fed intravenously and hunger for simple human touch that I will never receive. But enough about me.)

Following are the three IM-search providers and the IM services in which they operate.

- **Googolator:** This one works in AIM. Add Googolator to your Buddy list and send keywords whenever it's online. Five results are returned.

- **Googlematic:** This one works identically in AIM and MSN Messenger. Again, five results. In MSN Messenger, you need an entire e-mail address to locate a new contact. Look for `googlematic@interconnected.org`.

- **YIMGoogle:** This one is set for Yahoo! Messenger. The *YIM* stands for Yahoo! Instant Messenger, even though that's not really the name of the program. YIMGoogle is the screen name to look for and add to your Friends list. Query when it comes online to get five results.

To try any one of these, open the corresponding IM program and use the name from the list as a contact. In other words, send your keyword(s) as an instant message to that name.

Flash with Floogle

`www.flash-db.com/Google`

Here's an alternate Google with no added functionality. Floogle is an experiment in programming, and it delivers Google search results in the Flash environment.

Flash is a multimedia programming language usually used to display moving images and sound. In this case, it delivers static Google search results. The site does make fun beeping sounds, though, when the mouse cursor touches the Result Page numbers atop search results.

Searches are launched and results delivered within the same Flash frame residing in the Web page. You need Flash 6 for this to work. If you don't have Flash 6, the page tells you immediately and downloads it for you if you approve. Downloading and installation are transparent and automatic; just wait a minute or so (depending on your connection speed) until the search engine appears on the Web page. Figure 19-15 shows Floogle and its search results.

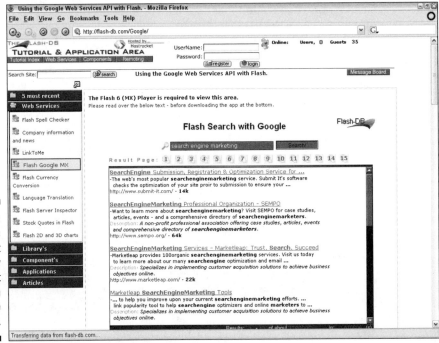

Figure 19-15: Floogle is fun but not particularly important as an alternative Google.

Simply enter a keyword string and click the Search! button. Note that pressing the Enter key to launch a search doesn't work here; doing so merely clears the keyword box.

Search results look fairly Googlish but without the Similar pages and Cached links. Oh, and without the entire top-page summary that Google provides. Floogle dishes up pure results and nothing but. Even the AdWords and sponsored links are missing. Click any result link to see the target page, opened in a new window. See results beyond the first ten by clicking a numbered button above the results pane — this is where the beeps are located.

Quotes with Your Search Results

The next entry, Boogle, is somewhat fun, undeniably trivial, and appears in this chapter more for the sake of comprehensiveness than because I particularly recommend it.

Boogle (`www.boogle.com`) provides a straight, simple Google Web search but adds a picture and a quote to the search page. The attribution of the quote is searchable — that's a nice touch. Click refresh to see a new picture and quote. Also stop into the forum linked on the front page. You might get hooked on the lively discussions and quote suggestions posted by fans.

Fabulous Searches with Xtra-Google

```
www.xtragoogle.com
```

I saved one of the best for last. Xtra-Google is a meta-search environment for Google, which simply means that you can access many different Google engines from one page. In that respect, Xtra-Google is like the Google Toolbar (see Chapter 12). But Xtra-Google goes beyond the Toolbar in its ability to fashion original and uniquely useful searches using combinations of search operators added automatically to your keyword or search string. (See Chapter 2 for more on search operators.)

Figure 19-16 shows the Xtra-Google home page. If you want to search the Google Web index, simply enter a keyword and click the Google Search button. There's no advantage in doing that over going to Google.com. You can see which Google engines are accessed by Xtra-Google by running your mouse cursor over the icons while keeping your eye on the Google logo; the logo changes to indicate which engine corresponds to that icon. (Figure 19-16 illustrates how the page looks when you touch the newspaper icon on the top row. Although you can't see the mouse cursor in the screen shot, you can see the Google News logo.) When searching non-Web Google indexes, use the icons as Search buttons: Enter a keyword, and then click the icon corresponding to the index you want to search.

Now consider two unusual icons that don't correspond with any Google engine covered in this book. They are the two icons at the left end of the bottom row. Run the mouse over them, and you'll see that one is MP3, and the other is Clips. MP3 is a music format. The Clips icon represents several types of video formats. Google doesn't have MP3 or movie indexes, and you can't perform a Google.com Web search for those file types using the *filetype* operator (see Chapter 2 for more about operators). So what gives?

Figure 19-16:
Xtra-Google invites searching many Google engines from one page, plus unique searches for music and movies.

Xtra-Google is doing something clever. By manipulating the keyword string with various operators that Google *does* support, it manages to produce Web-search results that often uncover MP3 and video files stored around the Internet. Some of these files are not meant to be found by search engines; Xtra-Google is tricking certain types of storage areas into revealing themselves. In particular, the altered search strings are designed to pry into FTP (file transfer protocol) locations that are not, technically, part of the World Wide Web, and are often used to store personal files. Downloading these files can technically break copyright laws, very much like all the file-sharing of music that you might have read about.

So if you're a law-abiding copyright citizen, you might wish to tread carefully or forget about these shenanigans altogether. On the other hand, the MP3 and Clips searches sometimes turn up completely legal, authorized music or movie destinations that you might not find by another means.

Chapter 20

Ten More Alternative Googles

Did you look at the previous chapter? Fun, eh? Well, I'm not finished yet. Nobody does fun like me. This chapter contains ten more sites that twist the Google we know and love into barely recognizable configurations. If anything, this collection is even more resourceful, ingenious, and visual than the previous group.

Google Cartography

```
richard.jones.name/google-hacks/google-cartography/google-
                    cartography.html
```

Google Cartography is probably the number-crunchingest Google alternative in the book. This application scours Google for references to any street address, builds a database of what it can glean about intersecting streets, and delivers a map (of sorts) that charts the tangled relationship of streets. Chapter 19 described the TouchGraph GoogleBrowser, which graphically displays networks of related sites. Similarly, Google Cartography displays networks of related streets.

Two points of note apply here. First, do not expect a normal-looking map. (See Figure 20-1.) Second, the intense gathering and collating of site references take time; a recent search required nearly five minutes to complete. One other point — all this is fairly useless. But remember what I said about fun? Well, here it is. You might have trouble recognizing it, but trust me: This is fun.

Google Cartography insists that users deploy their API License Key. These keys are available to anyone — you don't need to be a developer. See Chapter 19 to find out how to get one, and to cash in on the rampant fun of that chapter.

The Cartography site doesn't do a bang-up job leading new users through the application-launching process. Please follow these steps:

1. **Click the Cartography menu item in the left sidebar.**

2. **Scroll way down the page until you see a map with a <u>Your Area</u> link beneath it, and click that link.**

3. **Fill out the boxes in the pop-up panel (see Figure 20-2).**

   Enter your license key in the top box, and leave the two filled-in boxes as they are. Put a street name in the fourth box, and use the bottom box for a town and state combination. Use the post office abbreviation for the state.

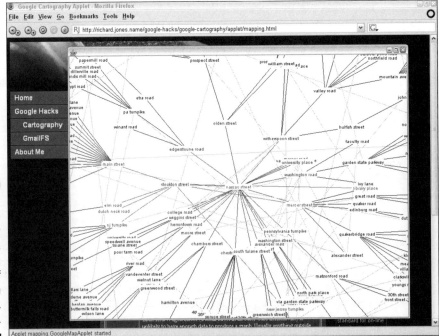

Figure 20-1:
Google
Cartography
in action,
depicting a
network of
streets in
Princeton,
N.J.

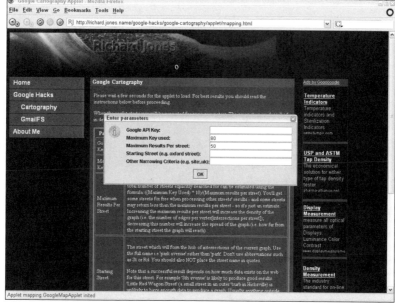

Figure 20-2:
Enter a
license key
and address
information
to get a
Google
Cartography
map.

4. **Click the OK button. And wait.**

   Keep waiting. Make some coffee; I'll take a cup, too. Watch your finger-
   nails grow. Plant a field of wheat and harvest it. The Cartography "map"
   will pop up when it's ready.

Your computer needs a recent version of the Java plug-in to run Google
Cartography. If the application fails for lack of that plug-in, a notification
appears. See the Google Cartography home page for a download link of the
required plug-in. Most recent browser versions have the necessary plug-in
built in.

Newsmap

```
www.marumushi.com/apps/newsmap/newsmap.cfm
```

Newsmap is a fabulous interface that reinvents Google News as a graphic
map of current events. Figure 20-3 shows a snapshot of Google News through
the Newsmap filter. The display is much more colorful than you can see on
this page. Each news section is represented by a different color, with darker
hues representing older stories. Hover your mouse cursor over any item in
the map to see the complete headline and a clip of the lead sentence, as in
Google News (see Chapter 5). Click any item to visit the source news page.

Figure 20-3:
Newsmap in its default view. Hover the mouse for details.

Newsmap archives seven days of Google News headlines, at four times during each day. Use the grid in the lower-left corner to change your point in time. Along the top, you can select different national editions of Google News.

The default layout shows squares, but you can also show the map as a series of vertical strips arranged in horizontal bands representing news sections. (Forget that confusing description and see Figure 20-4.) This arrangement, oddly, is called the standard view, and can be invoked using the link in the lower-right corner.

Thumbshots and Open Directory

```
open.thumbshots.org/
```

As I explain with tedious detail in Chapter 7, Google Directory is a repackaging of Open Directory, a nonprofit, all-volunteer Web-mapping project. A company called Thumbshots creates another repackaging of Open Directory in which search results are accompanied by thumbnail pictures of the target sites. The point is not to avoid clicking through to the target sites entirely but to get a gist of the target before clicking. Some disagreeable content can be avoided in this manner. More to the point, after you've tried the Thumbshots version of Open Directory, you might be unsatisfied with the ungraphical standard view.

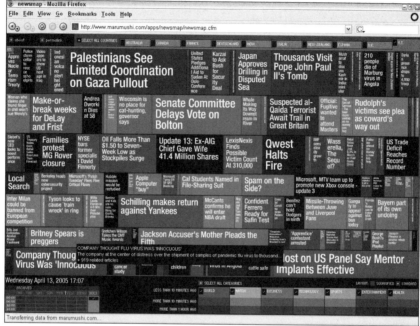

Figure 20-4:
The
Newsmap
in standard
view, with
news
sections
arranged as
horizontal
strips.

Note that Google's PageRank indicators are missing from the Thumbshots display, which isn't really the Google Directory. However, listings and search results are identical to Google's version. And it has pictures. This is all part of the ongoing fun.

Browsing the directory works just as well as searching; any page with site listings in Thumbshots Open Directory displays thumbnails.

SketchWeb

`blog.outer-court.com/sketchweb/index.php`

SketchWeb resembles a lightweight version of the TouchGraph Google Browser, described in Chapter 19. SketchWeb results are fewer and graphically simpler than in TouchGraph, as you can see in Figure 20-5, and the modules do not divulge any information when you double-click or right-click them.

The idea here is to show simple networks of related sites on a platform that doesn't require special software or a powerful computer. Is SketchWeb less fun than TouchGraph? Please. The contents of this chapter provide unrivalled fun. Complexity isn't everything.

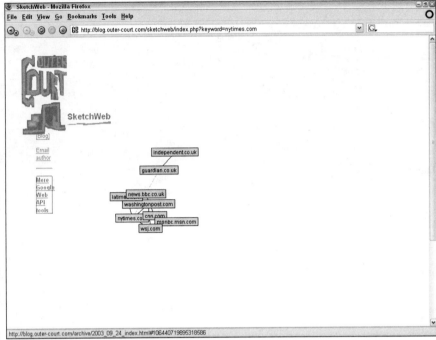

Figure 20-5:
SketchWeb
in action,
showing a
lightweight
network
of related
sites.

BananaSlug

www.bananaslug.com

The fun attains feverish intensity at BananaSlug, which adds random words to your search string. Related to the random searchers featured in Chapter 19, BananaSlug adds a layer of sophistication by allowing you to select a category from which the random word is selected. The entire keyword string consists of your words plus a category word.

The results can be startlingly interesting, as ideas that you might never have thought to combine get mashed together in the keyword string. Unlike other random-keyword generators, BananaSlug doesn't go for obscure words, which limit results to odd sites. The random word here is usually a common one, leading to substantial results that would be hard to find by normal means.

In one recent search, I chose *alan greenspan* for my keywords, and selected the Laws of Spirit button for the random word, which turned out to be *unity*. The results were startling and funny. Whenever you don't like the results, just choose another (or the same) category — your original keywords stay in play.

YaGoohoo!gle

`www.yagoohoogle.com`

The idea is simple. Smash the Yahoo! and Google search engines together. Begun as an April Fool's joke, YaGoohoo!gle has attained status as a metasearch engine with a great display. Figure 20-6 shows a typical search result.

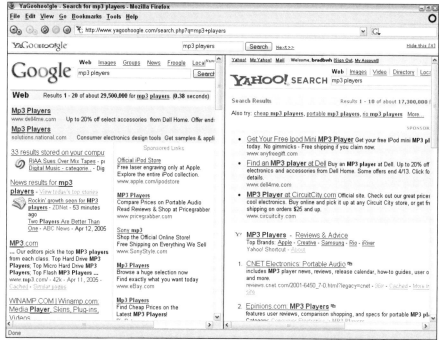

Figure 20-6: YaGoohoo!gle displays search results from both search engines.

One interesting feature of YaGoohoo!gle is the side-by-side display, which encourages you to compare how Yahoo! and Google package their search results. How many ads, news results, and miscellaneous information are crammed into the top of the page? The answer often depends on the search string. Things get really interesting when you *want* atypical results atop the page, such as reference answers and other basic facts (see Chapter 3). YaGoohoo!gle lets you put both engines to the test in head-to-head competition. (Beware: YaGoohoo!gle randomly switches the positions of the two sets of results.) Look at Figure 20-7 for an example: The point goes to Yahoo!'s immediate display of an address map.

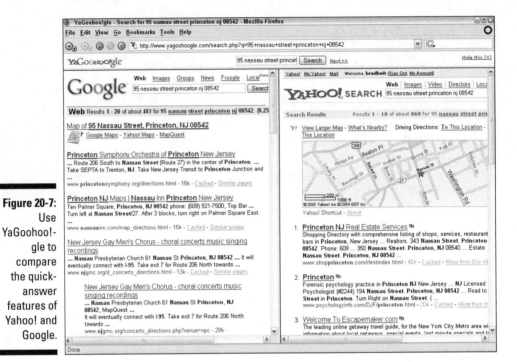

Figure 20-7: Use YaGoohoo!-gle to compare the quick-answer features of Yahoo! and Google.

LostGoggles

www.lostgoggles.com

If you like thumbnail-enhanced browsing as provided by Thumbshots, you might be attracted to LostGoggles, which extends the same sort of display to the entire Google Web-searching experience. LostGoggles used to be called MoreGoogle, but Google objected — to the name, not the application.

LostGoggles is a little program that works only with Internet Explorer (version 5 or later). You download and install it like any other program, and it takes residence quietly within Internet Explorer, waiting for a visit to Google. Then, whenever you perform a Google Web search, the results are displayed with accompanying thumbnail images of the target sites (see Figure 20-8).

LostGoggles is free, and absent of adware and spyware. The program has been around since August 2004 and enjoys a good reputation.

Figure 20-8:
LostGoggles
inserts
thumbnails
of Google
results.

Soople

`www.soople.com`

Soople is spectacular; that is the simple truth. Chapter 19 describes the Google Ultimate Interface, which is a wonderful advanced search screen that outshines Google's own Advanced Search page (see Chapter 2). But nothing comes close to Soople for unleashing the power of Google. I fully expect some readers, finding out about Soople on these pages, to substitute Soople for Google entirely. If Soople ever built a toolbar, I think Google would have to buy the company. Soople's results come from the Google engine and are presented on Google pages. But Soople's search forms go way beyond Google or any other interface in flexibility and idea generation.

Some studies have indicated that most people's searching success is hobbled by poor keyword selection. (To improve your keyword skills, see Chapter 2.) Soople helps by dividing operators into separate search fields, suggesting many topics to search, providing a wide array of keywords, aggregating groups of sites to search, and allowing you to save a personal page that displays just the tools you need.

Figure 20-9 shows the front page, which is just the beginning. Even so, you can see the breadth of search intelligence presented and the attractiveness of the design. You can launch a basic Google Web search here, but do yourself a favor by exploring all the options; clicking the *explain* link for feature descriptions.

Figure 20-9:
The Soople home page, a gateway to innovative Google searching.

The three main feature innovations at Soople are these:

✔ Suggested topics

✔ Suggested keywords

✔ Personalized page

Click the Topics tab to see how Soople handles search topics. The site has assembled about fifty popular search subjects, some of which are visible in Figure 20-10. Click any topic, or use the keyword box to search for a Soople topic.

Figure 20-11 shows a topic page — note that you can select individual keywords by checking boxes or bundles of keywords with a single click. When you're ready to run the search, simply click the search button near the middle of the page. (You must either check at least one check box or type a keyword into the Your own Keywords box to get any results.)

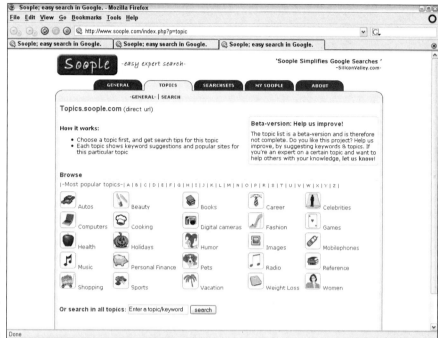

Searchsets are Soople's preset bundles of topic-relevant sites. In the Searchsets tab, you can find all the presets and build your own sets. You need to register for this, but it's free and painless. (Registration is required so that the site can remember your sets between visits.) Creating a searchset is a simple matter of assigning Web sites and naming the group. Using a custom searchset is a powerful way to keep up-to-speed in topics of interest, using sites you trust. Figure 20-12 shows the Searchsets tab with a couple of personal sets placed in it. Click any set to view the sites in that set. Use the corresponding keyword box to search any set.

Figure 20-12: Custom searchsets encourage users to put several trusted sites in a single search basket.

Use the My Soople tab to assemble a page with your favorite Soople tools. Only preset tools are available — in other words, any specific search function on the home page (the General tab). Topics and searchsets must be selected in their respective tabs.

WebCollage

www.jwz.org/webcollage/

WebCollage is a big poster that plucks pictures from Google Images, softens their edges, and displays them as a collage. The page automatically refreshes every minute or so, changing one or two of the pictures. After about ten minutes, the entire collage has changed. Meaningful? No. Productive? Hardly. (In fact, don't bring up this page at work. Keep your kids away from it, too. WebCollage is not "safe searching" by any means.)

Click any image in WebCollage to visit the site from the image was taken.

Babelplex

www.babelplex.com

Babelplex is a multilingual marvel that takes a search query typed in one language, translates it to another language, and then displays Google results in both languages. The two sides of the search are separated into frames.

The value of Babelplex is not merely linguistic. The site actually searches international editions of Google, so the non-American results are very different from the English side of the page, if English is one of your languages. It needn't be the starting language; use the drop-down menu on Babelplex's home page to choose your two languages.

Chapter 21

Ten Google Games

Google users and third-party developers are an imaginative, playful bunch. And some of the most Google-happy activities that sweep faddishly through the Internet are represented in this chapter. I am repeatedly impressed by the ingenuity of regular folks who take something as monolithic as a search engine, and turn it into an ingredient of a game.

In this chapter, you find a collection of Google games that whack and skewer the great index in deliriously time-wasting ways.

In Pursuit of the Googlewhack

www.googlewhack.com

It started a few years ago and has grown as an underground-cum-mainstream time-waster. The game is called Googlewhacking, and its goal is to obtain just one Google result for a two-word keyword string. A few legendary triumphs (they're not mine) follow:

ambidextrous scallywags

squirreling dervishes

fetishized armadillo

anxiousness scheduler

More recent milestones are

kneeboarding skywards

confluence urping

quakeproofed woman

naptime quaalude

You'd think that last one might return more than one Google result. And, by the time you read this, it might.

There is nothing official about Googlewhacking, so rules might seem excessively officious. But you won't get a whack recorded on the Googlewhack site unless it conforms to certain guidelines:

- ✔ **No quotes:** Using the exact phrase operator (see Chapter 2) makes it too easy to get a whack. Forcing unrelated words to exist right next to each other, as a phrase, instantly reduces results. Letting the words exist anywhere on the Web page brings in many more hits, making the game tougher.

- ✔ **No other search operators:** Although not listed as a Googlewhacking rule, it makes sense. Any of the operators described in Chapter 2, standard or specific to Google, narrow results artificially and should be considered cheating. Use pure, unfettered keywords thrown into the entire Web index.

- ✔ **No scripts allowed:** If you're resourceful enough to write a little software program that automatically queries Google with randomly combined words, don't use it. It violates the spirit of the game, but more important, this sort of quasicheating takes the fun out of cudgeling your brain for almost-impossible search strings.

- ✔ **Web searches only:** You might want to experiment with image searches, Groups searches, or news searches (Directory searches are too easy), but as of now, results of these variants are not considered true whacks.

✔ **Real keywords only:** The Googlewhack arbiter is Dictionary.com.

✔ **Real result(s) only:** If you manage to produce a single result (which is harder and more gratifying than finding a four-leaf clover), that result page must be legitimate and meaningful. Pages that contain mere lists of words, or gibberish, don't constitute a whack.

Play the game at Google, but visit the Googlewhack site for inspiration, history, and to read successful whacks and their humorous definitions. The inventive definitions of whack strings are almost the best part of Googlewhacking. In one particularly brilliant set of whackinitions, the site fabricated all-Enron explanations for recent whacks (see Figure 21-1). Reading through the whacktionary is both amusing and inspiring.

If you are so lucky (talented?) as to successfully whack Google, go to the Googlewhacking site and click the <u>Record Your Whack!</u> link. Googlewhack provides Google search boxes to verify your success. Don't use these boxes to try out new whacks. Their only purpose is to verify whacks already established through Google.

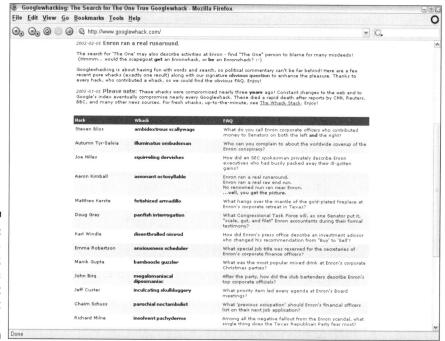

Figure 21-1: Google-whack definitions are almost the best part of the game.

Unfortunately, whacks are rarely permanent. Their transience is due not to the ever-changing Google index but to the urge to brag. If you promote your own whack, or record it on the Googlewhack site, that instantly creates a second page with your two keywords. Google will probably find it eventually. The Googlewhack site is already in the index, of course, so within a month at the longest (the usual length of Google's major update cycle) your whack will be ruined.

Googlewhackers are a strict bunch, but they look kindly on artificially ruined whacks as described in the previous paragraph. In fact, the name Heisenwhack has been applied to such disruptions in the quantum whackfield, after the physicist Werner Heisenberg. He, along with Niels Bohr, theorized that nothing exists without measurement, and the sheer act of measuring a phenomenon alters it. Hence, there is no objectivity. (This, however, is not the Heisenberg Uncertainty Principle, despite what some Googlewhacking sites tell you. The Uncertainty Principle is about the impossibility of measuring both the position and momentum of a particle.) The lack of objectivity relates to the unwhacking of keywords through the simple act of observing them (mentioning the whack on a Web page).

You can cut through a ruined whack by searching for the two keywords with the added negative keyword -googlewhack (using the *NOT* operator as described in Chapter 2). That should deliver the original single search result, verifying the un-Heisenwhacked whack.

The Random Googlelaar

www.northernlake.com/googlelaar/

In the preceding section on Googlewhacking, I mentioned that using automated, random-word search generators was cheating. Googlelaar, which generates one-word, two-word, and three-word searches in English or Dutch, provides perfect examples of why these things don't yield legitimate whacks.

When I first encountered Googlelaar, I got a Googlewhack in my first random search: *pained pentanone*. Cheating or not, it's amazing to see that "1 of 1" in the summary bar.

Googlelaar, and other random-word Google interfaces, are frivolous to the extreme. But there's something trivially satisfying about making Google chase its tail. Figure 21-2 shows Googlelaar's page — it's simple enough. Click the drop-down menus to select the number of words and language, and then click the Hit me! button. Google delivers the search results. Click the Back button to try another search.

Figure 21-2:
Googlelaar
provides the
keywords;
you just
choose how
many and
which
language,
English or
Dutch.

Googlelaar prowls through Webster's *Second International Dictionary* to find its keywords, and presumably the entire dictionary is in its memory. Most of the words I get are unfamiliar — and I know a lot of words. This means that either English has more exotic words than I realized or Googlelaar skews the keyword selection toward obscurities. In any event, a common results total for two- or three-word searches through Googlelaar is 0.

Another frequent result is Google asking if you didn't mean a slightly different spelling of your keyword string. I find this amusing. Recently Googlelaar generated the phrase *artiad skirted unbenetted.* Google responded — did you mean: *artiad skirted unbelted?* Yes, of course! *That's* what I meant!

Using Googlelaar for one-word random searches is more diverting. And this is where a little keyboard tip gives the exercise some rhythm. Googlelaar launches a search with a press of the Enter key — you don't need to click the Hit me! button. So you can bounce back and forth between Googlelaar and the search results page with repeated Enter-Back-Enter-Back sequences. There's never a need to type a keyword, of course.

Googlism

www.googlism.com

Googlism uses tricky (and undivulged) keyword manipulations to ascertain what Google "thinks" about people, places, and things. Although the keyword chicanery is hidden, the results are clearly scraped from actual Web pages Google finds in relation to your keyword(s). But don't mistake this site for an information resource — it's mostly entertainment. Googlism swept through the Usenet newsgroups when it was introduced, and everyone was delighted to discover the supposed revelatory truth about their online acquaintances.

Googlism works in plain fashion. Figure 21-3 shows the Googlism home page. Type a keyword, click the appropriate option (Who, What, Where, or When), and then click the Googlism! button. What follows is a list of sentence frag- ments and occasional complete phrases lifted from Google search results. The amusement factor is due to the phrases being taken out of context, as if they were always meant to be as declamatory as they appear in Googlism. Take, for example, this short sample from the Googlism on Microsoft:

> Microsoft is calling you
>
> Microsoft is losing its grip
>
> Microsoft is calling you a lab rat
>
> Microsoft is

The last one seems complete unto itself.

Run a Googlism on yourself, but remember that results must come from Web pages that include your name. Of course, getting hits on your name that belong to an identically named stranger is fun, too.

Want to know where a particular Googlism comes from? Even the silliest sound- ing ones are not made up; they come from some Web page. Simply type the Googlism into Google (not into Googlism) and check the results. Put quotes around the Googlism if the original search results show any confusion.

Capture the Map

www.capturethemap.de

One of the more recent, and most ingenious, Google games yet created, Capture the Map pits two players (one of which can be the computer) in a game of world domination. Where does Google fit in? You capture portions of the world by craftily generating search results that include Web sites located in those portions of the world. It's not easy to think of keywords with this strategy in mind. Simply entering names of places doesn't always work as well as you might hope. The keyword strategizing is toughest when the game is in the late stages and a few remaining territories are up for grabs.

Figure 21-3: Googlism finds out everything about people, places, and things.

Figure 21-4 shows a game in progress. A magnifying glass can be dragged around the world map for a close-up view of each player's holdings. Any held territory can be captured by the opponent, unless it covers an area of three-by-three squares.

Squabbling Keywords

Google's reputation as an arbiter of cultural relevance makes it the perfect source for a game that pits keywords against each other. Who is more important, Sean Connery or Harrison Ford? And if one gets more Google results than the other, does that really tell us something? The question seems ludicrous on the face of it, but considering the size and scope of Google's index, and the depth with which it catalogues human interest as expressed on the Web, there might be something to the idea.

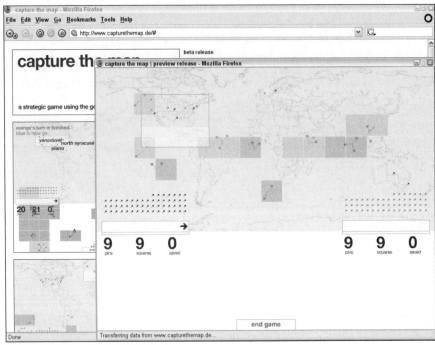

Figure 21-4:
A game of
Capture the
Map in
progress.

Anyway, nobody is trying to write a doctoral dissertation on the thesis. Again, the point here is entertainment. Here are the three sites in question:

- GoogleFight at `www.googlefight.com`
- Google Smackdown at `www.onfocus.com/googlesmack/down.asp`
- Google Duel at `www.googleduel.com`

The three sites are more similar than different, but each has strong and weak points. Figure 21-5 illustrates the home page of Google Smackdown. As with the others, the interface invites you to enter two keywords, phrases, or names. The engine then tabulates the results totals and throws away the actual results, leaving you with a count of the number of hits for each of the competing keywords or keyword strings.

This is great fun. During a political season, pit one *American Idol* candidate against another. Who is really more popular, Carrie Underwood or Bo Bice? (Hint: Count those telephone votes again.) Plug in any two names, concepts, expressions, objects, or locations. Put your hometown against your friend's hometown. Let Plato and Socrates fight it out in the Google index.

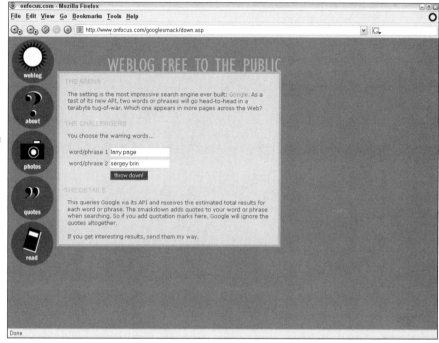

Figure 21-5:
Google
Smack-
down, one
of three
popular
keyword
battle sites.
In this shot,
Larry Page
fights
Sergey Brin.

Astute Google users might be tempted to put quotes around their keyword phrases to keep them intact, yielding more accurately competitive results. No need. Each of these three sites automatically adds quotes to your phrases (though you don't see the quotes) when they throw the search into Google. If you add your own quotes, around the invisible quotes, Google ignores the whole mess and treats your keywords individually. Then you get more but less accurate results.

Google Smackdown and Google Duel request that you use your own Google developer's key; it's only polite to provide your own key when a site provides space to enter it. (See Chapter 14 for information about getting a key.) Googlefight has a pleasing interface that puts your two keyword phrases in different colors.

When it comes to displaying results, my favorite is Google Duel, which renders an illustrative graph of the results, in addition to dishing up the raw numbers (see Figure 21-6). Notice the link to an advanced version of Google Duel called GoogleDuel Ultra, which encourages users to enter descriptive adjectives in addition to names (see Figure 21-7). The results are filtered by the extra information.

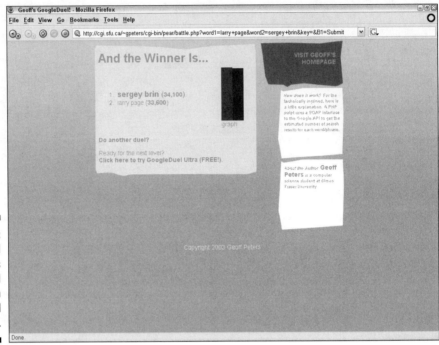

Figure 21-6:
Google Duel displays keyword fights in graphical format.

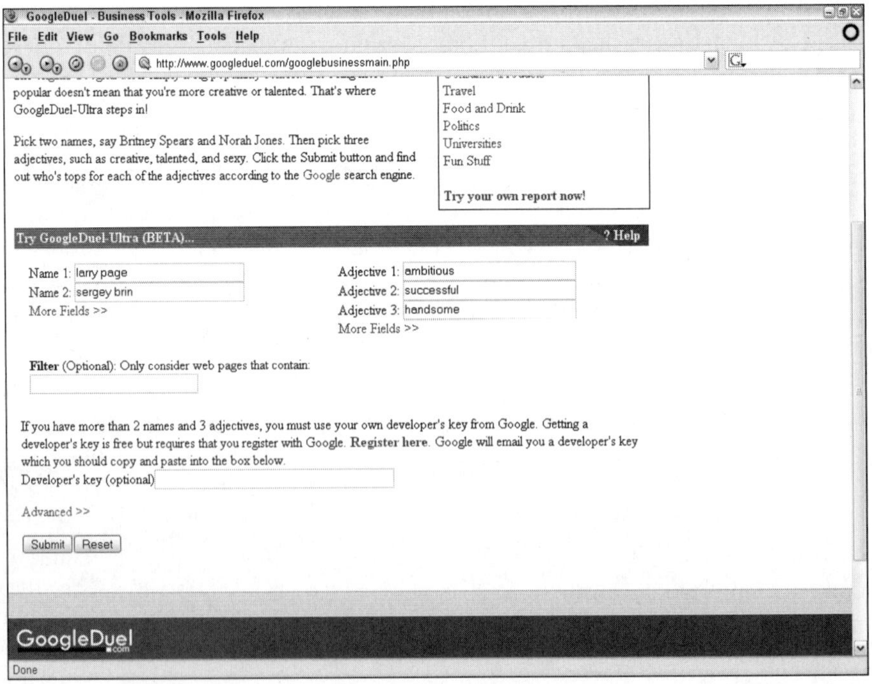

Figure 21-7:
GoogleDuel Ultra adds descriptive adjectives to filter the competition results.

Overall, when in the mood for a keyword fight, I find myself going to Googlefight more than the others. The interface is the least pleasant, in my opinion, but I like the archive of interesting and amusing keyword matchups.

More Random Searching

Earlier in this chapter I describe Googlelaar, which randomly generates keywords and shows you Google's search results for those words. In this section, I introduce three engines that also randomly contrive keywords but take the happy meaninglessness of random searching to the next level by leaping directly to the first result site for those words.

Two main features distinguish the best of these sites from the not-as-good:

- **Keyword customization:** Even though it's the engine's job to generate random keywords, the sites below all allow the user to specify the number of keywords used. Clearly, the greater flexibility in this department, the more fun the engine is. One of the sites described here even lets you set the maximum length of the keywords.

- **Frames:** Frames on Web pages can be a disagreeable design choice, but in this case they really help. Some sites throw the target page into your browser window without an anchor frame, forcing you to backtrack if you want to try a new random search. The better designs display the randomly found page below a horizontal frame containing the means to launch a new search.

The danger of random searches — besides being a stultifying waste of time — is that you're likely to stumble into site types that you'd ordinarily avoid. If you don't like opening PDF files, for example, you might be upset when one comes screaming in, unannounced. Adult sites are not out of bounds, either, unless you click the SafeSearch box — provided the search engine furnishes one.

Mangle

```
www.mangle.ca
```

Mangle — nice name for a site, isn't it? And not really descriptive: Mangle doesn't destroy keywords; it invents them. Hoping to please everyone, Mangle offers a choice of interfaces — frames or no frames. On the search page (see Figure 21-8), you can choose up to five keywords (the default setting is three). You can also select a country and language, or leave the gates wide open for everything. (Use the Region Mangle and Custom Mangle links.) Random searches become particularly useless if conducted in a language you don't understand. The engine is naturally biased toward English and generally delivers English-language sites in default mode.

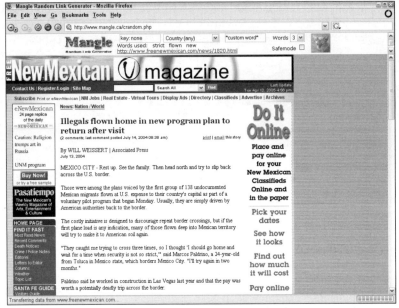

Figure 21-8:
Mangle in search mode, displaying the first search result from randomly chosen keywords.

Note a few features of the Mangle search frame:

✔ Click the cat picture (upper-right corner) to launch a search. Pressing the Enter key doesn't do it.

✔ Check the Safemode box to apply Google filtering to Mangle's search results.

✔ Use the drop-down menu to change the number of keywords. You may choose between one and five keywords.

✔ The keywords used by the engine are displayed just below the drop-down menus.

✔ The displayed page's link is below the keywords.

For truly empty-headed searching, click the archive search link on Mangle's home page. You get a random page from Mangle's storehouse of previously randomized results. So not only are you searching in the dark, you're taking random results from other people's blind searches. Good times!

Random Google page

www.bleb.org/random

One of the simplest random search pages is appropriately named the Random Google page. Two distinguishing features mark this site. First, you can generate up to ten keywords. That many keywords, more often than not, leads to zero results, but what's more fun than trying over and over until you find a page that matches ten keywords? The second feature is a list of recent search results (including yours) at the bottom of the home page. Each link allows you to recreate the search, as if once weren't enough.

Random Web Search

www.randomwebsearch.com

If there's one site that puts together all the important features of the others, and adds some of its own, for a thoroughly time-wasting and gloriously unproductive Google experience, it's the Random Web Search page. Figure 21-9 shows the options available on the home page. This site can act as a standard Web-search interface to Google. Just type your keywords and click the Google Search button. For random searching, click the Generate Random Word(s) button. You get one word most of the time, but the engine will throw you a phrase when you least expect it. And you can add your own keywords to the randomly generated word.

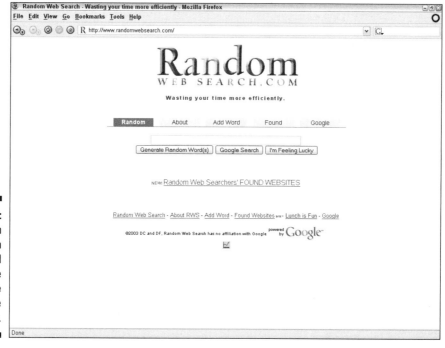

Figure 21-9:
The Random Web Search page, proud to waste your time more efficiently.

Click the Google Search button for standard results or the I'm Feeling Lucky button to see the first result site. Frames are not used when displaying target sites, so click the Back button to return for another search.

Click the Add Word tab to contribute a brilliant keyword to the site's archive. That word will begin appearing, randomly, on other people's screens.

Best of all, click the Found tab to see randomly found Web pages with short descriptions. This collection justifies the entire random-search movement. Maybe. At the very least, when using Random Web Search, you will be — as the site proclaims — "Wasting your time more efficiently."

Google Backwards

www.alltooflat.com/geeky/elgoog/

elgooG emulates Google in every respect, but in reverse. This site puts a literal spin on the concept of *mirror site*. Most mirror sites replicate their originals in every detail. elgooG replicates Google as a mirror image. Go to the elgooG page and try a search (see Figure 21-10) to see what I'm talking about.

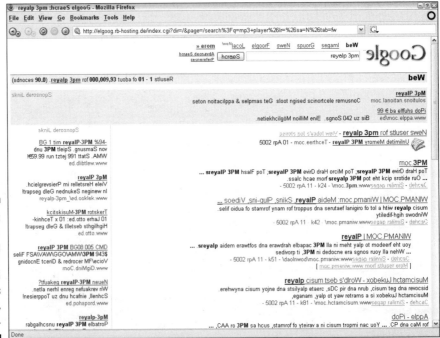

Figure 21-10: This is not a printing mistake! elgooG mirrors Google, literally.

The reversal is thorough. Search results pages come out as backwards as the home page. elgooG used to make users type their keywords in reverse but, perhaps having mercy on us, now reverses the characters after we type them in the correct order. (Typing backward still works, too.)

elgooG carries this conceit through all Google interface pages — Advanced Search, Preferences, Language Tools, the whole lot. News, Groups, Directory — all backwards. (In the Directory and Google Groups, pages that are at the second level and lower revert to a normal display.) Oh, and search results are reversed, too. When you click any result to leave Google, your screen reverts to its normal display.

Of what possible use is elgooG? The same might be asked of. In both cases, science has not yet found an answer.

Gettin' in the Hood with Gizoogle

```
www.gizoogle.com
```

Of the many Google games I've suggested in my Google Weblog, this one has received the most enthusiastic response. Gizoogle translates normal Google results to the brand of rap-speak invented and popularized by Snoop Dog. Figure 21-11 illustrates what you can expect from a Gizoogle search.

Figure 21-11: Gizoogle translates Google search results to a hip dialect.

Gizoogle isn't a G-rated site, just as hip, urban, rap-influenced speech isn't always wholesome. You might not want to enjoy the snappy and scatological phrases peppered through Gizoogle results with kids looking over your shoulder, or at work.

Gizoogle translates any material that you dump into it. Click the Textilizer link and type or paste sentences or paragraphs into the entry box, and then click the Tranzilate This Text button. When I did so with the paragraph preceding this one, I got this result:

"Gizoogle isn't a G-rated site, just as H-to-tha-izzip, urban, rap-influenced speech isn't always wholesome. You miznight not wizzay ta enjoy tha snappy n scatalogizzles phrases peppered through Gizoogle results wit kids look'n over yo cracka or at wizzork."

Isn't that what I said the first time?

A Google Time Machine

Google hasn't been in existence for very long in the grand scheme of things. But since it indexes many pages dealing with historic events, the Google brain can express the arc of human events to some extent. Describing that arc is the purpose of the FindForward engine. FindForward is a misnomer, because the engine actually finds backward, reaching into one of two fifty-year blocks of time (1900–1950 or 1950–2000). The FindForward site contains several search options; this time-machine gadget is merely the one I'm interested in here.

Start by going to the FindForward site:

```
www.findforward.com
```

On the front page, pull down the menu and select one of the two time periods. Generally, I find that better results come from the more recent period: 1950–2000. When I say "results," I don't mean typical Google listings. Instead, FindForward delivers a graph representing the newsworthiness of your keywords in each year of the time period. Figure 21-12 shows the results for the key phrase *moon landing*. Note that the year 1969 shows the peak of interest in those keywords, corresponding to the first manned lunar landing. Then, sadly, interest declines.

It takes a little while (up to a minute sometimes) for FindForward to display results. The site is not broken. Just cool your Internet-fueled jets and wait.

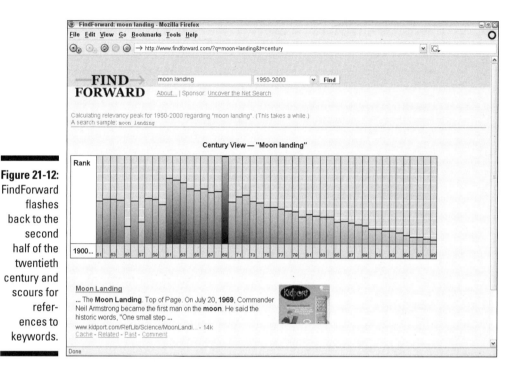

Figure 21-12:
FindForward
flashes
back to the
second
half of the
twentieth
century and
scours for
refer-
ences to
keywords.

Google Poker

www.library.vcu.edu/cfapps/jbc/instruct/google/game

At the site, this game is blandly (and self-importantly) called Google Game. But it's actually a sort of poker in which you bet whether your hand (provided by the site — you don't have to do anything) will beat the site's hand. A hand consists of three keywords, and one of the site's keywords is hidden. You bet on the high or low side, depending on your confidence that your hand of keywords will yield more or fewer results than the opposing hand. Each set of three keywords is thrown into the Google index as a single search string, not as three separate searches.

Figure 21-13 illustrates the results of one hand, and the setup of the next one. I bet low and won, and I'm going high in the next hand. (I won again. I rule.)

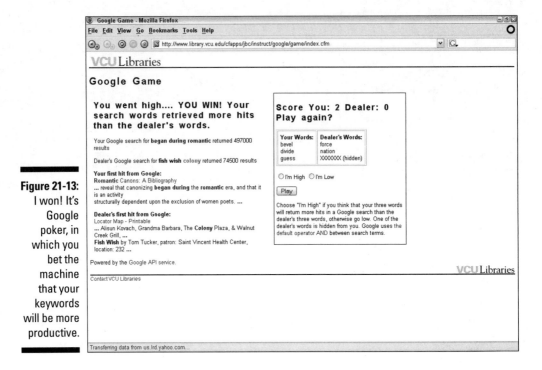

Figure 21-13:
I won! It's
Google
poker, in
which you
bet the
machine
that your
keywords
will be more
productive.

Chapter 22

Ten Sites and Blogs about Google

*T*he three broad areas of Google obsession are

✔ The search engine itself, and all of Google's related services

✔ Alternate Google sites and interfaces, described in Chapters 19, 20, and 21

✔ Analysis and discussion of Google and its extraordinary effect on our online lives

This book is mostly concerned with hands-on, heady interaction with the Google index through all its interfaces, both official and unofficial. This one chapter, however, points to sites in the third group. These sites *about* Google range from the technical to the journalistic, from the critical to the laudatory.

The Unofficial Google Weblog

google.weblogsinc.com

This one is mine, and I'll keep the plug brief. The Unofficial Google Weblog is part of Weblogs Inc., where I cover the search industry and a few other topics.

This blog is where I dump my daily commentary on Google news (a couple of examples of which are shown in Figure 22-1). It's a good place to keep up-to-date with new Google features and discover what other bloggers and journalists think of them. I, and occasional guest bloggers, take a broad approach to the subject, reporting and analyzing everything from perceived changes in the index to the evolution of Gmail, from Google stock to the rare utterances of Sergey Brin and Larry Page, Google's founders.

Come visit!

Google Watch

```
www.google-watch.org/
```

Google Watch is an extremely critical and well-researched site that offers a tonic to blind Google mania. Google Watch believes in its words, "There's a struggle going on for the soul of the web, and the focal point of this struggle is Google itself."

Figure 22-1: The Unofficial Google Weblog, written by the author of this book, comments on all kinds of Google news every day.

Google Watch has problems with Google's dominance and the influence it wields. The site also takes issue with the PageRank system, claiming that it unfairly adds to the prominence of popular sites that don't necessarily deserve their popularity. Further, Google Watch dislikes Google's use of cookies to track user behavior through the site. Google Watch even believes that Google's cached copy of Web sites is illegal, not to mention problematic for Webmasters. Google's general secretiveness is raked over the coals at Google Watch.

Google Watch is an investigative site, a scathing indictor of Google's operations, an explainer of technical arcana, and a loud whistleblower. At the same time, the site's importance is diminishing. Google Watch is not updated frequently and not varied enough. Its in-depth negative treatment of Google issues prevents the sort of quick, down-and-dirty treatment Google gets from blogs. Google Watch is starting to seem old, dated, and whiny.

Furthermore, Google-bashing is no longer a novelty. Google's initial stock offering brought the company and its products to the forefront of media coverage for several months, during which all remnants of reverence were stripped away from most people's perception of the company and its services. That's not to say Google isn't still greatly admired, but it is also commonly criticized, just like any other highly visible media company.

Google Watch probably won't make it in the next edition of this book. But now it is still worth a visit.

Webmaster World: Google

```
www.webmasterworld.com/forum30
```

Webmaster World's Google forum is one of the most visited sites for serious Google watchers. This forum is populated by Webmasters — site owners trying to maximize their exposure in the Google index and on search results pages. Much of the conversation is fairly advanced and technical.

Topics in this forum include bettering one's PageRank; understanding and coping with the Google dance; anticipating the deep crawl and preparing a site for it; and luring the Google spider, making it happy, and enduring its occasional wrath.

Webmaster World has developed several forums for discussion of Google features, including separate pages for messages about AdWords, AdSense, and Froogle. Use the following link to see the index of all Google-related Webmaster World destinations:

```
www.webmasterworld.com/category30.htm
```

Google PageRank

```
pr.efactory.de
```

PageRank is arguably the most important search technology to hit the Web in years. The ranking of Web pages based on popularity, as defined by the amount of backlinking directed toward them, lies at the heart of Google's effectiveness. Yet determining PageRank is not a simple matter of counting links. Google deploys algorithms that are both highly technical and partly secret.

This site explains PageRank with a depth only a truly ambitious Google fanatic can appreciate. Here you find a mathematical description of the Google algorithm as taken from the university papers of Google's founders. Eight other sections delve into the details of how PageRank is implemented, the role of incoming and outgoing links, ranking distribution issues, and quite a bit more, the description of which would make me appear quite foolish.

Google Weblog

```
google.blogspace.com
```

The Google Weblog provides a simple, nontechnical update of Google news. There's nothing controversial or difficult here. Even the typeface is childishly huge. Pro-Google perhaps to a fault, the Google Weblog is nonetheless objective enough to be a credible news source.

Elgoog

```
www.elgoog.nl
```

It's Google spelled backwards, get it? I didn't think it was clever, either. But Elgoog is a potent directory to Google-related sites. Prefaced as an "ode to Google," the site is less poetic than methodical and is possibly the most comprehensive directory of online Googlish destinations.

The inner workings of the directory exhibit a somewhat slapdash organization, with considerable duplication among the subjects. But never mind that. Many riches lurk within.

Googlepress

groups-beta.google.com/group/googlepress/

Google distributes press releases to anyone who wants them. These bulletins contain news about Google's services and features, and are, of course, free.

Curiously, Google uses a Google Group to collect memberships in the distribution list. Normally, Google Groups is used to build online communities around a certain topic, and it enables message-board discussions, chat rooms, shared calendars, posted pictures, and other fun features. Google has all those features turned off and uses the group strictly for e-mailing newsletters.

You sign up for Google's press releases by joining the Googlepress group. Please get your head into Chapter 6 if you have questions about navigating around Google Groups.

Search Engine Showdown

www.searchengineshowdown.com

If only the Search Engine Showdown site were updated more frequently. If only all the nations of the world would just get along. Oh well. Search Engine Showdown combines reviews, tutorials, and comparison charts to give visitors an intriguing view of the topography of the keyword-query industry. The topography of the keyword-query industry? Where do I come up with this buzzbabble? I'm just frustrated because the nations of the world don't get along. Anyway, my point here is that Search Engine Showdown is a great place to compare which search operators work in different engines, which search indexes are larger than others, and how to make better choices and conduct better searches. There is also a blog, but it's not updated frequently, and it rarely discusses world peace. I've got to get off this conflict of nations thing — it's depressing.

Google Blog — Live

www.google.com/googleblog/

New since the first edition of this book is Google's own blog, written by company employees. This is where you go for new product announcements and glimpses into the daily life at the Googleplex — Google's corporate campus.

Oddly, Google's in-house blog isn't that good. It compares unfavorably, in my opinion, with the blog written by engineers at Yahoo! Search. Google's blog is fluffy, often lacking substantial information and even more bereft of thought-provoking entries. You'd think that one of the most intense aggregations of brainpower in corporate America could do better, but Google Blog — Live is too often about promotion. It uses the word *cool* with uncool frequency, like a parent trying too hard. The blog is often behind the news curve, even about its own products.

Still, there it is — uniquely Google's. It must reside in your newsreader or bookmark list.

Google also produces a monthly newsletter. Well, almost monthly. Not quite monthly. Not even close to being monthly. Fourteen months elapsed between the last two editions, as of this writing. But the archives make interesting browsing (on a slow day), and I am told that the newsletter might awaken to a more frequent schedule. Here is the archives page:

```
www.google.com/googlefriends/archive.html
```

Click the Google Newsletter link on that page to find the e-mail subscription form.

Google Blogoscoped

```
blog.outer-court.com
```

One of the great, landmark, Google-centric blogs, Google Blogoscoped is a daily source of news and comment for many unquenchable Google watchers.

More than an information source, Google Blogoscoped produces a multitude of Google tools and API developments, such as The Google Family Tree and The Google Encyclopedia, as well as the FindForward engine described in Chapter 21. Everyone who follows Google as an interest, an obsession, or a professional requirement is in touch with Google Blogoscoped.

Index

• U •

• V •

• X •

• Y •

• Z •

Notes